Interdisciplinary
Views on Abortion

Interdisciplinary Views on Abortion

Essays from Philosophical, Sociological, Anthropological, Political, Health and Other Perspectives

Edited by
Susan A. Martinelli-Fernandez,
Lori Baker-Sperry *and*
Heather McIlvaine-Newsad

Foreword by Sue V. Rosser

McFarland & Company, Inc., Publishers
Jefferson, North Carolina, and London

LIBRARY OF CONGRESS CATALOGUING-IN-PUBLICATION DATA

Interdisciplinary views on abortion : essays from philosophical, sociological, anthropological, political, health and other perspectives / edited by Susan A. Martinelli-Fernandez, Lori Baker-Sperry and Heather McIlvaine-Newsad ; foreword by Sue V. Rosser.
     p.   cm.
    Includes bibliographical references and index.

    ISBN 978-0-7864-3494-7
    softcover : 50# alkaline paper

    1. Abortion.   2. Abortion — Moral and ethical aspects. 3. Abortion — Religious aspects.   I. Martinelli-Fernandez, Susan A., 1951–   II. Baker-Sperry, Lori, 1971–   III. McIlvaine-Newsad, Heather, 1967–
HQ767.I58   2009
362.19888 — dc22   2009001475

British Library cataloguing data are available

Cover image ©2009 Shutterstock

Manufactured in the United States of America

McFarland & Company, Inc., Publishers
  Box 611, Jefferson, North Carolina 28640
  www.mcfarlandpub.com

We dedicate this book to the women of Western Illinois University, who live with, around, through, and sometimes under the reality of reproduction. We also dedicate this book to our students who gave life and breadth to the initial course. Special thanks goes to the women of Illinois and around the world who loaned their voices to this volume. We also wish to acknowledge the hard work of a longtime administrative assistant for help in seeing this project to fruition. Finally, our heartfelt gratitude to Polly F. Radosh, whose steadfast loyalty and vision made our discrete intellectual commitments and lives become collectively one, and individually richer.

Table of Contents

TABLE OF CONTENTS

Foreword

How This Book Exemplifies the Best of Women's Studies

SUE V. ROSSER

Women's health served as a major impetus for the second wave of feminism and the women's movement in the 1960s, with access for women to safe, legal abortion, contraception, and medical school heading the agenda. After years of feminist activism and political coalition building, women's health now occupies a position in the mainstream of national medical research and education agendas. Women make up about half of medical students. Although few new methods of contraception have appeared in recent years and a campaign for abstinence from intercourse has occupied the national focus, contraception remains legal and widely used. In contrast, abortion has become increasingly unavailable, with some doctors who perform abortions having lost their lives to "pro-life" terrorists, and abortion is unlikely to be the focus of research and publications that can be used in the classroom or even discussed in educational institutions.

Women's studies became the academic arm of the women's movement, with many of the first courses, readings, and programs initially developed in the early 1970s. As one of the individuals involved in the first year of the Women's Studies Program at the University of Wisconsin in 1974–75, who then went on to serve as a director of women's studies for twenty-three years at three very different types of institutions in different states, I recall very well four of the criteria we applied in approving courses and selecting readings for women's studies. A central focus on women (and later gender) stood as the primary criterion that could not be violated, since the major rationale for women's studies was bringing women into curriculum and research from which they had previously been overlooked or excluded. The focus on women led relatively easily to the other criteria such as development of courses, research questions, and materials on new and controversial subjects not traditionally part of academic research and curricula. For example, little research and almost no courses on sexuality, including lesbianism, rape, domestic violence, and menopause existed before women's studies. Interdisciplinary approaches became significant since the approaches and theories of one discipline proved inadequate to understand these complex topics involving biology, psychology, sociology and culture. Because women's experience and activism had proved central in understanding these subjects and in making a place for them in the curriculum, activism and experience were valued along with theory, in women's studies.

Interdisciplinary Views on Abortion exemplifies these four criteria:

Focus on women: With the topic of abortion, one might assume that the focus would always be directly on women. As several authors, and particularly Aimee Shouse point out, much of the debate on abortion centers on the fetus, the rights of the father, or the rights of the state to control the process. This volume seeks to bring the focus back to women and abortion.

Controversial topic excluded from the curriculum: No one wants to have an abortion. After the Civil War in the U.S., most states passed laws overturning the traditional right of girls and women to abort during the first trimester of pregnancy. These laws passed in the late 19th C. allowed licensed physicians only to perform abortions when the pregnant woman's life was in danger, due to a medical condition. Until about 1950, most hospitals performed legal abortions frequently and routinely for a number of medical conditions, including severe psychiatric disorders. Beginning in the 1950s and extending until Roe v. Wade made abortion legal in all states in the U.S. in 1973, medical-technological advances and improvements in obstetrics divided the medical profession over abortions. Thinking of pregnancy as an added burden that women with certain diseases and mental conditions could not withstand became more difficult as improvements in technology and medicine decreased the situations in which the pregnant woman's life was clearly in danger. Abortion rates in the 1950s and 1960s decreased significantly over the rates earlier in the 20th C. (Solinger, 1993). The legalization of abortion in 1973 in Roe v Wade, reaffirmed by the Supreme Court decision on Casey in 1992, made abortion, with some restrictions, likely to be legal for the foreseeable future. As Polly Radosh documents, in recent years the number of abortions has decreased significantly under the Bush administrations by difficulties with access to abortion. Currently many obstetrician gynecologists are not trained to perform the procedure in medical schools.

As Susan A. Martinelli-Fernandez and Lori Baker-Sperry underline in the Introduction, an impetus for the volume came from the fact that no interdisciplinary text on abortion existed. The current politicization and controversy surrounding abortion in the United States has led to a dearth of research, courses, and even discussion about abortion in educational institutions. This dearth does not mean that women do not have abortions, it simply means that they have less information before the procedure, have little knowledge of the experience of other women who have had abortions in similar or very different circumstances from theirs, and as Heather McIlvaine-Newsad reveals, possess scant knowledge of how other cultures and countries view abortion. *Interdisciplinary Views on Abortion* helps to fill this dearth by providing a tremendous resource of information and viewpoints on abortion based on research and on women's experiences in both the United States and other countries.

Interdisciplinarity: As the controversy surrounding abortion demonstrates, abortion is more than a medical procedure in the United States. As it had in the first wave of feminism, a force motivating the wave of feminism begun in the 1960s was women's health concerns. Women sought the right to control their own bodies through access to safe birth control, abortion, and information about their physiology and anatomy, to define their own experiences as a valid aspect of their health needs, and to question the androcentric bias found in the hierarchy of the male-dominated health care system and its approach to research and practice.

The interdisciplinary nature of most issues in women's health and disease formed the *raison d'être* for health care professionals and researchers from diverse specialties, professions, and disciplines to interact. They recognized that the traditional territory of obstetrics/gynecology failed to include much of women's health beyond the defined limits of reproductive issues, and they expanded women's health to include differences in frequency, symptoms, and effects of diseases found in both sexes. The expanded definition also requires linkages with researchers in liberal arts to understand women's health. Behavioral and social sciences, particularly psychology, sociology, anthropology, and women's studies, provided basic research theories for domestic violence, eating disorders, and sexual and/or physical abuse, now recognized as central to women's health. These interdisciplinary approaches need to be expanded further to include theology, philosophy, political science, and cultural studies when considering abortion.

Fusion of activism with theory: Activist individuals, encouraged partially by the women's movement in the late 1960s, brought legal challenges, including class action suits, against medical schools which had quotas on the numbers of women, as well as racial and ethnic minority men, admitted. Their legal challenge of the quota system stood as one of the first of many critiques women presented to the medical profession. Women activists can claim responsibility for initiating a demographic shift within the medical profession that increased the percentage of women medical school graduates from about 7 percent in the mid–1960s to almost 50 percent today.

Much of the impetus for women's health arose from community activists in the women's movement in the 1960s. In 1970 the U.S. Senate held hearings on the contraceptive pill, organized in response to Barbara Seaman's 1969 Book, *The Doctor's Case Against the Pill*. In 1972, Belita Cowan created *Herself,* the leading newspaper of feminist health, and Phyllis Chesler wrote *Women and Madness*, critiquing sexism in the mental health system. These individuals, along with Mary Howell, the first female dean at Harvard Medical School and author of *Why Would a Girl Go into Medicine?* became founding members of the National Women's Health Network in 1975 in Washington, D.C. (Pearson and Seaman, 1998). Consumer, community-based organizations such as the National Women's Health Network (NWHN), the National Breast Cancer Coalition (NBCC), and the Boston Women's Health Book Collective (BWHBC) remain very active today.

Women's health activists had proven key in the lead-up to Roe v Wade in getting over-turned the century of criminalization of abortion that existed from the late 19th Century when the American Medical Association (AMA) successfully introduced statutes in all states by 1880 criminalizing abortion unless performed by a "regular" doctor in a hospital. Some of these health activists had set up underground networks that helped the estimated 1.2 million women who sought "illegal" abortions each year before Roe v Wade (Hunt and Joffe, 1994) to obtain safer abortions or aid women needing medical attention from botched abortions.

The editors and contributors to *Interdisciplinary Views on Abortion* have taken an activist approach to this controversial topic of abortion, using a variety of disciplinary lenses to re-focus the attention back on women and abortion. The scholarly community in general, and women's studies in particular, owes them a debt of gratitude for creating this invaluable text that exemplifies the best of women's studies criteria.

References

Hunt, Jean, and Carole Joffe. (1994). "Problems and Prospects of Contemporary Abortion Provision." In Alice Dan (Ed). *Reframing Women's Health: Multidisciplinary Research and Practice*. Thousand Oaks, CA: Sage Publications.

Pearson, Cynthia, and Barbara Seaman. (1998). "When Were We Founded? And Just What Were We Doing Back Then Anyway?" *The Network News 3*.

Solinger, Rickie. (1992). "Race and 'Value': Black and White Illegitimate Babies, in the U.S.A., 1945–1965" *Gender & History 4*.

Introduction

SUSAN A. MARTINELLI-FERNANDEZ
and LORI BAKER-SPERRY

This book is the product of a semester-long course on abortion offered in the women's studies program at Western Illinois University. The genesis of this course can be traced to a desire for a new, exciting course for students and a forum for women's studies faculty to share ideas, expertise, and concerns in the areas of feminist research and feminist pedagogy. We determined that the "perfect" venue would be a semester long seminar on a topic of particular interest to feminist and women's studies faculty and students alike. Various faculty members who have taught in the women's studies program were contacted to contribute a lecture and assume responsibility for a particular class session. Additionally, a new faculty member was chosen to coordinate the course readings and its activities. Because there was no interdisciplinary text available on the topic, each faculty member participating in the seminar compiled information pertaining to her discipline on recent research on abortion, with an eye to some theoretical issues addressed by various disciplines such as embodiment, autonomy, rights, and oppositional ways of carving out intellectual and personal positions on the issue of the permissibility of abortion. The information compiled became the basis for this book.

Hence, this collection of essays is offered to provide an in-depth summary of some of the issues that arise when considering the topic of abortion itself. In addition, some essays reflect original research and theoretical approaches. Only the issue of abortion is covered in this text, although it is situated within a wider understanding of the impact of reproduction on women's lives as well as on the lives of those who they hold dear. The objectives of this book are threefold: (1) To trace issues surrounding abortion and abortion practices in the United States through the lens of multiple disciplines; (2) to provide a readable and accessible summary of the recent research on this topic and (3) to offer additional insight into the issue of abortion through scholarship generated as a result of preparation for the course. The interdisciplinary nature of this book parallels the interdisciplinary nature of feminist and women's studies, for it provides the reader with a variety of disciplinary approaches, which together contribute to a broader and deeper understanding of the complexity of the general issue of abortion. Also, many of the articles include personal reflections on the challenges of striking and maintaining a balance between personal and professional attitudes, beliefs and commitments.

In this text, the authors represent different academic disciplines including sociology, anthropology, philosophy, community health and health services management, counseling, biology/theology and political science. The first three essays, offering sociological, medical, and political perspectives set forth theoretical issues as well as provide a general overview of the origin and evolution of the abortion debate. McIlvaine-Newsad's anthropological essay on women's views on abortion and family planning in rural Illinois serves as a bridge to the remaining essays, providing a turn from theory to academic practices that utilize as well as reflect upon that theory.

Several of the essays included in this volume can be understood as providing the "facts" of abortion. These include Radosh's "Abortion: A Sociological Perspective," Fischer and Goff's "Health and Medical Aspects of Abortion," and Shouse's "The Many Faces of U.S. Abortion Policy: How Government Structure Results in Multiple Policies." Presenting the origins of the American abortion debate, Polly Radosh discusses the sociological factors that affected the late 20th century shift in the central issues of the debate. In addition, this essay covers contemporary debates over abortion and discusses the downward trend in the number of abortions performed each year. As a feminist sociologist, Radosh provides an historical evaluation of the social acceptability of abortion. Her argument traces the ways that the male medical model (American Medical Association) co-opted the practice of abortion for a number of reasons, not the least being a right to control/dictate women's bodies, experiences, and autonomy. In a patriarchal society, this is implicitly understood as an unquestioned natural right of many men.

Kathy Fischer's and Sarah R. Goff's essay, "Health and Medical Aspects of Abortion," provides an overview of the various abortion methods from a health and medical perspective. Both medical and surgical abortion methods are addressed, including specific health risks for each method. Special emphasis is placed on the recent increased availability of early medical abortion methods. A brief description of emergency contraception is provided for the purpose of distinguishing it from medical abortion. Predictions are then made regarding the implications of the increased availability of medical abortion and emergency contraception for the patient and the provider.

Fischer and Goff also emphasize the importance of questioning current physician-guided care and illustrate the need for an understanding of occurrence rates and clinical procedure. Partial-birth abortion is an example of a "poster issue" with little statistical support, masking the reality of abortion procedures in the construction of abortion as common practice of unlawful death and not an issue of female control.

In "The Many Faces of U.S. Abortion Policy: How Government Structure Results in Multiple Policies," Aimee D. Shouse evaluates the strategies of pro-choice and pro-life interest groups as they try to influence the political policy at the state and national levels. Using online legislative databases, the author provides examples of state and national laws related to abortion and discusses why pro-life and pro-choice groups might focus their efforts at different levels and branches of government.

Shouse's essay on the construction of the political debate today highlights the social and public nature of the abortion debate and the communal contestation of legal abortion. Understanding the impact of groups involved, and the ways that they contribute to shaping and defining the debate, is imperative. Furthermore, a description of the policies and practices that influence lawmakers is especially important in light of female access to political process.

Moving from "facts" to testing theoretical assumptions, Heather McIlvaine-Newsad's "Hidden in Plain View: An Overview of Abortion in Rural Illinois and Around the Globe" draws upon first-hand anthropological research to examine women's views on abortion and family planning in rural Illinois. Her inquiry begins with the premise that anthropologists believe that both biological evolution and culture have shaped perspectives on and practices relating to reproductive issues. Her evaluation of the issue of experiences of rural women illustrates the importance of evaluating race, class, and gender in the abortion system. Her studies give rise to and address various questions: How do the female voices of McIlvaine-Newsad's research indicate the extent to which the issue of abortion is cultural, while patriarchy (literally

9

the "rule of the fathers") is alive and well in all known cultural systems? Are certain issues, even past the larger problem of inaccessibility, coloring rural women's choice to exercise a right? Whose voices can be determined to resonate with theirs or in their interests? And, simultaneously, whose voices can be determined to influence their actions? McIlvaine-Newsad argues that to understand the motivations of and reasons why women have or do not have abortions based on a seeming dichotomy and an oppositional categorization such as pro-life or pro-choice is unhelpful. Rather, the choice whether to have an abortion is more meaningfully understood by reflecting on women at various points in their lives and the concomitant desires, challenges and goals of those times.

As a Kantian, feminist, and reconstructionist, Susan A. Martinelli-Fernandez finds a middle ground between notions of autonomy, freedom, care, other-regardingness, and respect for human as well as non-human nature. By demonstrating how Kantian moral obligations arise out of particular relationships, she demonstrates how typical objections of abstraction, impartiality and universality might be blocked using the example of terminal selection. In so doing, she shifts the discussion from a rights-based discussion to one where relational elements are considered.

Althea K. Alton's essay on the biological and theological concerns related to abortion is a clear break to the more traditional considerations of the abortion question. Multiple theoretical elements and evaluation of key concepts such as human, person, life, death, and authority are framed by the author's perspective as both a biologist and a theologian. Her discussion of the mind/body dualism of Western thought mirrors the tension between her own dual academic perspectives. A theology of embodiment may be seen as a possible way to negotiate competing religious and scientific evaluations of pregnancy and abortion within a feminist framework.

Focusing on the constructed nature of abortion in a social context, Lori Baker-Sperry addresses the complexity of U.S. abortion debate today by examining the degree to which the popular text turned film *The Cider House Rules* reflects the current social ethos surrounding abortion and reproduction. Baker-Sperry uses this text in her college classroom, and argues that *The Cider House Rules* is a litmus for the social opinion and normative beliefs about abortion today. The author identifies themes in the text (pro-choice as status quo, sin and penitence, pro-life perspective, the public fetus, how the individual scenario sways opinion, and the business of abortion) that support the argument that abortion is a complex and contentious topic. Baker-Sperry argues that, even given multiple perspectives, abortion is always brought to level of the personal story, and that story has the most power to influence the individual belief or opinion on the subject. This is well-illustrated in the text *The Cider House Rules*.

Gayla Elliott's essay presents a feminist case study focusing on an abortion that was psychologically problematic for one woman, and how these issues were helped or alleviated through counseling. Elliott argues that a counselor must be open to evaluating the contributing factors in a given situation, some individual and some social, and that, while many women do not experience psychological distress after abortion, the experience of abortion is individual and must be treated as such. Elliot finds, in this case, that the lack of power and control over life in general and reproductive health, specifically, strongly influences one woman's experience of abortion.

Through the lens of Elliot's case study, we see that the notion of choice is itself challenged, given the realities of physical and psychological limits. How we understand choice is instrumental not only in understanding reproductive and abortion issues; this understanding is key in determining whether women are, in fact, free and equal members of social, political, and moral communities.

The essay entitled "Pedagogical Considerations for an Interdisciplinary Course on Abortion" by Baker-Sperry describes the process of producing and delivering a feminist course on abortion through the lens of many fields including sociology, political science, philosophy, and community health. With no appropriate composite reader available for the course, the individuals presenting adopted essays and combined readings with materials collected on the topic to present a thorough exploration to the students. This book is a result of the work begun in that interdisciplinary course on abortion.

In the concluding essay, McIlvaine-Newsad also reflects on the process of creating an interdisciplinary text on abortion and considers the common themes in these varied essays. Additionally, she addresses the need for a reader of this scope and reiterates the arguments for the current study of abortion. McIlvaine-Newsad closes by reviewing each essay through the unique lens of an anthropologist's perspective.

In the next section of the introduction, Martinelli-Fernandez and Baker-Sperry reconstruct initial conversations with each other about the purpose of this reader, and each particular essay One defining component of such conversations is each editor's disciplinary point of view; therefore each speaks in her own voice, as philosopher and sociologist, as well as individual women with a myriad of different experiences, personally and professionally.

A Philosopher's Story (Susan A. Martinelli-Fernandez)

Many people believe that a woman's political right to choose to have an abortion is unquestionable. Yet, in reality, the "right" to an abortion is restricted. This right to choose to have an abortion is grounded in the 14th amendment, which involves a right to privacy. Looking at the history of the legal permissibility of abortion in Roe v. Wade (1973) and Planned Parenthood of Central Missouri v. Danforth (1976), we see that a woman can fully exercise her right to choose only in the first trimester of a pregnancy. In the second trimester, the State has paternalistic supervision and in the third trimester, the State can interfere as parenspatrial (of the fetus). This suggests, from a political point of view, a woman does not have the full rights of a citizen to freely determine the course of her life. From a moral point of view, the woman is not seen as a full-fledged moral agent, who is responsible for her own decisions and leading her own life.

I start this introductory conversation with an emphasis on the difference between political and moral points of view because these perspectives are too often conflated. Given this potential for conflation, readers need to be aware of their own predisposition toward the topic of abortion and reproductive issues. Further, while some of the essays might be read as making specific normative recommendations, the purpose of each essay is to contribute to a scholarly discussion about the immense complexity of trying to discuss this topic. The topic of abortion is not tidy; it is messy. Yet, in their very messiness, abortion and reproductive issues allow us to explore underlying attitudes about who we are and what we hold valuable as individual women, as members of various relationships, as human beings, and as fellow citizens.

My own essay, "Abortion, Polyphonic Narratives and Kantianism: Quality of Life Matters," attempts to isolate the moral problem embedded in personal decisions about the desirability of abortion from the political one. Rights-focused discussions about the permissibility of abortion seem to con-

tribute little to the moral deliberations of women deciding whether to preserve or terminate a pregnancy. This is especially troublesome given that
modern advances in reproductive technology often result in pregnancies
involving multiple embryos.

Further, the idea of using abortion techniques to preserve a pregnancy
helps us appreciate the paucity of talking about rights (generally understood
as legal), when considering the morality and moral implications of abortion.
Two initial arguments are advanced. First: I suggest that quality of life is
more morally relevant than rights-based considerations, when looking at the
issue of abortion from an interested individual point of view. Second: I
demonstrate how quality of life may be subsumed under the broader concept of autonomy, understood as a Kantian moral concept. Specifically, I
hope to show how the second formulation of the Categorical Imperative and
its demand for people to treat each other as ends-in-themselves presuppose
a "relational" autonomy that requires respect for individuals' quality of life.
By integrating the concept of a polyphonic narrative with a deeper understanding of Kantian autonomy and respect for quality of life, I suggest that
a feminist Kantian perspective can be constructed. If my arguments are successful, both Kantian and feminist theory will be strengthened.

A Sociologist's Story (Lori Baker-Sperry)

I was professor of record for the interdisciplinary course on abortion
offered in the Women's Studies program. As a junior faculty member at the
inception of this book, a sociologist, and a professor of women's studies, what
is my addition to a clearer understanding of the issue of abortion in the U.S.?
There is the tendency for many to think that all recently trained young feminists are third wave. I am not sure that is what I bring to the table, although
I am certainly concerned with problems of essentialism in feminist study,
generalizing about the intrinsic, essential "nature" of women as shared by all
women. Essential nature defines and determines the person, which, in the
case of a pregnant woman has strong bearing on individual autonomy. These
shared essential characteristics are static, unchanging, and ahistorical and the
assumption of sameness across women is problematic in general, and
specifically in terms of reproduction, pregnancy, and abortion. This perspective pervades the everyday construction of women, even in the face of clear

evidence that women may not demonstrate such essential qualities. Juxtaposed to this, environmentally constructed "characteristics" and/or expectations created by social, political, and economic forces define and describe the individual position in the social structure (Martinelli-Fernandez, 2000).

Although anti-essentialism does question long-standing views, and calls for a re-thinking of traditional categories of women, I am always surprised when a feminist older than myself (I was twenty-nine when the course ran) tends to expect very revisionist politics or, sometimes, the opposite (a nod to the "malaise of third wave feminists," the idea that we enjoy the benefits of first and second wave activism but do not carry the good fight ourselves). In fact, I often feel that I have one foot squarely in both second wave feminist ideology and the anti-essentialist politic of the third or "no " wave feminist movement, a position reflective of my training and personal experience.

My colleague and co-editor, Susan A. Martinelli-Fernandez (of "A Philosopher's Story"), has been teacher, mentor, and friend. Susan A. Martinelli-Fernandez and Polly F. Radosh, who initiated the abortion project, speak of their feminism as a journey, as developing with the years of teaching and scholarship. The co-editors and the contributors have formed relationships during the development of this book, as well. These relationships have provided opportunities to learn and to teach, to negotiate opinions and personal beliefs, and to explore the reflexive nature of feminist study and the individual experience. We hope similar experiences occur for readers. This process has also provided another new place for feminist unity across disciplines at our particular institution that will, hopefully, only strengthen and grow. At a more general level, the power of affiliation in a network of relationships is certainly one "feminist way."

We are interconnected, all of us in Western society, by certain notions about life, death, and morality. These are shifting notions, but ones born in a particular cultural climate which encourages us to think about issues, such as abortion, in particular ways. The connections between life and death are not just opposites (as often characterized); rather, they represent a struggle of regeneration and the continuity of a group. Life, death, and therefore abortion, do not happen in a vacuum. The text, *The Cider House Rules*, which I evaluate in my contributing essay, illustrates this point. Abortion is not simply the clinical termination of pregnancy. Pro-life, pro-choice, anti-choice, and the ever curious notion of an "anti-life" position — what do those terms mean, outside of the context of the social world? We construct our terms, name our terms, place value and meaning to those words only in the context of our lives with one another. Where the construct ends and begins again is certainly a philosophical question, but also a sociological one, in that histories change meaning. Historical time, the construction of our "social stories," and the lived experience of group (social) life must be examined to realize abortion as an issue dependent upon time and place. It is also very much a feminist question, in that defining the physiological pregnant body in relation to an historically situated male (standard) body is past and current practice, regardless of the particular form the construction of masculinity takes in any given period. In this way, women's and men's choices and rights and respective autonomy are historically defined, and socially created, as well as manifested in ways infused with meaning and value. But this does not occur in a powerless void and without the control of such. Sexuality, reproduction and the female body are cultural constructs based on power relations, not the natural, observable fact embodied by the essentialist view. Therefore a discussion of abortion is never appropriate without context, without an understanding of the value placed upon meaning through the lens of power and privilege.

In the concluding section of "Abortion, Polyphonic Narratives and Kantianism: Quality of Life Matters," Martinelli-Fernandez stresses the importance of voice by asking "Whose voice?" I would reiterate by asking "Whose construction of meaning is valued?" Who has the power to create meaning in the abortion debate? Do the voices speak truth? Are the statements representative of real women's experiences? Of the experiences of all involved? Or are we more comfortable with those voices that resonate with the status quo, those voices who do not ask that we step outside of our (sometimes pregnant) selves and evaluate the struggle — for that is what it is — that surrounds the relationship between the born and the unborn, between the bearer, the to-be-born, and those selves reflected at the heart of the discussion (sometimes a part of the woman/pregnancy, at other times not).

In my essay, "Orphans, Abortions, and the Public Fetus in *The Cider House Rules*," I explore the complex nature of abortion as it occurs in a text situated in the not so distant past where much has changed but much has remained the same. A close reading of *The Cider House Rules* encourages particular questions, such as "Do we vilify abortion for some women, in some places — both historical and geographical — and not others?" We speak for the rights of the unborn, the fathers, the mothers, and for those who do not wish to be a parent, as well, in our answers. We speak for and also as these individuals. When we speak, we must also consider whose story we tell. Much of the argument is not necessarily embodied in contemporary mainstream or academic evaluations of autonomy, human agency, and personal choice, but is, instead, enmeshed in the historical importance of control over the construction of the argument. The issue no longer becomes an understanding of intentional oppression for oppression's sake (to "keep women down"), but as a much more complex system of casting women into dichotomous roles. Therefore, we need to examine the historically situated, contextualized version of the truth illuminated by a feminist analysis of *The Cider House Rules*. Along these lines, my concern over abortion rights and the control of female sexuality is often difficult to address when evaluating at only the individual or only the social levels. How much of our individual motivation to preserve a pregnancy or seek abortion or information about abortion is influenced, even unconsciously or as a normative unspoken, by issues of rights and control? To evaluate abortion socially, medically, biologically, and politically, is an extremely valuable activity, one of the main reasons why an interdisciplinary perspective is important. Only then are we able to explore the systematic relationship between abortion and women's overall social rights.

One might find that focusing away from the individual is certainly an obvious reaction of a sociologist, seeing the social in the individual. Many might argue it is essentialism in sociological research rearing its head. My point in emphasizing the public nature of the abortion debate is not to start disciplinary wars. It is important to understand abortion as a public and a personal issue and as a topic in need of analysis and focus of study.

Martinelli-Fernandez outlines the importance of recognizing that women negotiate multiple issues when considering abortion as a personal option. She argues that this evaluation is not limited to a view formulated in the more traditional rights-based language of philosophy, but also encompasses an affiliative notion of responsibility (in particular, levels of responsibility and obligation) in which beneficence is defined as a form of obligation based upon a particular relationship or set of relationships. This leads her to an exploration of a polyphonic narrative to describe the multiple voices that influence the abortion decision. Using the unusual and illuminating example of multiple embryos to illustrate (test) the Kantian concept of autonomy, Martinelli-Fernandez demonstrates that an understanding based on a quality of life argument does not negate a more traditional notion of rights and autonomy, but instead expands that formulation to include a feminist understanding of an ethics of care and "relational autonomy."

In fact, the "multiple voices" of the polyphonic narrative are at odds, in some ways, with any hegemonic view of the normative constraints and beliefs on the issue of abortion and here is a struggle. Normatively, abortion is discussed in terms of right and wrong, for and against, as Shouse illustrates in her analysis of political interest groups and the rhetoric of the abortion debate. But, as Martinelli-Fernandez outlines, we often take many factors, including the desire of others, into account in an abortion decision. We might begin to sort the normative from the interactional influence of multiple voices as we consider McIlvaine-Newsad's essay on rural women in Illinois. Furthermore, there are currently connections to the understanding of individual considerations and social forces (Radosh) and the subtlety (and sometimes covert nature) of the normative expectation and its origins. Issues of access and the politics of the procedure(s) (Fischer and Goff) further inform the reader as to the tension between the normative arguments surrounding abortion and the real lived experience of pregnancy and/or the termination thereof. These are certainly resonated in Alton's piece focusing on the tensions between the biological and the theological perspectives on abortion. A follow-up to the more clinical and "objective" (an interesting term I use tongue-in-cheek given the authors of the medical and biological pieces were personally, a nurse and a theologian), is Elliott's piece from a counseling perspective, where the focus is the psychological health and well-being of the person, with biological arguments about when life begins and medical procedure firmly in the periphery.

As Martinelli-Fernandez previously notes, each essay works holistically to provide a picture of the issue of abortion in the U.S. as it has been discussed and is currently debated. The obvious importance of an interdisciplinary, theoretical, and substantive exploration of the topic of abortion cannot be over-stressed.

Abortion

A Sociological Perspective

POLLY F. RADOSH

Abstract

For most of the second half of the 20th century Americans debated the morality of abortion. After the 1973 legalization of abortion in the famous Roe v. Wade U.S. Supreme Court decision, the opponents to legal abortion became increasingly militant in their efforts to reduce the scope of this legal option or to roll back the decision through a Constitutional amendment. Militancy, demonstrations, blockades, bombings, and murder of abortion providers characterized the 1980s and 1990s as the rights and legal restrictions were debated and resolved in the late 20th century. Prior to the Roe v. Wade decision most of the advocacy for change had been on the side of the proponents of legal abortion. The issue of abortion remains an important political topic and one in which religious and moral values are hotly debated. The late 20th century furor over this issue is unusual in the long history of abortion, however, and may illustrate other more pertinent concerns associated with women's rights and emerging changes in gender expectations than about the actual practice of abortion.

Almost all societies have practiced abortion at some time, and in the U.S. abortions were relatively common and not punished or censured until the mid 19th century. The 19th century movement to criminalize the procedure centered not on the morality of the practice, but on who should perform the service. As the American Medical Association formalized the regulations for medical practice, services that had at one time been provided by unlicensed female providers, such as obstetrics (midwifery) and abortion were subsumed under the practice of medical doctors. The debate was not over whether abortions should be performed, but over control of the practice and procedures. Through the first half of the 20th century doctors and

19

hospitals performed abortions if approved by a therapeutic board. The debate did not begin to take on its present tenor until the 1960s, when it became more difficult for women to obtain approval for a variety of reasons.

This essay covers the origins of the American abortion debate. The sociological factors that affected the late 20th century shift in the central issues of the debate are discussed. In addition, this essay covers contemporary debates over abortion and discusses the downward trend in the number of abortions performed each year.

Nineteenth Century Changes in Abortion Practices

Abortion in the United States was not regulated until the mid part of the 19th century. Abortions were performed by midwives prior to organization of the American Medical Association (AMA) in 1847 (Luker, 1984). Midwives used herbs, such as ergot which is derived from a fungus on rye grain, tansy, pennyroyal, savin derived from juniper berries, or aloe, to induce abortion through contractions of the uterus (McGregor, 1998, p. 119; Dayton, 1991, p. 19). As in most cultures in the world, abortion was not considered to be a moral dilemma if the pregnant woman had not yet experienced "quickening," or become aware of movement of the fetus. Historically and across cultures, the moment of quickening, which occurs in the fourth or fifth month after conception, has been used as the method for determining pregnancy. Women's knowledge of their own bodies and acknowledgement of their pregnancies has been the measurement used most consistently when it was necessary to terminate a pregnancy. Common folklore in the early 19th century stressed that quickening indicated that the pregnancy as "alive." A late menstrual period prior to quickening was often referred to as a "blockage" which could be removed with herbs or manual manipulations by a midwife (Tone, 1997, p. 26). An 1812 Massachusetts court ruling affirmed that common law upheld a woman's right to abortion prior to quickening, as did common practice throughout the United States (Tone, 1997, p. 26). Abortion was a private matter and not subject to regulation, if performed shortly after a missed menstrual period.

Abortion was of little concern to most people prior to the organization and subsequent expansion of the AMA. The use of herbs to bring on a late menstrual period was quiet, personal, and not subject to debate until the

AMA began to try to prevent competitive practitioners from providing medical advice in the latter half of the 19th century. The AMA was organized primarily as a social club, with only about 100 members, in 1847. As late as 1900 they had only 8400 members (Weibe, 1967, p. 115). In 1859 the AMA approved a resolution condemning the practice of abortion (Luker, 1984, p. 191). This action initiated a shift in the abortion debate. Only 10 states had laws prohibiting abortion or limiting the herbs used as abortifacients prior to the AMA resolution (Tone, 1997, p. 138). These state laws reflected concern that women would be harmed by the herbal remedies, rather than with the moral question of abortion.

Professional medical practice in the United States emerged after the AMA began to advocate for higher standards of practice. Physicians in the 1850s had little scientific information upon which to build the practice of medicine. As the profession began to formalize one of the strategies employed by the AMA for improving public perception of physicians was to claim superior scientific knowledge. Physicians actually had little scientific knowledge and were often guided by superstition, religious belief, or ancient tradition. In fact, many physicians resisted new scientific theories or practices that challenged traditional methods. When the well-known 19th century physician, Charles Meigs, was presented with the theory of contagion, for example, he was insulted and refused to use the sanitary procedures that had been recommend by colleagues in European hospitals. He said:

> I have in numerous instances, gone from the bedside of women dying with childbed fever, whether sporadic, or to the most malignant degree epidemic, without making my patients sick.... I did not then, nor should I now, fear to be the medium of transmission.... I did not merit to be regarded as a private pestilence ... [Meigs, 1854, p. 103].

Meigs, like most physicians, advocated that education in medicine should rely on the apprentice system of practice under the guidance of an experienced practitioner. Until the discovery in 1860 of the bacillus that causes anthrax, medical practice was based upon the intuition of the practitioner and the folklore of treatment. Physicians had little evidence to differentiate diseases from symptoms (Friedson, 1970, p. 16). Educational requirements were minimal. Almost anyone with an elementary education could take a course of lectures, pass an exam, and become a doctor in the mid 19th century. In 1900 many medical schools admitted students who could not get into liberal arts colleges (Shryock, 1966, p. 152).

After Louis Pasteur's work on the anthrax virus, medical science and treatment techniques improved profoundly and medicine began to abandon folklore and rely on science as the foundation of practice. The issues of education, standards of practice, and maintaining dominion over the field of medicine dominated the foci of the AMA between 1880 and 1920. Not only was it necessary to improve the practice of medicine, but the public had to be convinced that doctors could do more for their patients than midwives, lay healers, herbalists, and other practitioners who had provided medical treatment that equaled or surpassed that provided by physicians at the time. As a result, much of the rhetorical reference to physicians in the late 19th century focused upon the superiority of their medical knowledge. By 1910 the AMA had increased its membership to 70,000, and to 60 percent of physicians by 1920 (Weibe, 1967, p. 115). The AMA was unified by goals that stressed educational requirements for all members, scientific research, superior medical care, and limited entry into the field of medicine. The practice of medicine was not as advanced as the rhetoric of the AMA and they fell short of the goal of "superior" medical treatment in many respects. Midwives, for example, lost fewer babies and had lower rates of maternal mortality than physicians through most of the early part of the 20th century, in spite of the fact that only European immigrant midwives were trained and most Americans had learned their trade through apprenticeship (Abbott, 1917, p. 147; Hardin, 1925, p. 347; Folks, 1902, p. 435). The AMA knew that physicians' care was equally as unskilled as lay practitioners, but the goal was to convince the public that physicians were superior:

> We can do very well without midwives, but physicians are indispensable. The sensible thing to do is eliminate midwives and educate physicians until they are capable of doing good obstetrics, and then make it financially possible for them to do it. Physicians cannot be properly trained in obstetrics, however, until they can have the work midwives are doing, since 75 percent of the clinical material otherwise available for teaching purposes now provides a livelihood for midwives [Ziegler, 1912, p. 1738].

> It will not get us anywhere to say that midwives do just as good work as the average doctor, which may be true. It should not be a question of the lesser of two evils. Neither is fit. We want something better, we want well trained doctors to attend women in confinement [Ziegler, 1922, p. 412].

The process of defining the profession of medicine required not only securing the venue of practice and eliminating competitors, but also convincing the public that physicians should make decisions regarding treatment. Time-honored practices had to be abandoned and old-world knowledge suppressed in favor of the new modern, scientific treatments offered by physicians. Decisions about treatment should not be left to women, whose lack of sophistication and ignorance of scientific knowledge could lead to disaster. Charles Meigs' description of women typified the condescension typical of the medical profession:

> [I]t is easy to perceive that her [women's] intellectual force is different from that of her master and lord.... She reigns in the heart; her seat and throne are by the hearthstone. The household altar is her place of worship and service.... Home is her place, except when like the star of day, she deigns to issue forth to the world upon all that are worthy to receive so rich a boon — and then she goes back to her home ... [Meigs, 1848, p. 40–42].

The AMA's resolution in 1859 to condemn abortion was part of a much larger effort to eliminate competitive practitioners, such as midwives, and to support the claim that only physicians could make decisions that had at one time been exclusively made by women. The goal was not to eliminate the practice of abortion, but to eliminate competition posed by the practitioners who provided abortions, and to secure this practice within the domain of obstetrical expertise provided by physicians. Much of the anti-abortion rhetoric of the late 19th and early 20th centuries focused upon the midwife as the source of morbidity and mortality among women who used such services. Death from abortion was targeted as a singular example of the inferiority of midwifery services. Midwifery would be abolished, by this reasoning, if the abortion services provided by midwives were illegal (Reagan 1997, p. 91). Elimination of midwifery would secure all obstetrical services, including abortion, for physicians.

Twentieth Century Changes in Abortion Practices

Through most of the first half of the 20th century abortions were available and provision of abortion services was neither a public issue nor a matter of medical controversy (Luker, 1984, p. 49). As long as the medical profession controlled the procedure, few people were concerned with the issue of abortion. In 1939 about two million abortions were performed, with about 1.7 million completed by physicians, 200,000 by midwives, and the remaining 100,000 performed by unknown practitioners (Tolnai, 1939, p. 425). A study completed by the New York Academy of Medicine found that most abortions were requested by married women with children. The fact that the most efficient birth control of the time had an effective rate of only 40 percent probably contributed to the fact that married mothers sought abortion more often than any other group of women. In the 1930s, abortion was illegal in most states, but fairly easily obtainable. If the mother's life or health were endangered by the pregnancy, physicians would perform an abortion. Six states had no prohibitions to abortion (Tolnai, 1939, p. 425).[1] Even illegal abortions, often performed in "abortion parlors," were rarely prosecuted. Penalties for death of a patient resulting from an illegal abortion ranged from one to twenty years in prison, depending upon state law. Prosecutions of physicians were very rare, however. Midwives were more likely to be prosecuted and punished than physicians, but even in cases of death, penalties were rare (Tolnai, 1939, p. 425).

In the 1930s concern over the number of women who died from illegal abortions was expressed in popular press publications and was denounced by the medical profession, but it appears that little was actually done to curtail illegal abortions. Legal abortion performed by a physician was also of little concern to the public or the medical profession. It was estimated in 1939 that about 10,000 women had died each year of the decade as a result of illegal abortions. The highest rates of fatality were among 35–39 year old women who had been pregnant six or seven times. Nearly all deaths from illegal abortion occurred among married women with three or more children (Tolnai 1939, p. 425).

Through the first half of the 20th century, women obtained most abortions from their physicians who determined whether it was necessary. Conditions that are treatable today, such as chronic vomiting, cardiac problems, diabetes, toxemia, or renal problems, would have presented more serious medical concern and very likely were used as a rationale for medically necessary abortions through the 1950s (Luker, 1984, p. 37). By the mid part of the century, however, treatment of these conditions was more advanced and presented less reasonable justification for an abortion. In addition, another trend in medical care that had emerged throughout the first half of the 20th century had become the norm. In the early part of the century, most medical care occurred in the home of the patient. Only five percent of all births occurred in hospitals in 1900, for example. By 1930, close to one-third of births occurred in hospitals, but after World War II, most births had been moved to hospitals. The same was true of many other medical procedures. Abortions that were performed on the kitchen table of the woman's home in the early part of the century were gradually shifted to the physician's office or clinic by the 1930s, and then to hospitals in the 1950s (Luker, 1984, p. 654–56). Oversight by hospitals opened up the discretionary decisions of physicians that had previously been private. Review boards were established in the 1950s to determine the medical necessity of abortion (Luker, 1984, p. 58; *Time,* 1962, p. 52).

By the early 1960s, the number of legal abortions had dropped precipitously and hospital review boards had become increasingly strict in application of criteria that dictated medical necessity. Some hospitals used a quota system, so that abortions would be denied if the quota for the month had already been reached; others used a criteria system with a checklist of medical reasons that had to be met prior to approval by the board; and others used a market system that approved abortions for well-connected, affluent patients, but denied poorer applicants with fewer resources (Luker, 1984, p. 57).

Other social factors also influenced a sharp decline in the number of abortions that were approved as medically necessary. Catholic opinion, which had voiced papal opposition to abortion as early as 1869, became more vocal. Catholic hospitals did not perform abortions, but articulation of Catholic opposition in the documents of the Second Vatican Council in 1965, statements by Pope John XXIII and by Pope Paul VI brought the opposition of the Catholic Church to public debate. An issue that had previously been characterized as a medical decision was transformed into a moral debate in the 1960s.

California was the first state to formalize in statute the particular modern standards to justify the procedure. Issues of physical and mental health of the mother, deformity in the fetus, and termination of a pregnancy that resulted from rape or incest were incorporated into California law in 1967 (Luker, 1984, p. 88). Abortion on demand was not approved, but the California law became the most liberal in the nation prior to the *Roe v. Wade* U.S. Supreme Court Decision in 1973.

After *Roe v. Wade,* abortion as a moral dilemma was increasingly debated in public and political discourse. Opposition to abortion has focused on the life that is not lived as a result of the terminated pregnancy, while proponents of abortion rights advocate the woman's absolute right to make decisions about her own body. Feminist critics of abortion opponents have pointed out that issues of control are still a central theme in the anti-abortion campaigns. Notification laws, waiting periods, mandated supply of information about consequences of the procedure, prohibition of discussion of abortion in federally funded facilities, and other recently legislated restrictions on abortion rights have been aimed at shifting control of the circumstances surrounding abortion services to those who would discourage abortion on moral grounds.

The *Roe v. Wade* decision opened a deep division between those who support abortion rights and those who oppose. The 1980s and 1990s were characterized by violent protests, bombings of abortion clinics, and murder of practitioners who provided abortion services. Militancy was most pronounced among those who opposed abortion on moral or religious grounds. Women who sought abortions and doctors who performed them were characterized as "killers." Public opinion polls since *Roe v. Wade* have indicated fairly consistent national attitudes about abortion, in spite of political positioning on the issue, however. In 1975, Gallup Polls indicated that 22 percent of the American population believed that abortion should never be legal, and 22 percent of Americans believed it should never be legal in 2005 (Pastore and Maguire, 2008). Similarly, support for abortion on demand, or under some circumstances, has remained at about 78 percent of the American population for 30 years.

Political opposition to abortion has been a lightening rod for right wing conservative and fundamentalist politicians since the mid 1970s. In spite of prevailing national attitudes that indicate the majority of Americans believe that abortion should be available, at least under certain circumstances, most states have moved to restrict access through regulation of services. One of the most important political moves to restrict abortion services was the Hyde Amendment, passed in 1978, which cut off Medicaid funds for abortion unless the mother's life was in danger or in cases of rape or incest. Medicaid funded abortions had dropped by 99 percent within 19 months of passage of the bill (Jaffe, Lindheim, and Lee, 1981, pp. 141–147). In 1977, prior to the Hyde Amendment, abortion rates for Medicaid recipients were three times higher than for more affluent women. Critics of the Hyde Amendment often point out that restriction of funding ultimately limits poor women's access to abortion services. Abortion has become, in other words, an option for the affluent.

In addition to the Hyde Amendment, a 1987 U.S. Department of Health and Human Services ruling, usually called the "gag rule," specified that family planning clinics which receive federal funds may not offer abortion counseling, or discuss abortion as an option in family planning in any way. While numerous court rulings have affirmed state control over abortion services, including parental consent laws, spousal notification, compulsory anti-abortion lectures, waiting periods, specific restrictions on the places where abortions are performed, and numerous additional limits, the gag rule stands out as second to the Hyde Amendment in significance in restricting poor women's access to abortion. The rule was in effect until lifted by President Bill Clinton in 1993. In 2001, President George W. Bush reinstated the gag rule as one of his first official acts in office.

Abortion as an Issue of Power

Prior to the formation of the AMA, decisions related to pregnancy and abortion were made primarily within the domain and control of women. Midwives and the pregnant women they served decided the best course of action within extant knowledge of pregnancy. Most people did not view what would currently be called a first trimester abortion as a significant moral issue. Common reference to menstrual abnormalities, dysfunctions, and "blockages" or "obstructions" in historical sources suggests that folklore dictated that women would be restored to balance if the obstruction was removed by herbal remedy. Most people in the 19th century believed that women were especially susceptible to uterine abnormalities that needed treatment. A woman's awareness of quickening indicated a real pregnancy. Some have estimated that between 20–35 percent of 19th century pregnancies were terminated as a means of restoring "menstrual regularity" (Luker, 1984, p. 18–21). About 20 percent of pregnancies were aborted as late as in the 1930s (Tolnai, 1939, p. 425).

With the previously discussed professionalization of medicine, control of abortion services shifted to the predominantly male medical profession, but was largely unregulated until the second half of the 20th century. While shifts in the place of medical treatment from home to office to hospital were influential in tightening control over abortion decisions, there were other pertinent cultural issues that were also influential. The fact that restriction in abortion availability coincides with the modern women's movement, or the second wave of feminism, is significant. Hospital boards in the 1950s approved abortion in most cases. In the 1960s the approval boards became more restrictive, prohibitive, and authoritative at the same time that women began to advocate for other reproductive rights. The 1965 Supreme Court ruling in Griswold v. Connecticut, for example, specified that state law prohibiting use of contraception violated constitutionally guaranteed rights to privacy.[2] Availability of birth control would, presumably, make abortion less necessary, but hospital boards were increasingly reluctant in the 1960s to give permission for abortion even in cases of fetal abnormality (*Time*, 1962a). Issues of morality had been raised by the Catholic Church, and critique of family organization and reproduction rights were a source of social and political debate as the public became more aware of the issues raised by women's rights groups.

As private decisions about reproduction were publicly debated and decided in courts, issues of morality in reproduction were also debated. Previously private decisions now became a matter of national concern. Moral questions about family planning were called into question by the sexual revolution, increased divorce rates, higher rates of single parenthood, challenges to traditional family structures, and ultimately by religious teachings about family. Those with traditional views of family and religion were often most vehemently opposed to increasing reproductive choices, which many believed to be the source of higher rates of divorce and pre-marital pregnancy.

As women advocated for more rights, advocacy for restriction of abortion services became more apparent among those who held tightly to traditional roles for women. The nearly all male medical profession, state legislatures, Congress, law professions, and clergy were undoubtedly threatened by women's increased advocacy for control over their own reproductive rights. Just as the medical profession of the 19th century wrestled control over childbirth and abortion from midwives, medical professionals and lawmakers in the 1960s fought to maintain decisions about abortion services within the domain of their professions. In both cases women lacked influence in the decision making process. Nineteenth century women lacked the right to vote and they were excluded from the AMA. Twentieth century women had almost no representation in the medical, legal, or legislative professions, nor among the clergy, as decisions about reproductive rights were debated in these venues.

Additionally, as women in the 1960s and 1970s advocated for opportunities to participate in many social and cultural activities that had previously been closed to them, resistance to changing social patterns was persistent. The effects of efforts to improve women's opportunities to participate in education, occupations, professions, and to achieve equal social status with men are well known as a cultural trend in the late 20th century. The backlash against women is not so well documented, however. Restriction of abortion services falls within the realm of this backlash and has become a struggle over power in reproductive decisions. Those who advocate most vehemently against abortion rights commonly hold highly traditional views about women's roles in society and in the family. Not surprisingly, those who advocate for abortion rights usually hold very liberal views about women's rights.

In the first year after the 1973 *Roe v. Wade* decision, there were over 50 bills introduced to restrict the right to abortion, and the onslaught of opposition to this legal option has not faltered since 1973 (Faludi, 1991, p. 412). Anti-abortion proponents since *Roe v. Wade* have characterized those who support abortion options as anti-family, radical feminist, baby killers who are destined to destroy the nation (Faludi, 1991, p. 411–413). The fact that abortions have been a normative solution to unplanned pregnancy for thousands of years is irrelevant in the present rhetorical assault on women's rights. To advocate for abortion choice was to advocate against the family in the post *Roe v. Wade* political polarization. Most leaders of the anti-abortion political movement have been men, including leaders of Operation Rescue, Focus on the Family, Americans United for Life, the Christian Coalition, Life Dynamics, Inc., the Pro-Life Action League, and the National Right to Life. In the words of Operation Rescue leader, Randy Terry:

> Radical feminism gave birth to child killing ... radical feminism, of course, has vowed to destroy the traditional family unit, hates motherhood, hates children for the most part, and promotes lesbian activity. [Margaret Sanger] was a whore, an adultress, and slept all over the place, all over the world, with all kinds of people [quoted in Faludi, 1991, p. 408].

Leaders of these organizations are often men who believe deeply that family life requires a divinely ordained system of patriarchy. Women who support these organizations also believe that women are biblically required to serve men in marriage and that abortion not only interrupts a divinely ordained order, but also challenges the God-man-woman hierarchy. Certainly there are those who oppose abortion rights exclusively on the basis of moral values about the origins or meaning of life, but those who have been most vocal, militant, and widely publicized have espoused feminist critique of patriarchy as immoral and abortion rights as the symbol of feminism.

Issues of power still dominate the abortion debate; only the domain of power has shifted. Those who advocate for abortion rights still maintain that the power to choose whether to parent should rest with women who must bear the physical responsibility of reproduction. Those who advocate against abortion rights are no longer only those who want to control the procedure, but now also include those who want to control women's lives and options. The 19th and early 20th century debates concerned who should provide services; the current debate focuses upon who should control women's lives. Those who advocate against abortion rights often believe in traditional restrictions on women's opportunities. To affirm abortion is, symbolically, to affirm social, economic, political, and reproductive choice, which is usually incompatible with the values and beliefs of those who oppose abortion rights. While moral issues related to life, conception, and divine intervention in the initiation of life are at the forefront of anti-abortion arguments, the moral issues in the second tier of the debate generally return to social, political, and reproductive freedoms for women, which threaten traditional views.

Current Trends in Abortion

Since *Roe v. Wade*, the courts have continued to affirm women's rights to abortion, but also to allow states to limit or restrict access on a variety of grounds, as previously discussed. The current climate, under appointments made by President George W. Bush, is for increased restrictions. His reinstatement of the gag rule on his first day in office, January 22, 2001, foreshadowed subsequent appointments to federal office that worked to reduce access to abortion and contraceptive services for American women. President Bush's removal of contraceptive coverage for federal employees from his first federal budget (2001), and subsequent appointment of "abstinence only" proponents to key public health offices and international agencies, such as the Office of Health and Human Services, the United Nation's Children's Summit, and the State Department Bureau of Population, indicate ongoing administrative efforts to roll back access to abortion and contraceptive services. Among the most important actions of the Bush administration has been support of legislative initiatives to redefine the meaning of "fetus," such as those in the Children's Health Insurance Program (CHIP), the Unborn Victims of Violence Act (2001) and the Child Custody Protection Act (2002), which assign particular rights to "unborn" children (Planned Parenthood, 2003). Proponents of abortion rights believe that separate administrative and legislative actions that assign rights to the unborn will eventually be used *in totem* as a mechanism for overturning *Roe v. Wade.*

The rate of abortions in the United States has been declining for several years. In 2005 it reached its lowest level since 1974, at 19.4 abortions for every 1000 women aged 15–44, or about 1.2 million abortions (Guttenmacher Institute, 2008; *New York Times*, 2008). Over 95 percent of abortions are performed in the first trimester of the pregnancy. The majority of women who have abortions are white (70 percent), not married (60 percent), and about half already have children (Planned Parenthood, 2003). Reasons for the decline are mixed. Some believe that increased effectiveness and better access to contraceptives may decrease the need for abortions. As some states have expanded family planning services under Medicaid, abortions have declined, which suggests that when women have better access to birth control they are less likely to need abortion as an alternative family planning method (Reuters, 2003). Proponents of restricted access to abortion believe that increased obstacles to attaining abortion have discouraged women from using this option, which encourages further efforts to restrict abortion alternatives.

Conclusion

Abortion rights issues have taken on their current format only since the 1973 legalization of abortion in the *Roe v. Wade* decision. Ironically, abortion is probably less accessible today than it was two hundred years ago, when removal of "blockages" were routinely accomplished by herbal remedies. Modern birth control makes the need for abortion less urgent as a family planning tool, but even modern birth control is not always available, reliable, or accessible. Unplanned pregnancies and the responsibility of women to endure the physical consequences are still very real. Issues of power and control have remained central to the abortion debate for 150 years.

While death from illegal abortion has been problematic for American women for over 100 years, the majority of abortions performed in the United States prior to the 1950s were legal. The availability of legal abortion became increasingly restrictive between the late 1940s and *Roe v. Wade* in 1973. While legalization in 1973 may have solved the issue of an absolute right, efforts to control this right began immediately after the decision, and have continued since the 1973. Fundamental issues include not only the problem of access to abortion, but also definitions of women as independent, autonomous agents. Efforts to control abortion are frequently tied to attempts to limit women's rights to act independently in other areas of modern life. As is evident from much of the anti-abortion rhetoric, abortion is not only a matter of reproductive choice, but also a symbolic point of departure from traditional gender roles.

Notes

1. Florida, Louisiana, Massachusetts, New Hampshire, Pennsylvania, New Jersey.
2. Griswold v. Connecticut 381 U.S. 479 (1965).

References

Abbott, G. (1917). *The Immigrant and the Community.* New York: Century.

Dayton, C. H. (1991). Taking the Trade: Abortion and Gender Relations in an Eighteenth-Century New England Village. *William and Mary Quarterly,* 3d Ser. 48 (1), 19–28, 40–49.

Faludi, S. (1991). *Backlash: The Undeclared War Against American Women.* New York: Anchor.

Folks, R. (1902). Obstetrics in the tenements. *Charities and the Commons,* 9 (18), 429–438.

Friedson, E. (1970). *Professional dominance: The Social Structure of Medical Care.* New York: Atherton.

Guttenmacher Institute (2008). Facts on Induced Abortion in the United States. http://www.guttmacher.org/pubs/fb_induced_abortion.html (June 18, 2008).

Hardin, E. R. (1925). The Midwife Problem. *Southern Medical Journal,* 18 (5), 347–350.

Luker, K. (1984). *Abortion and the Politics of Motherhood.* Berkeley: University of California Press.

Jaffe, F. S., B. L. Lindheim, and P. R. Lee (1981). *Abortion Politics: Private Morality and Public Policy.* New York: McGraw-Hill.

McGregor, D. K. (1998). *From Midwives to Medicine: The Birth of American Gynecology.* New Brunswick, NJ: Rutgers University.

Meigs, C. (1854). *On the Nature, Signs and Treatment of Childbed Fever.* Philadelphia: Lea and Blanchard.

New York Times (2008, January 26). Editorial: Behind the Abortion Decline. http://www.nytimes.com/2008/01/26/opinion/26sat2.html (June 23, 2008).

Pastore, A. L., and K. Maguire (2008). *Sourcebook of Criminal Justice Statistics.* Washington, DC: U. S. Government Printing Office, Table 2.100.2005. http://www.albany.edu/sourcebook/index.html (June 23, 2008).

Planned Parenthood (2003) http://www.plannedparenthood.org/library/facts/030114 (June 9, 2003).

Reagan, L. J. (1997). *When Abortion Was a Crime: Women, Medicine, and Law in the United States 1867–1973.* Berkeley: University of California Press.

Reuters (2003, January 15). "Abortion Rate Down but Abortion Pill More Popular," *Perspective on Sexual and Reproductive Health,* 35, 6–15.

Shryock, R. H. (1966). *Medicine in America, Historical Essays.* Baltimore: Johns Hopkins.

Time (1962, July 13). Abortion and the Law. 80, 52–53.

Time (1962a, August 3). Abortion and the Law. 80, 30.

Tolnai, B. B. (1939). Abortions and the Law. *Nation,* 148 (April 15), 424–427.

Tone, A. (1997). *Controlling Reproduction: An American History.* Wilmington, DE: SR Books.

Weibe, R. (1967). *The Search for Order, 1877–1920.* New York: Hill and Wang.

Zeigler, C. E. (1912). Elimination of the Midwife, Proceedings of the American Association of the Study and Prevention of Infant Mortality. *Journal of the American Medical Association,* 59 (9), 1738.

Ziegler, C. E. (1922). How Can We Solve the Midwifery Problem? *American Journal of Public Health,* 12 (5), 405–413.

Health and Medical Aspects of Abortion

KATHY FISCHER *and* SARAH R. GOFF

Abstract

This essay provides an overview of abortion from a health and medical perspective. First, a brief overview of fetal development is presented. Next, both medical and surgical abortion methods are described, including specific health risks for each method. Special emphasis is placed on the recent availability of early medical abortion methods. A brief description of emergency contraception (EC) is also provided for the purpose of distinguishing it from medical abortion. In addition, predictions are made regarding the implications of the increased availability of medical abortion and emergency contraception.

The 1973 *Roe v. Wade* Supreme Court decision reaffirmed a woman's right to privacy under the ninth and fourteenth amendments, and protected a woman's right to seek a safe and legal abortion in the United States (Pichler & Golab, 2007). Not only did the legalization of abortion provide women with the freedom to seek abortion services from trained physicians in safe and sterile environments, but also it virtually ended the back alley botched abortion horrors of the past. Since the 1973 ruling, however, pro-choice and pro-life advocates have vehemently clashed on many issues regarding abortion, including a woman's right to control her body, the morality of abortion in early and late stages of pregnancy, fetal rights, and controversial legislation such as parental notification and consent laws, waiting periods, and federal funding restrictions. As a result, the disputes over abortion and the politics surrounding the debate are far from resolved (Kolander, Ballard, & Chandler, 2008; Pichler & Golab, 2007).

Approximately one-half of pregnancies in the U.S. are unintended, and over 40 percent of these pregnancies are terminated by abortion each year. Of the women who obtained abortions in 2002, the majority were either Black or Hispanic, younger than 25, and identified themselves as never-married. Women living below the federal poverty level were more than 4 times as likely to have an abortion as women above 300 percent of the poverty level (Guttmacher Institute, 2006). Facing an unintended pregnancy can be an overwhelming and even devastating event in a woman's life regardless of her race, age, marital status, religion, or financial circumstances. Not only must a woman deal with the initial shock of acknowledging her pregnancy, but also she must face the often difficult decision of whether to become a parent, choose adoption, or have an abortion. For some, the word "abortion" can evoke fearful images of pre–Roe back-alley butchers, septic infections, and uncontrollable bleeding. It is essential that women who elect to have an abortion be provided with accurate information regarding the various abortion procedures, possible complications, and aftercare instructions. Accurate and unbiased information dispels myths and eases concerns regarding the safety of abortion, as well as promoting an empowering — rather than shameful — abortion experience.

This essay provides an overview of abortion from a health and medical perspective. First, a brief overview of fetal development is presented. Next, both medical and surgical abortion methods are described, including specific health risks for each method. Special emphasis is placed on the recent availability of early medical abortion methods. A brief description of emergency contraception (EC) is also provided for the purpose of distinguishing it from medical abortion. In addition, predictions are made regarding the implications of the increased availability of medical abortion and emergency contraception.

Overview of Fetal Development

This brief overview of fetal development is provided strictly from a health and medical perspective. Ethical and spiritual aspects of abortion will be discussed elsewhere in this book.

The entire duration of a pregnancy, from implantation to birth, is 266 days or 38 weeks — although up to 40 weeks gestation is common. The gestational period is divided into three phases called trimesters, consisting of approximately 3 months each (Alexander, LaRosa, Bader, & Garfield, 2007).

Once fertilization of the egg by the sperm occurs, it takes 3–5 days to travel from the fallopian tube to the uterus. When the cluster of cells reaches the uterus to implant itself, its size is smaller than the head of a pin. Once implantation occurs, it becomes known as an embryo. The amniotic sac soon develops and envelopes the embryo. Amniotic fluid provides protection from shock and bumps, and helps maintain homeostasis. The placenta soon forms, supplying the embryo with nutrients and oxygen and ridding it of waste products. During the first month, the embryo grows to about ½ ounce in weight. By the end of the 8th week, the embryo becomes known as a fetus and weighs about ⅙ ounce. By 12 weeks gestation, the sex of the fetus can be determined, the heart beats, and the kidneys begin producing urine. By 14 weeks gestation, bones have developed, the head and extremities are formed, and the major organ and nervous system are formed. The fetus now weighs just over 1 ounce (Alexander et al., 2007; Kolander et al., 2008).

During the second trimester, fetal growth becomes much more rapid. Beginning with the 4th month, the mother can feel fetal movements and heart sounds can be monitored with external instruments. During the 5th month, detailed formation of bodily structures (e.g., eyebrows and fingernails) occurs and the fetus now weighs between .75 and 1.4 pounds. By the end of the 6th month, the fetus kicks and turns over, has wake and sleep cycles, and has a developed sense of hearing. It is between 10 and 11.5 inches long and weighs about 2.1 pounds. If the fetus is born during the 6th month, survival is possible if intensive neonatal care is provided (Alexander et al., 2007; Kolander et al., 2008).

By the end of the 7th month, the fetus weighs between 2.5 and 3 pounds, and if it is born it is generally able to survive. Growth continues to occur at a rapid pace. By the end of the 8th month, it weighs between 4 and 5.5 pounds. Bones become harder and the skin has a wrinkled appearance. During the 9th month, the fetus gains about an ounce of weight per day. By the end of the 9th month the baby weighs between 6 and 9 pounds and is between 16 and 22 inches long. The skin has become filled out and smooth. It is ready for survival outside the womb (Alexander et al., 2007; Kolander et al., 2008).

Surgical Abortion Methods

There are four surgical abortion methods that are available depending on the length of pregnancy or size of the fetus; they include vacuum aspiration, dilation and evacuation (D&E), intrauterine installation with saline, and hysterotomy (Planned Parenthood, 2007a). A fifth method, dilation and extraction, was an option, but was banned in a 2007 ruling by the U.S. Supreme Court in all cases except to save the life of the mother (Barnes, 2007).

Vacuum Aspiration

Eighty-nine percent of all surgical abortions are performed using the vacuum aspiration and dilation and evacuation methods to terminate pregnancies between 6 and 16 weeks gestation, with the vast majority of these using the vacuum aspiration method (Centers for Disease Control and Prevention [CDC], 2006; Knowles, 2002). This procedure is provided on an outpatient basis, usually in a clinic or doctor's office, and generally includes the following: laboratory tests to confirm the pregnancy and to verify the woman's Rh factor type (positive or negative); counseling provided by a professional staff member; and the reading and signing of an informed consent form. The vacuum aspiration abortion is performed by administering a local anesthetic, cleaning the inside of the vagina with an antiseptic solution, dilating the woman's cervix, and inserting a suction cannula through the cervical opening (os) to aspirate the contents of the uterus. The procedure is completed in 5–10 minutes and generally causes menstrual-like cramping during and immediately following the abortion (Knowles, 2002).

After the abortion is complete, the patient is monitored at the facility for 30–60 minutes, directed to rest that evening, and is provided with after-care instructions. Most women can expect to experience variable bleeding, clotting and cramping for 1–3 weeks after the procedure, and are advised to refrain from heavy lifting and strenuous work and exercise for 5–7 days. A post-abortion examination, including a low-sensitivity pregnancy test, is recommended (but not required) 3 weeks following the procedure (Knowles, 2002). Although the complication rate for a vacuum aspiration abortion is extremely low (less than 1 percent), possible complications can include allergic reactions to drugs, infection, retained tissue, hemorrhage, cervical tearing, or uterine perforation (Planned Parenthood, 2007a; Guttmacher Institute, 2006).

Dilation and Evacuation

A dilation and evacuation (D&E) procedure is used to terminate a pregnancy between 14 and 24 weeks gestation (CDC, 2006; Knowles, 2002). The D&E is almost identical to the vacuum aspiration abortion but requires greater dilation of the cervix, as well as the use of a curette to scrape the uterine wall and forceps to remove the products of conception (POC) (Knowles, 2002). This procedure can be performed in one or two days, and often requires the use of laminaria (also called osmotic dilators) to gradually dilate the cervix (Knowles, 2002). Laminaria consist of medically prepared seaweed that is sterilized and compressed into the shape of small rods. After being inserted into the cervix, the laminaria absorb moisture from the woman's body and gently expand to slowly dilate the cervical os. The woman may feel moderate to heavy cramping during the insertion, as well as light to moderate cramping prior to and during their removal. Depending on the length of the pregnancy, some women may need two or more laminaria insertions to adequately dilate the cervix (Lowdermilk, Perry, & Boback, 2000). The D&E abortion can be performed using either a local anesthetic or conscious sedation, and takes approximately 10–20 minutes to complete the procedure. Although the woman may be advised to rest for up to 2–3 days, the other aftercare guidelines (including the post-abortion exam and possible complications) are identical to the vacuum aspiration abortion (Knowles, 2002).

Intrauterine Installation with Saline

The third surgical abortion procedure, intrauterine installation with saline (also known as a labor induced method), is very rarely performed and accounts for only 0.3 percent of abortions (CDC, 2006). This method is used after the 16th week gestation and occurs in a hospital setting under local or general anesthesia. The intrauterine installation with saline abortion is performed by removing 200 mL of amniotic fluid and replacing an equal amount of hypertonic solution (concentrated salt water) by injection. The injection takes approximately 15 minutes to administer, and the patient will begin labor after several hours. The pregnancy tissue is normally delivered within 24–72 hours, and pain management is required to counteract the discomfort of contractions (Reeder, Martin, & Konicek-Griffen, 1997). Possible complications of the intrauterine installation with saline method include infection, retained tissue, failed abortion, and hemorrhage (Lowdermilk et al., 2000).

Hysterotomy

Like the intrauterine installation with saline method, the fourth surgical abortion method, hysterotomy, is rarely used (CDC, 2006). This procedure is performed in the second or third trimester of pregnancy, usually after other methods have failed. A hysterotomy is in effect the same as a cesarean section, and can be performed either vaginally or abdominally (Reeder et al., 1997). The procedure requires a general or spinal anesthesia, and includes all the risks of major surgery (Reeder et al., 1997).

Dilation and Extraction (D&X, Intact D&E)

The dilation and extraction abortion method (also called D&X or intact D&E) involves the dilation of the cervix and extraction of the intact fetus. It is often referred to by pro-life groups as a "partial birth" abortion, a political term not recognized by the medical community (Religious Tolerance, 2004). Specifically, the D&X procedure entails widely dilating the cervix and delivering the fetus in the breech position, while simultaneously collapsing the fetus' skull by extracting the brain tissue to reduce the chance of injury to the cervix (Grimes, 1998; Religious Tolerance, 2003a). When this procedure is used, it is almost always during the latter part of the second trimester. Based on the most recent statistics, the Guttmacher Institute estimated that in the year 2000, 2,200 D&X procedures were performed — constituting only 0.17 percent of all abortions performed in that year (Guttmacher Institute, 2007b).

In 1996, the American College of Obstetrics and Gynecology issued a statement maintaining that in rare cases a D&X may be the most appropriate procedure to save the life or preserve the health of a woman, and only the doctor, in consultation with the patient, can make this decision (Religious Tolerance, 2003a). Likewise, in 1997, the American Medical Association issued a position statement that it does not condone this procedure except in rare cases where it would be safer than the induction method (e.g., severe hydrocephalus where the fetus' head is extremely large, or the fetus is dead or severely malformed) ("AMA recommends," 1997). This begs the question, "Why not let the medical community regulate itself?" However, a realistic concern with self-regulation is the possibility that unscrupulous physicians could perform unjustified D&X procedures, falsely claiming "protection of the health of the mother" as the criterion. In fact, there is evidence that in the past, a physician in a hospital in New Jersey violated his medical association's regulations by performing numerous late second-trimester and even third-trimester abortions for non-medical reasons (Religious Tolerance, 2004).

Emotional reactions to the D&X procedure, concerns regarding fetal viability and fetal ability to perceive pain, and concerns regarding the ability of the medical profession to regulate itself (as discussed above), repeatedly generated controversial legislation attempting to place a ban on the D&X procedure at the state and federal levels during the 1990s and early 21st century (Religious Tolerance, 2007a; Religious Tolerance, 2007b). In fact, some witnesses gave disturbing testimony during some of these hearings — e.g., accounts of viable fetuses being aborted using the D&X method (Gonzales v. Carhart et al., and Gonzales v. Planned Parenthood Federation of America, Inc., et al., 550 U.S. 05–380 and 05–1382, 2007). During this time period, several versions of the bill known as the *Partial Birth Abortion Ban Act* were vetoed by former President Bill Clinton and stricken down by the U.S. Supreme Court, based on ambiguous language as well as the exclusion of any provision to allow for the procedure in cases to save the life of the woman. However, in October 2003, the House of Representatives and the Senate passed a new version of the *Partial Birth Abortion Ban Act,* and the legislation was signed into law by President G.W. Bush in November of 2003 — thus declaring the use of this method illegal (Religious Tolerance, 2003b).

In April 2007, in a 5–4 vote, the U.S. Supreme Court upheld the federal *Partial Birth Abortion Ban Act* (Gonzales v. Carhart et al., and Gonzales v. Planned Parenthood Federation of America, Inc., et al., 550 U.S. 05–380 and 05–1382, 2007; Guttmacher Institute, 2007b). The Court ruled that the ban is constitutional, deeming that: (a) it is not vague; (b) it does not unduly restrict abortion access (since there are other available methods); and (c) it does not need to have a health exemption since there is no consensus among physicians about the necessity of the D&X procedure (Gonzales v. Carhart et al., and Gonzales v. Planned Parenthood Federation of America, Inc., et al., 550 U.S. 05–380 and 05–1382, 2007; Religious Tolerance, 2007c). It is anticipated that the Supreme Court decision will stimulate increased political efforts by groups on both sides of the abortion issue — e.g., advocacy, lobbying, and campaigns to support like-minded candidates for Congress and the Presidency (Vaida, 2007). This ruling also opens the door for more state policy makers to revisit abortion procedure bans (Krisberg, 2007). In other words, the political battle over the "partial birth abortion" issue is not over.

Issues Related to Prevalence of Surgical Abortion

In the year 2003, 1.28 million surgical abortions were performed in the U.S. (Finer & Henshaw, 2006b). While overall abortion rates continue to decline, the abortion rates among low income and minority women are significantly higher than among college educated women, white women and those with modest incomes (Finer & Henshaw, 2006a; Boonstra, Gold, Richards, & Finer, 2006). More than half of all abortions occur within the first 8 weeks gestation, 88 percent occur within the first 12 weeks, and almost 99 percent occur within 20 weeks gestation (Guttmacher Institute, 2006). Abortions are increasingly being performed in the early stages of pregnancy for several reasons. First, blood and urine pregnancy tests have become more accurate and can identify a pregnancy by 1 or 2 weeks after conception, respectively (National Women's Health Information Center, 2003). In addition, many abortion providers (37 percent) have begun to offer abortion procedures at 4 weeks gestation or earlier due to the availability and more widespread use of the manual aspiration technique that uses a hand-held suction syringe instead of the conventional aspiration machine (Goldberg, 2003; Guttmacher Institute, 2006). Furthermore, improvements in ultrasound equipment allow for pregnancy detection as early as 4 week and 3 days gestation. These technological advances not only provide women with more options, but also allow providers to perform abortions with greater accuracy and fewer complications (Goldberg, 2003).

Over 140,000 abortions (11 percent of all abortions) are performed during the 2nd trimester of pregnancy each year (Boonstra et al., 2006). Women who decide to seek abortions later in their pregnancy do so for several reasons, including the following: (1) genetic defects are generally identified using amniocentesis, a procedure that cannot be performed until the second trimester of pregnancy (Planned Parenthood, 2000a). (2) Some women — particularly those in their teens — may experience denial or not realize they are pregnant until their pregnancy progresses into the second trimester (Boonstra et al., 2006). (3) Some women may have difficulty gathering money quickly enough to pay for a first trimester abortion. To illustrate, the average cost of a first trimester abortion (at 10 weeks gestation) is approximately $372 (Boonstra et al., 2006). Most clinics require clients to pay for their abortion prior to receiving the procedure, accept only cash or credit card, and are unable to offer any significant financial assistance (Boonstra et al., 2006). (4) Other reasons that women may delay seeking abortion services include issues related to parental notification or consent laws, and problems locating and traveling to a provider (Boonstra et al., 2006).

Although 93 percent of surgical abortions are performed in small clinics or doctors' offices, the number of surgical abortion providers has declined steadily in the past 30 years (Boonstra et al., 2006; Guttmacher Institute, 2006). As of 2000, 87 percent of U.S. counties lacked an abortion provider, forcing many women — especially those in rural areas — to travel distances of 100 or more miles to seek services (Boonstra et al., 2006; Guttmacher Institute, 2006). This lack of access is particularly challenging for lower income women who cannot afford to travel, must arrange for childcare, and/or might need the utmost discretion (Boonstra et al., 2006).

Medical Abortion Methods

Medical abortion, which accounts for eight percent of all abortions, involves the use of medications to terminate a pregnancy up to 49 — 63 days after the first day of a woman's last menstrual period (CDC, 2006; Planned Parenthood, 2006). There are currently two medical abortion methods used in the U.S.: (1) mifepristone (known as RU–486 in Europe) and misoprostol, and (2) methotrexate and misoprostol (American College of Obstetrics and Gynecology [ACOG,] 2001). The Food and Drug Administration (FDA) approved mifepristone and misoprostol in September 2000 (National Abortion Federation, 2001). Prior to that time (from the years 1994 — 2000), medical abortions had been increasingly performed using the off-label method methotrexate and misoprostol, the only method of medical abortion then available (ACOG, 2001; National Abortion Federation, 2001). Any physician who provides medical abortions must have the capability of assessing the gestational age of a pregnancy via an ultrasound or sonogram, diagnosing an ectopic pregnancy (a pregnancy that develops outside the uterus, most commonly in the fallopian tube), and providing the patient with a surgical intervention in the case of a failed abortion (ACOG, 2001).

Mifepristone and Misoprostol

A medical abortion using mifepristone and misoprostol generally requires three separate visits to the clinic or doctor's office. On the first visit, the woman is required to do the following: provide a full medical history, submit to laboratory tests (including a pregnancy test), have a physical exam and ultrasound, discuss her decision with a clinical staff member or physician, and sign an informed consent form. The first medication, mifepristone (an anti-progesterone drug that blocks the effect of progesterone on the uterine lining), is taken orally at the clinic to begin the abortion process. Forty-eight hours later, the woman returns to the clinic (or remains at home, depending on the physician's and/or the patient's preference) to insert the second medication, misoprostol (a prostaglandin hormone that causes uterine contractions), vaginally. Once this drug is administered, the pregnancy is usually terminated within 4 hours (ACOG, 2001; Planned Parenthood, 2001).

Side effects from the combined medications include moderate to heavy abdominal pain and cramping, bleeding, clotting, and gastrointestinal distress (i.e., nausea, vomiting, and diarrhea) (National Abortion Federation, 2001). The third visit, which occurs two weeks following the date of the first visit, includes a follow-up exam, ultrasound, and pregnancy test to ensure the completion of the abortion (ACOG, 2001; Planned Parenthood, 2001).

Between 92 and 97 percent of women who take mifepristone and misoprostol will abort their pregnancies successfully; on the other hand, approximately 1–4 percent will require a surgical abortion to complete the process (Planned Parenthood, 2006). Complications associated with medical abortion include retained tissue, allergic reactions, severe bleeding, uterine infection, and in rare cases, death (Planned Parenthood, 2007a). Another possible complication is a ruptured ectopic pregnancy. Doctors should make efforts to diagnose an ectopic pregnancy prior to administering medical abortion; however, they can be difficult to diagnose (Planned Parenthood, 2007a; "Reports posted on abortion pill," 2002).

There were no life-threatening complications reported until August 2002. Since that time, one woman died after having suffered a ruptured ectopic pregnancy after receiving a medical abortion, and six women died after experiencing severe infections from the rare bacterium Clostridium sordellii (Gardiner, 2006); however, one of those women did not receive mifepristone during her abortion. While the FDA is still investigating the nature of the infection-related deaths, it was reported that misoprostol was administered vaginally, not orally (as is recommended by the FDA), which may have played a role in the infections (Rovner, 2006). As with any medical procedure, it is of utmost importance that medical professionals are diligent in detecting and treating any possible complications.

Methotrexate and Misoprostol

The procedure for medical abortion using methotrexate and misoprostol is very similar to that of mifepristone and misoprostol; however, it is slightly less effective, and women may experience more undesirable side effects. Also, this method always requires a minimum of three appointments to the clinic or doctor's office (Planned Parenthood, 2001). The protocol for the first visit is the same as for the mifepristone/misoprostol method, the exception being that she receives methotrexate instead of mifepristone. Methotrexate causes cellular damage to the chorionic villi (the precursos or the placenta) and is administered through an injection. Three to seven days later, the woman returns to the clinic to receive misoprostol vaginally (ACOG, 2001). The abortion usually occurs within 24 hours after the misoprostol insertion but may take up to 48 hours in some cases. Approximately 50 percent of patients expel their pregnancies the same day the misoprostol is administered, and an additional 35 — 40 percent will complete their abortions within the week. The entire process can take anywhere from 14 to 28 days. Two weeks following the abortion, the woman returns to the clinic for a follow-up exam and pregnancy test (Planned Parenthood, 2001).

Approximately 90 percent of women who receive the methotrexate and misoprostol abortion will abort their pregnancies (ACOG, 2001). If the abortion does not occur or is incomplete, either additional doses of misoprostol can be given or a surgical abortion will be performed (ACOG, 2001). Bleeding generally lasts longer with this method, and the side effects may be more severe if additional doses of misoprostol are required. Complications are rare, but can include severe bleeding, uterine infection, low white blood count, and hair loss (ACOG, 2001; Managing Contraception, 2000). There have been no deaths associated with this method; however, because of the longer process involved with methotrexate, mifepristone is usually the preferred method for medical abortion.

Issues Related to Prevalence of Medical Abortion

It is estimated that in the year 2003, 55,048 women had medical abortions (CDC, 2006). Many abortion clinics have reported a considerable increase in their usage of medical abortion since its FDA approval in the year 2000 (Boonstra et al., 2006; Goldberg, 2003). For example, from 2001 to 2004, Planned Parenthood clinics reported a 15 percent increase in mifepristone use among women seeking early abortions (Boonstra et al., 2006). Although most medical abortions are offered at facilities that provide surgical abortion, "... nearly one-fifth of mifepristone sales are to providers that are not abortion clinics" (Boonstra et al., 2006, p. 18).

Comparison of Medical and Surgical Abortion

Although a medical abortion may be perceived as being the more "natural" or "easy" method, it is important for women who may be considering this procedure to know that a medical abortion involves much more than ingesting a couple of pills. The woman must be prepared to monitor her bleeding, check for the passage of pregnancy tissue, report any unusual or abnormal symptoms to her physician immediately, cope with possible side effects from the medications, and attend each of her scheduled appointments until her physician has verified that the pregnancy is terminated (Planned Parenthood, 2001).

The choice to seek a medical versus surgical abortion is a very personal decision and involves weighing the advantages and disadvantages of each method. For example, a surgical abortion is an invasive, one-day procedure with a 99 percent success rate (National Abortion Federation, n.d.). Clinics offer a local anesthetic and even conscious sedation, but the procedure is generally not available to those less than seven weeks into their pregnancy (National Abortion Federation, n.d.). A lack of privacy is a concern for some women, but the procedure is predictable and patients rarely require a follow-up exam to address complications (ACOG, 2001; National Abortion Federation, n.d.).

A woman who chooses medical abortion avoids the invasive procedure as well as the side effects of sedation medications. The success rate of 95 percent is slightly lower than a surgical abortion, and the procedure takes considerably longer to complete (Managing Contraception, 2000). Medical abortions are restricted to early pregnancies and require a follow-up exam to ensure the completion of the abortion (National Abortion Federation, n.d.). The procedure involves multiple appointments, but many women are comforted by the potential for more privacy as they abort their pregnancies at home. The costs for the procedures are comparable, averaging $372 for a surgical abortion and $490 for a medical abortion (Boonstra et al., 2006).

In summary, a comparison of medical abortion and surgical abortion follows: Medical abortion: (1) usually does not involve an invasive procedure or anesthesia; (2) can be used any time in early pregnancy; (3) requires two or more visits; (4) requires days to weeks to complete; (5) requires patient participation in a multi-step process; and, (6) has a success rate of about 95 percent. On the other hand, surgical abortion: (1) involves an invasive procedure and may involve the use of sedation; (2) often, cannot be performed until 7 weeks gestation; (3) usually requires only one visit; (4) is completed in a predictable period of time; (5) requires patient participation in a single-step process; and (6) has a success rate of 99 percent (ACOG, 2001).

Impact of Medical Abortion in the U.S.

The Impact of Medical Abortion on Overall Prevalence of Abortion

Some anti-abortion activists had predicted that the widespread availability of mifepristone would lead to an increase in the overall number of abortions. Thus far this has not been the case (Boonstra et al., 2006). This should come as no surprise if one considers the impact of mifepristone on the abortion rates in France, Great Britain and Sweden. Following the introduction of mifepristone in those three countries, the overall abortion rate remained unchanged. However, it did bring about a change in the timing of abortions; a larger percentage of women in each of those countries are now having abortions at an earlier stage of gestation. One might speculate that the same phenomenon will eventually occur in the U.S. (Boonstra et al., 2006).

The Impact of Medical Abortion on Overall Accessibility of Abortion Services

As previously mentioned, the provision of medical abortion has been limited mostly to specialized clinics (e.g., Planned Parenthood). But among those specialized clinics, the use of medical abortion has increased dramatically. For mifepristone, drug sales in the first quarter of 2002 were up 39 percent as compared with the first quarter of 2001. Over time, the proportion of abortions performed with mifepristone is expected to increase steadily, if the history of its use in Europe is any indication. Some abortion rights advocates had hoped that mifepristone would be used by large numbers of physicians in private practice, who could thus provide abortions in previously unserved areas; however, thus far this has not occurred in overwhelming numbers (Boonstra et al., 2006). Speculated reasons for this include the fact that physicians must meet certain requirements that may create barriers (e.g., skill in diagnosing ectopic pregnancy, the purchase of ultrasound equipment) (Boonstra, 2002a).

Emergency Contraception

Although not an abortion method, emergency contraception (EC) is discussed here for the purpose of delineating it from abortion, as well as to provide understanding of the recent impact of EC on the abortion rate in the United States. Emergency contraceptive pills — nicknamed "the morning after pill" — contain the same hormones used in oral contraceptives, but in larger doses. If used within 5 days of unprotected intercourse, they significantly reduce the risk of pregnancy (Johnsen, 2006).

Even though large doses of certain brands of oral contraceptives have been prescribed as EC for over 30 years, their use was very limited until the late 1990s because until then there was no medical protocol. This necessitated prescription by a method called "off label" use and even though this practice was not illegal, it posed certain logistic barriers for physicians and pharmacists (Planned Parenthood, 2000b). But in 1998 the first product, *Preven* (a combination of synthetic estrogen and progesterone), was FDA-approved and marketed expressly for post-coital contraception. Subsequently in 1999, *Plan B* was approved as the first progesterone-only emergency contraceptive. *Plan B* has the advantages of being slightly more effective and having a significantly lower rate of side effects (Planned Parenthood, 2000b; Johnsen, 2006). A new development occurred in August of 2006 when Plan B was approved for over-the-counter (OTC) use for women over the age of 18 (National Women's Health Information Center, 2006). In the year that followed, sales of Plan B doubled — increasing from about $40 million a year in 2006 to almost $80 million for 2007 (Stein, 2007).

EC is widely misunderstood by the American public. One widely held myth is that EC is a form of medical abortion (which is not true since it is taken early, before a pregnancy occurs). Depending on what time of the cycle unprotected intercourse occurs, in most cases EC is thought to prevent pregnancy by inhibiting ovulation and, less often, by preventing fertilization (Weiss & Golub, 2006). Recent studies demonstrate that progestin-only EC (e.g., Plan B) works strictly by preventing ovulation or fertilization and has no effect on implantation. However, combination-hormone EC (e.g., Preven) may, in some cases, work by altering the endometrium, thereby inhibiting implantation (Planned Parenthood, 2003). In this case it does not prevent conception — in which case some may question whether combination-hormone EC is an abortifacient. The answer to this question depends on one's definition of when pregnancy begins. The American College of Obstetrics and Gynecology defines the beginning of pregnancy as implantation — not conception (Murphy & Allina, 2003). However, there are those who disagree with this definition, believing that pregnancy begins with conception, in which case they would not discount the notion that combination-hormone EC can act as an abortifacient in some cases (Religious Tolerance, 2002). However, considering the fact that the predominant type of EC being dispensed in the United States today is Plan B, this is a moot point in the majority of cases.

The sooner after unprotected intercourse that a woman uses EC, the greater is the likelihood that it will be effective. If progestin-only EC is used within 72 hours of unprotected intercourse, it reduces the risk of pregnancy by 89 percent. If used within 24 hours, it reduces the risk by 95 percent. Combination-hormone EC has a slightly lower effectiveness rate (Weiss & Golub, 2006).

EC is a very safe medication. The most common side effects — nausea and vomiting — are typically mild (Johnsen, 2006). One commonly asked question is whether EC can negatively affect an existing pregnancy (e.g., a woman takes EC not realizing that she is already pregnant). For example, could EC cause a miscarriage or cause birth defects? The answer is that EC does not pose any increase in risk for an existing pregnancy (NOT-2-LATE, 2003). The cost of EC varies widely. Plan B usually costs between $10 and $45, depending on the type of clinic or pharmacy where it is dispensed (Johnsen, 2006).

In spite of the fact that Plan B is now over-the-counter for women age 18 or older, barriers to access still exist. Obviously, the most formidable barrier for women under the age of 18 is the fact that they must obtain a prescription. This can cause delays in obtaining the medication, which can decrease the chances that it will be effective (Guttmacher Institute, 2007a). But even for women age 18 and older, lack of availability of Plan B can be a problem. Some individual stores have refused to keep EC in stock. However, in April 2007, Wal-Mart announced that nationwide, its pharmacies would stock EC and dispense it without discrimination and without delay. A number of other drugstores have made similar commitments (e.g., CVS, Walgreens) But there are other drugstores where consistent accessibility is not yet a reality (Planned Parenthood, 2007b).

Lack of education about this relatively new method of birth control is another major barrier. Many women and men still do not even know about EC; much more needs to be done to increase public awareness (Guttmacher Institute, 2007a). According to one recent study, doctors are overwhelmingly failing to utilize opportunities to educate their patients about emergency contraception. Even though it is now OTC, health care providers still need to educate their patients about it (National Women's Health Information Center, 2007). Cost is another potential barrier — especially for low income women. Many insurance companies do not cover the cost of OTC drugs, and only a few states cover EC for women on Medicaid without requiring a prior visit to a doctor or clinic — which can cause delays in obtaining the method (Guttmacher Institute, 2007a).

But in spite of barriers, the impact of emergency contraception usage on the abortion rate is already being realized. According to estimates by the Guttmacher Institute, in the year 2,000 alone, EC prevented as many as 51,000 abortions (Wind, 2002). It is estimated that the future potential for EC is even greater; it could potentially prevent 1.7 million pregnancies and 800,000 abortions every year (Boonstra, 2002b). Compared to medical and surgical abortion, EC is substantially cheaper and safer, more convenient and private, and considerably less stressful.

In summary, the advent of emergency contraception as a widely available means of post-coital contraception has had a significant impact on the incidence of abortion in the past several years. And as the usage of EC continues to increase in the next few years (as is expected), an even greater decline in the annual abortion rate is likely to occur. Emergency contraception is a relatively safe and extremely valuable addition to women's options for pregnancy prevention. More information about EC can be obtained by accessing these websites: *www.plannedparenthood.org*, *www.agi-usa.org*, or *www.NOT-2-LATE.com*.

Conclusion

The following conclusions can be drawn from the essay's discussion: (1) The annual abortion rate is decreasing due in part to increased use of emergency contraception. (2) Increased awareness of, and availability of, emergency contraception could theoretically prevent the need for the majority of abortions. (3) The majority of second and third trimester abortions could be prevented by increasing awareness of (and access to) emergency contraception and first-trimester abortion. (4) Medical abortion and surgical abortion are relatively safe. Women's preference of method depends on a variety of factors, some of which are not medical in nature. (5) Although medical abortion offers some advantages over surgical abortion, it is not likely to resolve access issues for rural women or economically disadvantaged women. (6) Experts predict the continued increase in the incidence of medical abortion and use of emergency contraception. (7) The political debate over the dilation and extraction ("partial birth") abortion method, as well as late-term abortions in general, is expected to continue.

References

ACOG American College of Obstetrics and Gynecology. (2001, April). Clinical Management Guidelines for Obstetrician-Gynecologists. (Practice Bulletin No. 26). Washington, DC: Author.

Alexander, L., J. LaRosa, H. Bader, and S. Garfield (2007). *New Dimensions of Women's Health* (4th ed.). Sudbury, MA: Jones and Bartlett.

AMA Recommends Alternatives to So-Called 'Partial Birth' Abortions. (1997, May 14). *AllPolitics.* Retrieved on March 29, 2001: *http://www.cnn.com/allpolitics/1997/05/14/ama.abortion/*

Barnes, R. (2007, April 19). High Court Upholds Curb on Abortion. *Washington Post.* Retrieved on July 20, 2007: *http://www.pqasb.pqarchiver.com/washingtonpost/access/1256808381:1256808381:&F*

Boonstra, H. (2002a). Mifepristone in the United States: Status and Future. *Guttmacher Report on Public Policy.*

Boonstra, H. (2002b). Emergency Contraception: Steps Being Taken to Improve Access. *Guttmacher Report on Public Policy.*

Boonstra, H., R. Gold, C. Richards, and L. Finer (2006). Abortion in Women's Lives. Retrieved July 19, 2007: *http://www.guttmacher.org/pubs/2006/05/04/AiWL.pdf*

CDC — Centers for Disease Control and Prevention. (2006, November 24). Abortion Surveillance — United States, 2003. *Surveillance Summaries,* MMWR 55 (SS11).

Finer, L. and S. Henshaw (2006a). Disparities in Rates of Unintended Pregnancy in the United States, 1994–2001. *Perspectives on Sexual and Reproductive Health,* 38(2): 90–96.

Finer, L. and S. Henshaw (2006b). Estimates of U.S. Abortion Incidence, 2001–2003. Retrieved on July 19, 2007: *http://www.guttmacher.org/sections/abortion.php?pub=stats*

Gardiner, H. (2006, May 12). Seventh Death in Medical Abortion. *The New York Times.* Retrieved on July 19, 2007: *http://query.nytimes.com/gst/fullpage.html?sec=health&res=9C03E4D7173EF931A25756C0A9609C8B63*

Goldberg, C. (2003, January 23). Women Having Earlier Abortions: 'Morning After' Pill Use Rises. *The Boston Globe.* Retrieved on January 23, 2003: *http://www.boston.com/dailyglobe*

Gonzales v. Carhart et al. and Gonzales v. Planned Parenthood Federation of America, Inc., et al., 2007, 550 U.S. 05–380 and 05–1382.

Grimes, D. A. (1998). The Continuing Need for Late Abortions. *Journal of the American Medical Association, 280,* 747.

Guttmacher Institute. (2006). In Brief: Facts on Induced Abortion. Retrieved on July 19, 2007: *http://www.guttmacher.org/pubs/2006/05/04/AiWL.pdf*

Guttmacher Institute. (2007a). Have You Backed Up Your Birth Control? Retrieved on July 14, 2007: *http://www.guttmacher.org/media/inthenews/2007/03/20/index.html*

Guttmacher Institute. (2007b). Supreme Court Upholds Federal Abortion Ban, Opens Door for Further Restrictions by States. *Guttmacher Policy Review, 10,* 1–2. Retrieved on July 22, 2007: *http://www.guttmacher.org/pubs/gpr/10/2/gpr100219.html*

Johnsen, J. (2006). Emergency Contraception. Planned Parenthood Federation of America. Retrieved on July 14, 2007: *http://www.plannedparenthood.org/birth-control-pregnancy/emergency-contraception-4366.htm*

Kolander, C., D. Ballard, and C. Chandler (2008). *Contemporary Women's Health: Issues for Today and the Future* (3rd ed.). New York: McGraw-Hill.

Knowles, J. (2002). Surgical Abortion: Questions and Answers. Planned Parenthood Federation of America. Retrieved on October 5, 2002: *http://www.plannedparenthood.org/abortion/surgabort1.html*

Krisberg, K. (2007). Supreme Court Decisions are Shaping Efforts on Greenhouse Gases, Abortion. *Nation's Health, 38,* 1–18.

Lowdermilk, D. L., S. E. Perry, and I. M. Bobak (2000). *Maternity and Women's Healthcare* (7th ed.). St. Louis: Mosby.Managing Contraception. (2000). Pregnancy Termination: First Trimester (Early) Medical Abortion with Methotrexate and Misoprostol. Retrieved on March 21, 2002 *http://www.managingcontraception.com/choices/ch-pregt2.html*

Murphy, R., and A. Allina (2003, January/February). Improving Access to Emergency Contraception. *The Network News, 28,* 1.

National Abortion Federation. (2001). Early Options: A Provider's Guide to Medical Abortion. Retrieved on October 11, 2002: *http://www.earlyoptions.org/mifepristone.html*

National Abortion Federation. (n.d.). First Trimester Abortion: A Comparison of Procedures. Retrieved on June 13, 2003: *http://www.earlyoptions.org/fs/fs11.html*

National Women's Health Information Center. (2003). Pregnancy Tests. Retrieved on June 14, 2003: *http://www.4women.gov/faq/pregtest.htm*

National Women's Health Information Center. (2006). 'Morning After' Pill Approval Prompts Mixed Reactions. Retrieved on July 14, 2007: *http://www.womenshealth.gov/news/english/534598.htm*

National Women's Health Information Center: (2007). Plan B Not Always Available. Retrieved on July 14, 2007: *http://www.womenshealth.gov/news/english/604398.htm*

NOT-2-LATE. (2003). Emergency Contraceptive Pills: Frequently Asked Questions. Retrieved on December 29, 2003: *http://ec.princeton.edu/info/ecp.html*

Pichler, S., and D. Golub (2007). *Roe v. Wade*: Its History and Impact. Planned Parenthood Federation of America. Retrieved on July 15, 2007: *http://www.plannedparenthood.org/news-articles-press/politics-policy-issues/courts-judiciary/roe-v-wade.html*

Planned Parenthood Federation of America. (2000a). Fact Sheet: Abortion After the First Trimester. Retrieved on March 20, 2001: *http://www.plannedparenthood.org/library/facts/abotaft1st_010600.html*

Planned Parenthood Federation of America. (2000b). Fact Sheet: A Brief History of

Emergency Hormonal Contraception. Retrieved on March 20, 2001: *http://www. plannedparenthood.org/library/facts/echist500done.html*

Planned Parenthood Federation of America. (2001). Medical Abortion: Questions & Answers. Retrieved on March 21, 2002: *http://www.plannedparenthood.org/library/ facts/medabort_fact.html*

Planned Parenthood Federation of America. (2003). Fact Sheet: Emergency Contraception. Retrieved on December 29, 2003: *http://www.plannedparenthood.org/library/ BIRTHCONTROL/EC.html*

Planned Parenthood Federation of America. (2006). First Trimester Options — Medication Abortion, Vacuum Aspiration Abortion — a Comparison. Retrieved on July 19, 2007: *http://ppfa.org/birth-control-pregnancy/abortion/first-trimester-options.htm*

Planned Parenthood Federation of America. (2007a). Abortion Risks and Side Effects. Retrieved on July 19, 2007 from *http://www.plannedparenthood.org/birth-control-pregnancy/abortion/risks-and-side-effects.htm*

Planned Parenthood Federation of America. (2007b). Planned Parenthood Activists Get Wal-Mart to Change Its Birth Control Policy at Pharmacies. Retrieved on July 14, 2007: *http://www.plannedparenthood.org/news-articles-press/politics-policy-issues/ walmart-policy-13564.htm*

Reeder, S. J., L. L. Martin, and D. Koniak-Griffen (1997). *Maternity Nursing: Family, Newborn and Women's Health Care* (18th ed.). Philadelphia: Lippincott.

Religious Tolerance. (2002). Emergency Contraception: Birth Control or Abortifacient? Retrieved On December 29, 2003: *http://www.religioustolerance.org/abo_emer2. htm*

Religious Tolerance. (2003a). D&X/PBA Procedures: Introduction. Retrieved on June 10, 2003: *http://www.religioustolerance.org/abo_pba.htm*

Religious Tolerance. (2003b). D&X/PBA Procedures: Attempts to Pass a Federal Law, Years 2002 & 2003. Retrieved on December 27, 2003: *http://www.religioustolerance.org/ abo_pba2.htm*

Religious Tolerance. (2004). How Are Late-Term Abortions Performed? Retrieved on August 5, 2007: *http://www.religioustolerance.org/abo_late1.htm*

Religious Tolerance. (2007a). Can an Embryo or Fetus Feel Pain? Federal and State Laws Concerning Fetal Pain. Retrieved on August 5, 2007: *http://www.religious tolerance.org/abo_pain3.htm*

Religious Tolerance. (2007b). Can an Embryo or Fetus Feel Pain? Statements by Physicians and Researchers. Retrieved on August 5, 2007: *http://www.religious tolerance.org/abo_pain2.htm*

Religious Tolerance. (2007c). D&X/PBA Procedures. Federal law: Supreme Court Activity. Retrieved on August 5, 2007: *http://www.religioustolerance.org/abo_pba10.htm*

Reports Posted on Abortion Pill. Medical Letter on the CDC & FDA. (2002, May 26). Retrieved from HealthInfo database.

Rovner, J. (2006, March 18). FDA Investigating Two Deaths from Abortion Pill. National Public Radio. Retrieved on July 19, 2007: *http://www.npr.org/templates/story/story. php?storyId=5287775*

Stein, R. (2007, July 13). Plan B Use Surges, and So Does Controversy. *Washington Post.* Retrieved on July 15, 2007: *http://www.washingtonpost.com/wp-dyn/content/article/ 2007/07/12/AR2007071202146._pf.html*

Vaida, B. (2007). Abortion Wars Return. *National Journal, 39,* 28–32.

Weiss, D., and D. Golub (2006). Emergency Contraception. Planned Parenthood Federation of America. Retrieved on July 14, 2007: *http://www.plannedparenthood.org/news-articles-press/politics-policy-issues/birth-control-access-prevention.html*

Wind, R. (2002, October 8). U.S. Abortion Rates Continue to Decline, Especially Among Teens. Guttmacher Institute. Retrieved on July 14, 2007: *http://www.agi-usa.org/pubs/archives/nr_340502.html*

The Many Faces of U.S. Abortion Policy

How Government Structure Results in Multiple Policies

AIMEE D. SHOUSE

Abstract

Although abortion policy in the United States is often considered as a single policy area, the reality is that there is a wide range of actual policies across the country that deal with abortion. In fact, a woman's access to abortion can be influenced greatly by the state in which she happens to reside. The origin of this diversity in abortion policy falls back to two structures of American government: federalism and the separation of powers. There simply is no single place in government where abortion policy is made; instead there are multiple locations, including the three branches of the national government as well as the fifty states. This essay discusses how these two governmental structures have influenced abortion policy in the United States.

In a recent graduate seminar on American politics, I overheard one of my students ask her classmates whether they had ever noticed how "we talk about abortion in almost every class?" Upon realizing that I had walked into the room and overheard her, she added brightly, "There's nothing wrong with that, of course ... it really seems to relate to every topic we've considered!" Although I don't recall mentioning abortion during every class, I don't dispute that it's possible. The student was right in at least one of her assertions: the topic of abortion can be used to illustrate almost every topic typically considered in a course on American government and politics. Abortion is clearly both a personal and a political issue. When abortion is discussed in the United States, it's often considered in the context of public policy; we consider what is permitted, what is prohibited, who gets to make that decision, and who influenced that decision. These questions are consistent with the classic definition of politics as "who gets what, when, how" (Lasswell, 1936). It is not too strong to say that one cannot fully understand abortion in the United States without understanding government policies regarding abortion and the politics of creating abortion policies, including who makes those policies and the political influences on the policy making process. Thus, the discipline of political science provides a necessary contribution to any interdisciplinary consideration of abortion.

Abortion policy in the United States relates to numerous aspects of American politics. The topic could easily be used thematically for an entire class on American government and politics, providing depth to the study of the political behavior and attitudes of voters, parties, and interest groups; the role of political institutions, such as Congress, President, and the Supreme Court; and the structure of government, such as federalism and the separation of powers. And that's only in the realm of American politics; abortion certainly has relevance to the study of comparative politics and international relations, as well. Comparatively, one can look at abortion policy as a manifestation of different cultures and government structures. In regard to international relations, the issue of human rights, generally, and abortion, specifically, has influenced foreign policy decisions. In the United States, for instance, foreign aid appropriations have mandated that the funds not be used for the funding of abortions.

This essay, however, focuses exclusively on abortion in the realm of American politics. In the United States, abortion has become a political behemoth; it has, more than any other issue, been used to distinguish the two major political parties in the United States from one another, and it is an essential element in defining the liberal and conservative ideologies within the United States (Adams, 1997; Carmines & Woods, 2002). No candidate for state or national office can run a campaign without addressing this issue (Abramowitz, 1995), and the candidates' stance on the issue immediately demarcates many of their supporters from their opponents. It's easy to see the politics of abortion played out in political campaigns and partisan debates. It's easy to see the protestors and supporters of abortion policy square off over its legality and morality. More subtle, however, is how the very structure of American government has influenced abortion policy in this country.

James Madison, often referred to as the father of the Constitution, addressed the influence of government structure on political behavior in *The Federalist Papers*, Numbers 10 and 51. Madison explains that the very structure of the American system of government will affect the decisions made by government and the interaction of people with the government. This is because the structure of government constrains and limits the types of interactions that can exist with, and within, the institutions of government. In regard to abortion, the federalist structure of government and the separation of powers at the national level have a tremendous influence on the politics of abortion and abortion policy in the United States. This essay will address these two structures of American government, examining how both federalism and the separation of powers have affected the policy making process and the actual policies regarding abortion.

The Structure of American Government: Federalism

Politicians and political observers often refer to "abortion policy," in the singular. Yet, in the context of the American system of government, it is imprecise to refer to a single abortion policy because there is no one abortion policy for the entire country. Although this is not common practice, it is actually more accurate to refer to abortion "policies," in the plural, primarily because there is no single location at which abortion policy is made. The American system of government is complex, characterized by a vertical division of power between the national and state governments, called federalism, and a horizontal division of the powers of government at the national level, generally referred to as separation of power. It is important to understand the intent and function of both of these structures because they have contributed to a dynamic of policy making that has clearly shaped abortion policy in the United States.

The United States government is federalist in nature, meaning that the sovereign powers of government are divided between the national and the state governments. In simple terms, the national government has some powers, the state governments have other powers, and there is an area of overlap between the two.[1] Thus, in certain policy areas, such as education, most criminal law, and the regulation of certain professions, the states have the autonomy to make policy, leading to quite a bit of policy variation across the country. Conversely, the national government has authority over policy areas as outlined in the Constitution or that have been interpreted as falling within the constitutional parameters of the national government.

Federalism emerged from the framing of our government for both pragmatic and principled reasons. Pragmatically, any system of government devised for the United States was necessarily going to have to consider the role of the states, since the states were already in existence and had developed their own government institutions and traditions. In fact, several states had been colonies for over two hundred years prior to the Constitutional Convention of 1787 and it was clear to the framers that it was unfeasible, politically, to dispense with the states. As for a principled justification of federalism, the division of government power between a national government and various state governments prevented any part of government from having too much power over the people, something about which the framers of the Constitution were concerned. Further, state governments could represent regional interests while the national government could govern over issues of relevance to the country as a whole. This division of power between the national and state governments can mean that there is a great deal of variation across the states in a single policy area and that both the state and national levels of government may contribute different policies to a single issue of concern.

This division of power between the national and state governments gives those individuals and groups who want to influence the decisions of government multiple points of access into the policy making process. While the national and state levels of governments have their own governing authority, there is certainly some overlap in their authority over certain policy areas. Thus, individuals or groups can attempt to further their interests at the national level, or within the fifty state governments, or both, depending on where their chances for success are the greatest. For instance, if the political environment of one state is not particularly hospitable to a particular interest, such as advocates for abortion rights, proponents of that interest can simply target another state. Similarly, if focusing on the policy process of fifty different state governments is too arduous, setting one's sights on the national government may be a more reasonable approach to influencing government policy. In short, groups with an interest in abortion policy can often target the part of government most open to their views.

While this essay will later consider the effect of federalism on abortion, a brief example from another policy area, same sex marriage, illustrates the policy variation that can exist in a federalist system of government. Laws regarding marriage are a state function. Marriage licenses are issued by the state and each state can mandate the procedure for attaining a marriage license within its boundaries. The question of whether or not two people of the same sex can marry is thus decided by the states, and there is a lot of variation in how the states have addressed the question. Policies range from the tolerant to the restrictive. Specifically, Massachusetts legally permits gay marriage and New York is currently considering it, four states permit civil unions between two people of the same sex but stop short of permitting "marriage," eighteen states have passed laws defining marriage as between a woman and a man, and another twenty six have solidified this restrictive policy even further by including a heterosexual definition of marriage in their state constitutions. The source of this variation is complex, encompassing the richness of the political and social climates of all fifty states. However, the political and social climate of an individual state can affect which political interest groups are most successful in having their interests represented in public policy.

The national government also became involved in the issue of gay marriage when Congress passed the Defense of Marriage Act in 1996. As controversial as it was, this law clearly demonstrates the potency of federalism to influence the content of public policy. In essence, the law simply clarifies that when an entity of the national government such as Congress or a bureaucratic agency uses the term "marriage," it is referring only to a union between a man and a woman. One might conclude that this is rather little substance for such a controversial law. The explanation lies in our federalist system of government. Because the definition and regulation of marriage is constitutionally a state function, the national government could define marriage only for itself and its functions, not for the country as a whole. Thus, there is no single policy on what constitutes marriage in the United States. This can be said about numerous policy issues, including the mundane, such as speed limits and voter registration requirements, and the controversial, such as environmental regulation and abortion policy.

The Structure of American Government: Separation of Powers

In addition to federalism, the American government is characterized by a separation of powers at the national level. The term "separation of powers" is almost cliché in the United States, most often paired with the phrase, "checks and balances." These two structures of the national government are not synonymous; they refer to two related, but different, mechanisms for preventing the national government from becoming too powerful.[2] Separation of powers gives each branch of government its own sphere of influence, its own powers and responsibilities; it simply breaks up the legislative, executive, and judicial functions of government into different branches of government, so that no part of government can exercise too much power on its own. Checks and balances give each branch of government some authority over the powers of the others, such as the presidential veto or the Congress's ability to override a veto. Thus, it is more accurate to say that the Congress, President, and Supreme Court are "separated institutions sharing power," rather than three autonomous entities (Neustadt, 1990, p. 29).

With each part of the national government having a different function, each branch has its own influence and powers over public policy. Although this is an oversimplification of these powers, in short, Congress writes the law, the President and executive branch execute the law, and the judiciary interprets and applies the law when specific disputes over the law arise. In more detail, by writing the law, Congress gets to decide what is included and what is excluded in legislation. Although the ability to determine the language of legislation is its most potent power, Congress also has the authority to oversee the implementation of law and it has ultimate control over the government's budget. In its turn, the President can veto a bill passed by Congress or can sign it into law, if the bill is passed during his or her administration. However, for laws that already exist when the President assumes office, the President can influence the implementation of the law by appointing people to the executive branch who are sympathetic to the President's views of that law. Further, the President can give directives to the executive branch, called executive orders, on how the executive branch will carry out its functions, and he or she can bring up issues for the public's and Congress's consideration.

Both the President and the Congress can be proactive when it comes to public policy, in that they can take steps to initiate the policy process. The Supreme Court and other federal courts, on the other hand, are reactive, having to wait until a case is brought to them before they can act. However, once the court has a case to decide, its effect on policy can be significant. The Supreme Court not only can interpret and apply laws to particular cases, it can actually overturn laws that it perceives as violating provisions of the Constitution. This process, called judicial review, applies to laws that are passed either by states or by the national government and to actions by the executive branch. Although there are exceptions, court decisions generally explain what the national and state governments can or cannot do, rather than stating what they must do or how they will do it.

A brief example before turning to abortion policy may be helpful. President George W. Bush's education initiative, No Child Left Behind (NCLB), demonstrates how the three branches of government can each contribute differently to public policy. Although the passage of NCLB is primarily credited to President Bush, the law was an amendment, albeit a significant amendment, to an already existing law, the Elementary and Secondary Education Act. Thus, while the President initiated this proposal, it was ultimately Congress who had responsibility for drafting the legislation, a process that is characterized by compromise and revision. As such, Congress substantially revised President Bush's initial proposal, including provisions regarding school choice and the funding authorization for the policy. Ultimately, the bill that made it to George Bush's desk for his signature was not the same proposal that he had submitted for consideration, largely because separation of powers guarantees that Congress will have its own interests and these interests are often reflected in the drafting of legislation. Further, Congress is more open to various outside interests than is the President because of the large size and structure of the branch. In the case of NCLB, Congress simply had more voices with which to contend when considering President Bush's proposal.

After being signed into law, the President can have a great deal of influence over a bill's implementation. Namely, the President appoints people to positions of authority in the executive branch who share his views and interests in public policy. In the case of NCLB, Bush had appointed Margaret Spellings as Secretary of Education, head of the executive branch department responsible for drafting the rules and regulations necessary for states and schools to carry out NCLB. The Department of Education's regulations for NCLB offer guidelines on topics that range from same-sex classrooms, limited English proficiency students, to assessment testing for disabled students. These regulations provide more specific direction to states and schools, directions that are in line with the President's priorities, yet are also consistent with the law as written by Congress.

In most cases of public policy, not everyone will be pleased with the outcome or the outputs of the policy, and NCLB is no exception. If political actors such as interest groups have not successfully influenced Congress or the executive branch regarding a public policy, they often turn to the remaining branch of the national government, the judiciary, to exercise influence. For instance, NCLB spawned numerous lawsuits regarding the national government's level of funding to the states, primarily in regard to the assessment testing provisions of NCLB. Although none of these cases have yet to be settled, the Supreme Court may ultimately decide whether or not the implementation of NCLB has violated the law regarding funding. Further, the Supreme Court has ruled on other topics related to NCLB, such as with *Zelman v. Simmons-Harris* (2002), in which the Supreme Court decided that tax vouchers being used at private, religious schools did not violate the First Amendment's Establishment Clause regarding the separation of church and state.

Both the issues of gay marriage and of No Child Left Behind provide examples of the influence our government structure has on the politics and policies that emerge from the American political system. Clearly, the structures of federalism and the separation of powers can have a tremendous effect on the policies and the policy process within the United States. In regard to abortion policy, the influence of these structures is particularly pronounced. In fact, one cannot fully appreciate abortion policy in this country without understanding how it has been influenced by the very structure of government. It would be inaccurate to say that this is the only influence on abortion policy, given that both opponents and proponents of abortion rights, both in and out of government, have influenced abortion policy in this country. But the very tactics used by interest groups and government officials are fundamentally shaped by federalism and separation of powers.

The remaining section of this essay will consider how the structure of American government has influenced abortion policy and the politics surrounding abortion policy. In addition to a discussion of the influence that federalism and the separation of powers has had on abortion policy, this section also includes references to the various resources one can use for conducting research on government policy, including abortion policy.

The Effect of Federalism on U.S. Abortion Policy

While Americans generally consider the source of abortion policy to be the Supreme Court case *Roe v. Wade* (1973), it's important to reiterate that abortion policy is primarily under the jurisdiction of state governments. What *Roe v. Wade* accomplished was to apply the implicit right to privacy, found in the Bill of Rights and the Due Process Clause of the Fourteenth Amendment, to a woman's decision to end a pregnancy. In very practical terms, the court simply overturned a Texas law that had banned abortion, claiming that the law violated a woman's right to privacy, which then prevented other states and the federal government from making abortions illegal up until the point of fetal viability. However, short of making it illegal, states can do much to influence the actual practice of abortion. This relates to James Madison's point that regional variation can best be represented by state governments rather than by a single national government. Although we do see similarities across the states, with fifty states each making policies regarding abortion, it's impossible to identify one single abortion policy for the nation.

Currently, there are numerous on-line resources for researching abortion policy in the American states. These can range from organizations that advocate for a particular stance on abortion, to non-partisan organizations that provide objective current information about the practice and regulation of abortion. For instance, for information with a "pro-life" perspective, the organization National Right to Life provides a thorough website, as does Operation Rescue, which is also a very active pro-life organization with religious ties. Conversely, those interested in information with a "pro-choice" slant can turn to the National Abortion Rights Action League (NARAL) or the National Abortion Federation, both of which provide thorough information about abortion rights. There are many abortion websites that take a particular political or ideological slant, although the reader must be careful to evaluate the value of the information provided. Two excellent on-line resources available at the time this volume was published that provide non-partisan information about the abortion policies of each state are the Guttmacher Institute and the Kaiser Family Foundation. These two organizations monitor abortion policies, as well as other types of policies, to provide objective information about the practice of abortion in the United States. All the organizational websites mentioned above are accessible to anyone who has access to the Internet. For readers with access to on-line subscription databases through their library, Lexis Nexis State Capitol Universe is also an excellent resource for researching state laws on any subject, including abortion.

The websites devoted to abortion and abortion politics make clear the importance many people place on this issue. Yet, attitudes toward abortion vary widely across the United States, from the more liberal position protecting the rights of women regarding their reproductive health, to the more conservative focus on a fetus's right to its life. State public policies regarding abortion mirror the public's perspectives, ranging from states with more liberal, permissive abortion policies to those with more conservative, restrictive policies (Cook, Jelen, & Wilcox, 1993). While all states regulate the practice of abortion to some degree, the regulation can vary widely, from a focus on the physicians who conduct abortions, to a focus on the girls and women who seek an abortion. One interesting aspect of federalism is that a state can "learn" from other states and essentially copy what its policymakers consider to be a good idea from another state. Thus, while state policy on abortion can vary from state to state, one can see considerable overlap in the types of policies states adopt to regulate abortion.

The policies a state adopts in regard to abortion are related to the goals that the state's policymakers are attempting to promote. These goals can be largely routine and non-controversial, such as promoting the general public health, or they can be paternalistic and obstructionist, making abortion a less attractive, and even downright difficult, option. Policies related to abortion, however, all tend to relate to the concept of protection. States make policies to protect individuals from harm and to protect society as a whole. Of course, opinions on what and whom need protecting vary from person to person, and state to state. In regard to the more routine forms of regulation, all states act to protect public health by regulating the medical profession, including those within the profession who perform abortions. States regulate and license many occupations, from physicians and insurance agents to barbers and truck drivers, with the goal of securing public safety and well-being. In regard to abortion policy, these policies are directed at the people who perform abortions, rather than at the women who are seeking or having an abortion. For instance, thirty-nine states require that abortions be performed by a licensed physician. As such, anyone performing an abortion in one of these states who is not a licensed physician can be prosecuted. Further, a large minority of states require that abortions be performed in a hospital. In nineteen states, it is illegal for a physician to perform an abortion in her or his office, even though physicians in other states may be free to do so. This is an example of how federalism creates a virtual "patchwork quilt" of policies across the country. What is legal in one state may be illegal just over the state line.

A second goal of abortion policy is to protect the interests of "others," whose rights may be harmed by a woman's decision to have an abortion. For example, most states, currently thirty-five, require some sort of parental involvement if their minor daughter is seeking an abortion. Specifically, twenty-two states require that a parent gives his or her consent before an abortion can be performed, while eleven states simply require that one or both parents be notified. The laws of two states require that both parental notification and consent be obtained. Fifteen states either do not have such a provision in their statutes, or court orders have prevented them from being carried out. In the thirty-five states with this requirement, it is clear that the rights of parents to be involved in their child's healthcare decisions is promoted, even if that makes obtaining an abortion more difficult for the young woman. In cases where parental notification is impossible or inadvisable, most states with parental notification policies allow for some sort of court approval for the abortion, although this is a lengthy process. A few states allow a physician to waive the parental notification or court approval in certain circumstances, but this is rare.

Taxpayers are another group of people states attempt to "protect" by prohibiting the use of public funds for abortions. In 1977, Congress passed the Hyde Amendment, named for Representative Henry Hyde (Rep- IL), which prohibited abortions from being covered by Medicaid funds except when the life of a woman was endangered.[3] This restriction on Medicaid-funded abortions was loosened in 1993 when exceptions to the prohibition on funding were extended to cases of rape and incest. Because Medicaid is a program funded both by the federal government and the states, states have some latitude as to how the funds will be used in regard to paying for abortions. Consequently, there is some variation as to how rigorously the Hyde Amendment is implemented. Most states, a total of thirty-two, largely follow the federal government's lead of only funding abortions when the pregnancy endangers the woman's life, or is the result of rape or incest. Seven of these thirty two states have extended the exceptions slightly, including coverage of an abortion when there is an abnormal fetus or when the pregnancy would cause long-term harm to a woman's physical health. Seventeen states, however, fund all or most "medically necessary" abortions, a term that generally means any abortion that is performed by a medical professional who is licensed by the state to perform abortions. South Dakota will only fund abortions if a woman's life is in danger, in violation of the Hyde Amendment. A policy to fund medically necessary abortions offers low-income women much fewer restrictions for obtaining an abortion than a policy that follows the Hyde Amendment provisions.

A third goal of abortion policy is to protect the fetus from what the state considers to be unreasonable harm. States can set parameters as to when during a pregnancy an abortion can be performed. Although fourteen states have no restriction on when abortions can take place during a pregnancy, thirty-six do prohibit abortions in the latter stages of a pregnancy, unless the woman's life is at risk. This prohibition varies, ranging from fetal viability in twenty-three states, to the third trimester of pregnancy in five states, to the twentieth or twenty-fourth week of pregnancy in eight states. In half of the states prohibiting abortions after a certain point in the pregnancy, a second physician must be consulted before an abortion can take place if it is deemed that a woman's life is at risk. Several states have also prohibited a particular abortion procedure. Although rare, thirteen states have prohibited the "intact dilation and extraction" method of abortion, which is often referred to as "partial birth abortion" by opponents to abortion rights. The constitutionality of these laws have been questioned in several states, but the Supreme Court ruled in 2007 (*Carhart v. Gonzales*) that a federal prohibition on the procedure, the Partial Birth Abortion Ban of 2003, is permissible under its interpretation of the Constitution. This ruling may usher in greater adoption of this policy in other states.

A final goal served by abortion policies is to ostensibly protect the emotional well-being of a woman who is considering an abortion. While a woman's health is protected by the state's regulation of abortion providers, the state addresses a woman's emotional health by aiming policies toward the woman herself. These policies are often designed to delay the process of obtaining an abortion, to provide certain information about abortion, and to even deter a woman from having an abortion at all. Many states mandate that a woman seeking an abortion be counseled on the effects of abortion. The most common types of counseling, required by twenty-six states, relates to alternatives to abortion and the types of services available if the woman chooses to continue her pregnancy. Much less common is the requirement by three states that women be counseled on the emotional effects of an abortion, the requirement by four states that they receive information regarding the pain felt by the fetus during an abortion, and the requirement by three states that women be counseled on the incidence of breast cancer after an abortion.

Most recently, Georgia has passed legislation, the "Woman's Ultrasound Right to Know Act," which requires that physicians offer all women seeking abortion the opportunity to view the ultrasound image and hear the fetal heartbeat before an abortion takes place. A woman is not required to view the image or hear the heartbeat, but the physician is required to ask. According to the findings in the Georgia's law (H.B. 147), the law will ensure that a woman receive complete information on the "reality and status" of her pregnancy, that the fetus is protected from an uninformed decision, and that a woman is protected from the "devastating psychological consequences" of making an uninformed decision regarding abortion (Georgia H.B. 147). The overt intent of this policy is to deter women from having an abortion, on the assumption that hearing a heartbeat and seeing an image makes the fetus more human and "real" to the pregnant woman. Other states that have similar laws are Mississippi, Alabama, Michigan, and Arkansas. In March of 2007, the South Carolina House of Representatives attempted to take the policy a step further by requiring that women view an ultrasound image and hear the heartbeat of the fetus. Currently, the bill has not passed the state senate.

The above discussion gives an overview of the most commonly used state policies regarding abortion, although there are numerous variations from state to state when looking at the details of each law. As can be seen by these policies, the practice of abortion can be influenced dramatically by policy makers' goals and the policies they adopt to achieve their goals. It's also important to note that the goals they claim to promote may actually be designed to achieve other goals. For instance, is abortion defined merely as a healthcare procedure? If so, then the state's only interest is in making sure it's carried out by trained professionals in a safe environment. But defining abortion in this manner ultimately promotes abortion rights, even if that may not be the stated goals of policymakers. Further, is abortion a decision that affects only the woman who obtains the abortion? If not, whose rights take precedence over the woman's: parents, the fetus, society? (See the essay in this volume by Martinelli-Fernandez). By clarifying in policy that others may have a legitimate interest in the practice of abortion, the state effectively establishes barriers to women who seek an abortion. These barriers can be costly, in both time and money, for the woman seeking an abortion. For the healthcare professionals who provide abortion service, these barriers may be costly enough that they choose to no longer offer the service. In essence, the more the state requires of people who perform abortions, the more difficult it is to offer the service. Thus, abortion may be legal, but largely unavailable, in some states because of the policies that state has adopted regarding the procedure (See Rose, 2007).

Although this section has focused almost exclusively on the variation of state abortion policies allowed by a federalist system of government, it's important to note that federalism also includes consideration of the national government's role in policy making. While the national government is involved in abortion policy, there isn't just one source of policy within the national government. In fact, there are three sources of policy, found in the legislative, executive, and judicial branches of the national government, and these three branches do not always speak with a single voice or intent on policy issues. As with federalism, separation of powers makes it difficult to speak of a single national abortion policy. Rather, there are numerous policies related to abortion that have emerged from the national government. The next section addresses the effect the separation of powers has had on abortion policy in the United States.

The Effect of Separation of Powers on Abortion Policy

As already discussed, the United States' national government is characterized by a division of power which gives each branch its own powers and responsibilities. These powers overlap with those of the other branches however, which theoretically contributes to each branch being able to check the excesses of either of the other two. Not only does each branch have its own powers, but it is also differentiated from the other branches in terms of its members' method of appointment, their term of office, and the scope of their representative function. The founders of the Constitution reasoned that the members of each branch would have different interests than the members of the other branches because they would have to act differently to remain in office. For instance, a member of the House of Representatives must go up for reelection every two years and she represents a district of almost 700,000 people. Clearly, she would have to act differently to appeal to her constituents than would a U.S. Senator, who only faces reelection every six years and represents an entire state's population. Both the House member and the Senator would behave differently than the President, who faces reelection every four years, can be elected no more than two times, and represents the entire country. Even more unique, members of the federal judiciary have different incentives built into their office; they are appointed by the president, confirmed by the Senate, and serve life terms. Thus, theoretically, even if the same political party controls all three branches of government, the three branches will not always see eye to eye, simply because the incentive structures built into each branch differ.

Contributing to this effect is the fact that none of the branches are static; they change, depending on who is elected and which party is in power of each branch. Clearly the presidency of Bill Clinton was different from the presidencies of both George H. W. Bush and George W. Bush, his predecessor and successor. Similarly, as the party in control of Congress shifts from Republican to Democrat, so does its relationship with the other two branches of government. Given that the government changes over time, the policies that emerge from that government can also change over time. Thus, national abortion policy varies, depending on which branch is making the policy and the political circumstance of the time. This section will look at each branch in turn, discussing the various types of abortion policy that each has approved.

Among the three branches of the national government, the Supreme Court has played the most visible role in the national government's policy towards abortion. The Supreme Court has several powers at its disposal, including the interpretation and application of law when cases arise, the interpretation and application of the Constitution to state and national policies when the Constitution and the policy seem to be at odds, and the discretion to hear or not hear cases that are appealed to it. Court decisions generally outline what is permissible or impermissible within the confines of a statute or the Constitution's language. Rarely does a court decision say what must be done, but rather clarifies what can or can't be done. Unlike the Congress and the President, the checks on the court's powers are somewhat indirect. Probably the two most potent checks on its power include the reactive nature of its policy making, in that it can only make policy when a case is brought before it, and its inability to carry out its own decisions. In short, the court has to depend on others to implement its decisions, an act which becomes less assured if the decisions of the court are perceived to be illegitimate by the public that is affected by the decision or other parts of government.

The Supreme Court made one of its first forays into the issue of reproductive rights in 1965, when deciding the case *Griswold v. Connecticut*. In this case, physicians at a Connecticut Planned Parenthood clinic were prosecuted for giving information about contraception and selling contraceptive devises to married couples, which was in violation of Connecticut law at the time. In addition to the portions of the law directed at healthcare providers, the law also targeted the individuals who would use contraception. The appellants, who had been found guilty and fined in lower court, argued that the Connecticut law violated the Due Process Clause of the Fourteenth Amendment to the Constitution. The Supreme Court ultimately reversed the decision of the lower court, claiming in its opinion that the Connecticut law violated the Constitution's right to privacy, a right not explicitly mentioned in the Constitution but largely considered to be within the parameters of the other rights it provides. Because of the Court's broad reading of the Constitution, this state law was ruled unconstitutional and could no longer be used to limit access to or information about contraception. The application of the constitutional right to privacy to reproductive rights laid the groundwork for *Roe v. Wade* in 1973.

One of the most controversial cases decided by the Supreme Court, *Roe v. Wade* overturned state laws that prohibited abortion, using a similar rationale as offered in *Griswold v. Connecticut*, that the reach of government does not extend to a woman's right to make her own reproductive choices. As seen in the discussion of federalism, the decision still gave the states some discretion in regulating the practice of abortion, but the Court's opinion flatly stated that laws outlawing abortion prior to fetal viability were unconstitutional and thus, invalid. While the foundation of abortion legality established by *Roe v. Wade* remains intact, many have argued that the court has chipped away at abortion rights by allowing states to increasingly impose limitations on the practice of abortion, as seen in the discussion of state abortion policies above.

Why has this change in court decisions taken place? In short, the answer comes down to changes in the ideologies and views of the people who serve on the federal courts. With nine justices on the Supreme Court, currently appointed by four different presidents, it's not surprising that they do not share a single interpretation of law or the Constitution. As the people on the court have changed over time, as presidents appoint new justices who reflect their own political views, the interpretation and application of constitutional provisions often change. This has clearly influenced the judicial decisions being made in regard to abortion policy. While *Roe v. Wade* was a clear advancement of the national government's role in making abortion policy, the trend since this case has been to give the states more discretion in how they regulate abortion, short of making it illegal. However, even at its zenith, judicial abortion policy tends to be broad, making decisions as to what states can and cannot do regarding abortion regulation, not necessarily what they must do regarding abortion. That level of specificity from the national government comes from policies made by Congress and the Executive branch.

As the elected representative body within the national government, Congress ideally translates public opinion and interest into legislation. While laws can be written in broad language, the scope of legislative abortion policy tends to be significantly narrower than the policies made by federal judiciary. For instance, while *Roe v. Wade* broadly prohibits states from infringing upon a woman's right to privacy by making abortion illegal, Congress focuses on more discreet topics, such as whether the national government will fund abortions. However, like the courts, Congress is not immune to the effects of changing political party leadership, and since 1994, the party leadership of Congress has changed twice. Consequently, the focus of federal law regarding abortion has varied over time.

Currently, the database *Lexis Nexis Congressional* makes it relatively simple to see the various laws Congress has passed that include any consideration of abortion. Notably, since *Roe v. Wade* Congress has passed only twenty-nine laws that include any provisions regarding abortion. In fact, twenty-one of the twenty-nine simply include abortion as one item in a more comprehensive law that appropriates funds for some function of the government. For instance, in several of the laws appropriating funds for the Department of Defense, Congress has clarified that none of the appropriation could be used for purposes of abortion. Given the amount of talk devoted to abortion by candidates for congressional office, it is perhaps surprising that this is by far the most common approach to abortion policy by Congress. Looking at the twenty-nine laws passed since 1973, this prohibition against using federal funds for abortion services is as close as Congress gets to any kind of theme in abortion policy. The remaining eight laws that consider abortion address a variety of topics. These range between restrictions on certain types of abortions, such as the federal ban on late term abortions in the Partial Birth Abortion Ban of 2003, to the protection of women who are trying to access abortion clinics in the Freedom of Access to Clinic Entrances Act of 1994. The three most recent of these laws have implications for abortion rights, even if the subject of the law is not abortion, per se. In addition to the Partial Birth Abortion Ban of 2003, these include the Born-Alive Infants Protection Act of 2002, which clarifies that a baby who is born alive, after a failed abortion for instance, is considered a person under federal law, and the Fetus Farming Prohibition Act of 2006, which prevents the use of aborted fetuses for medical research. Beyond these three, there does not appear to be a common theme or approach to abortion in the remaining non-appropriations laws.

Generally, members of Congress pass laws when problems come to their attention and there is enough political support for the policy to pass. Thus, because new problems emerge over time, or our perceptions of problems change, it is difficult to see a consistent or coherent train of congressional policy regarding abortion, other than the prohibition on its funding. The difficulty in passing a coherent, consistent policy is exacerbated by several factors. First, Congress is a large institution which is divided between the House of Representatives and Senate, and for any law to pass, it must receive majority approval in each of the chambers. In fact, no bill can be sent to the President that has not been approved by both the House and the Senate, a difficult and time-consuming process in even the best of circumstances. But on a contentious issue like abortion, it can be extremely difficult to secure a majority vote, even when bills are drafted in such a way as to minimize conflict. A second difficulty in passing coherent policy over time is the role of political parties in providing leadership to each congressional chamber. If the political party in control of a chamber changes, not only may that chamber adjust its proposed solutions to problems, but the very conceptualization of what is a problem can change. Thus, abortion policy across time is influenced by the public's perceptions of abortion, who that public elects to Congress, what party controls the chambers of Congress, and what members of Congress are willing to do about an issue fraught with conflict. In short, the approach Congress has taken has been to refuse to pay for abortion with federal funds, a decision that is largely supported by the public, and to simply deal with individual issues related to abortion as they arise.

The last branch of the national government to be considered is the executive branch, and it too has its own influence over abortion policy. With one exception, the President's influence on abortion policy is more indirect than that of the other two branches of the national government. As the head of the executive branch, the President has the power to nominate all federal judges and justices as well as the leadership positions of the executive branch. Thus, when the President has the opportunity to fill a vacancy on the Supreme Court, the President can appoint people who share his or her views on numerous issues. Abortion has been one of the issues past presidents have considered when they have nominated people to the federal judiciary. While the President has to be conscious of attitudes in the Senate when he or she appoints someone to the courts, given that the Senate must confirm these nominations, a president still has a great deal of discretion in choosing someone who shares his or her political views on the role of the government in regard to the practice of abortion. The same discretion is granted to the President's power of appointment to officials in the bureaucracy, although the bureaucracy's influence over abortion policy is somewhat muted.

The President also has the power to veto legislation that comes to his or her desk from the Congress. This power has been used on two major occasions on abortion bills: during the administration of President Clinton, the Republican-controlled Congress passed the Partial Birth Abortion Ban twice, only to have it vetoed both times by the President. Both vetoed bills prohibited late term abortions unless the life of the woman was at risk, while President Clinton explained in his veto message that he would not sign the legislation unless there was an exception if a woman's health was also endangered. Congress was not able to get the law passed until the political environment had changed with the election of Republican President George W. Bush. Although Congress can override a presidential veto with a two-thirds vote, this overwhelming majority is extremely difficult to achieve and, as such, overriding a veto is very rare.

The most direct influence the president has on abortion policy is through the use of executive orders, which is the President's ability to direct the executive branch in matters not specifically addressed in law. During his administration, President Ronald Reagan issued an executive order that prevented any foreign aid for family planning to be distributed to clinics or governments that perform or counsel regarding abortion. Clinics worldwide could continue to discuss abortion as an option with clients, but they would relinquish necessary American aid if they did so. Although Congress had not considered this particular issue in law, the President does have the discretion to direct the executive branch as to how it must operate, as long as these directives do not violate law. In this case, Congress had appropriated funds for assistance to family planning clinics worldwide, but these appropriations had further limitations imposed on their distribution by the President. After President Reagan, this executive order was retained by President George H. W. Bush, but was promptly overturned by President Clinton when he took over the office. George W. Bush reinstated the order when he became President. Not only does the shift in policy affect the United States, but it has clear implications for reproductive policies worldwide.

By looking at each of the three branches of the national government, one can see that there is little coherent thread of public policy at the national level regarding abortion, except perhaps in regards to the prohibition of its funding. Given the federalist nature of our government, this is understandable. Abortion policy is largely the domain of the state governments. In the states, we do see a policy trend toward protectionism, although the subject of state protection (healthcare providers, the unborn, taxpayers, and women) varies across policies. However, the national government is limited, constitutionally, to certain types of action. How national funds can or must be spent, or not spent in this case, certainly falls within the discretion of Congress and the President. Beyond the issue of funding, however, abortion policy at the national level has been somewhat disjointed, made as issues emerge out of the current political environment. Separation of powers provides each of the three branches its own powers and motivations and its own mechanism for effecting policy. This governmental structure has clearly influenced the types of abortion policies coming from the national government.

Conclusion

The politics of abortion policy is complex and cannot fully be understood without addressing the roles played by political parties, interest groups, candidates, and elections in the creation of abortion policy. This essay has attempted to demonstrate that all other facets of abortion politics in the United States are shaped, at their foundation, by the very structure of the American government. Because the United States is geographically large and diverse, it would be impossible to identify a single "public opinion" in regard to abortion, since views vary so widely. These various views are reflected by our parties, by the political interest groups that work to influence abortion policy, and the candidates who run for office. But it is the structure of federalism and the separation of powers that allow that diversity of opinion to find purchase in public policy across the United States, expressed through the various laws and policies across all levels of the American government.

Notes

1. The Tenth Amendment to the Constitution states that the "powers not delegated to the United States by the Constitution, nor prohibited by it to the States, are reserved to the States respectively, or to the people."

2. In *The Federalist Papers*, Number 51, James Madison advocates "contriving the interior structure of the government as that its several constituent parts may, by their mutual relations, be the means of keeping each other in their proper places" (Madison 1961: 320). It's fascinating that the very structure of government was designed to keep each branch in its proper place. Madison believed that giving each branch of government its own powers would motivate those officials within each branch to jealously guard their powers from encroachment by the other branches. In fact, he assumed that it was the very desire to usurp the powers of the other branches that would ultimately keep each branch in its place. In Federalist 51, Madison famously articulates this assumption of political motivation for power by saying that "ambition must be made to counteract ambition" (Madison 1961: 322).

3. Medicaid is a health insurance program, created by the national government and administered jointly with the states, to provide health care services primarily to low income people.

References

Abramowitz, A. I. (1995, February). It's Abortion Stupid: Policy Voting in the 1992 Presidential Election. *The Journal of Politics*, 57 (1), 176–186.

Adams, G. (1997, July 1). Abortion: Evident of Issue Evolution. *American Journal of Political Science*, 41 (3), 718–737.

Carmines, E. G. and J. Woods (2002, December). The Role of Party Activists in the Evolution of the Abortion Issue. *Political Behavior*, 24 (4), 361–377.

Cook, E. A., T. G. Jelen, and C. Wilcox (1993, December). State Political Cultures and Public Opinion About Abortion. *Political Research Quarterly*, 46 (4), 771–781.

Georgia General Assembly, House Bill 107–147.

Guttmacher Institute. *http://www.guttmacher.org/*

Kaiser Family Foundation. *http://www.kaisernetwork.org/index.cfm#*

Lasswell, H. (1936). *Politics: Who Gets What, When, How.* New York: Meridian Books.

Madison, J. (1961). "Federalist 51," *The Federalist Papers*. New York: Mentor Books, 321–325.

National Abortion Federation. *http://www.prochoice.org*

National Abortion Rights Action League. *http://www.naral.org*

National Right to Life. *http://www.nrlc.org*

Neustadt, R. (1990). *Presidential Power and the Modern Presidents.* New York: The Free Press.

Operation Rescue. *http://www.operationrescue.org*

Rose, M. (2007). *Safe, Legal, and Unavailable.* Washington, D.C.: CQ Press.

Hidden in Plain View

An Overview of Abortion in Rural Illinois and Around the Globe

HEATHER MCILVAINE-NEWSAD

Abstract

Whether and under what circumstances abortion should be legal is highly debated in many parts of the world, with arguments based on religious, moral, political, human rights and public health grounds[1] (Alan Guttmacher Institute, 2003). Despite these arguments, induced abortion is a significant phenomenon in contemporary global society. Annually, one out of every fourteen women of reproductive age undergoes an induced abortion (World Health Organization, 1994). With an estimated 45–46 million abortions performed each year, (World Health Organization, 1998) abortion is a procedure that cuts across political, religious, economic, and ethnic lines. This essay presents a cross cultural view of abortion by providing the reader with a brief anthropological overview of the history and background of abortion, the reasons why women seek abortions, and the characteristics of women seeking abortions. The essay ends with a case study that illustrates how rural women in western Illinois view abortion given the current political, economic, and social climate.[2]

Abortion Around the Globe

Whether abortion is ethical or not, is a point upon which many individuals disagree. Some argue that abortion is a sin. Others may approve of it in theory, but may waiver when theory meets reality. Still others may denounce abortion altogether. No one can contradict however, the fact that abortion, whether a legal right or not, is a reality in all cultures and societies. As women and feminists, we must recognize that the lives of real women hang in the balance when it comes to this issue (Manivannan, 2008).

Anthropological Evidence of Abortion

Anthropologists have found evidence of abortion in every known culture throughout history (Devereux, 1976; Gallen, Narkavonkit, Tomaro, & Potts, 1981; Jöchle, 1974; Newman, 1985; McFarlane and Meier, 2001; Riddle, 1992). Mankekar (1973) cites written Chinese texts, dating back approximately 4500 years, as among the earliest recorded history of induced abortion. Greek philosophers are recorded as viewing abortion as a means to control population growth or as a way to end an unwanted pregnancy as early as 384 B.C.E. (Mankekar, 1973). In India, *Ayurvedic* medicine uses many plants as early term "morning after" means of abortion (Taylor, 1996, p. 89). Abortion was also an accepted practice in classical Europe. These abortions, like those in the *Ayurvedic* tradition, were most commonly performed by drinking an herbal concoction; although records of physical interventions are also present (Caldwell & Caldwell, 2003).

In the Arctic, the conservation of food resources for traditional peoples was a critical factor limiting the size and density of the population. For traditional nomadic peoples of the Arctic, the food supply was rarely dependable enough to allow them to settle in one place for long periods of time. If population size exceeded any given region's resources, starvation loomed. The Inuit, for example, considered many factors when trying to maintain a stable population size: predation, starvation, disease, accidents, and social mortality (McElroy & Townsend, 2004). Before the introduction of Christianity to the region, abortion and infanticide were prevalent forms of social mortality. According to Smith and Smith (1994, p. 595):

> Rates of female infanticide averaged 21 percent and ranged from 0 percent to 40 percent. Since the normal ratio of males to females born to humans is 105 to 100, this gender discrepancy reveals the high infanticide rate as well as possible neglect of female offspring.

According to McElroy and Townsend (2004, p. 27), "infanticide keeps a population stable in several ways: It is a direct check on the effective birth rate and reduces the number of potential reproducers in the next generation." In groups like the Inuit "...who experienced high death rates among the adult male population from hunting accidents and homicides, female infanticide served to balance the gender ratio over the long run, increasing the proportion of food-producing males to non-food producing females"

(McElroy & Townsend 2004, p. 27). According to Cohen (1989) and Posner (1992) infanticide and abortion are practices that can be substituted for each other. Both methods are meant to prevent unwanted births after contraception has occurred. Until recently in human history, after the establishment of orphanages for unwanted children, infanticide was more widely practiced because it posed less of a risk to the mother's health than abortion. Though clearly a widespread practice, infanticide has varied considerably among societies depending in large part on economic and cultural circumstances (Haas, 1994). As we can see from these examples, abortion has been and continues to be present in many cultures around the globe. However, despite the long and cross cultural history, it continues to be a subject that garners attention and controversy.

As contemporary cultures continue to place constraints on sex, the societal norms surrounding abortion vary greatly around the globe. Both the Kaiser Family Foundation (KFF) and the Alan Guttmacher Institute (AGI) have tracked societal norms and the status of women's health and abortion issues globally since the mid 1970s. In 2003, AGI issued a report on the status of abortion around the world. The AGI estimates that of the 46 million women who have induced abortions each year, 36 million women (or 78 percent) live in developing countries, and the remaining 10 million (22 percent) live in developed countries (Alan Guttmacher Institute [AGI], 2003, p. 25).

Table 1 (AGI, 1999) shows that regardless of whether a woman lives in a developed or a developing country, her likelihood of having an abortion is much the same. Research carried out by the World Health Organization (WHO) in 1994 suggests that abortion is practiced by one of every fourteen women of reproductive age annually. Global estimates from the WHO 1998 and AGI 2003 reports suggest that more women are obtaining legal abortions (approximately 26 million) than illegal abortions (an estimated 20 million). Abortion is legal in China and Eastern Europe, which have the highest number of women obtaining abortions. Because abortion is prohibited throughout Africa and Latin America, unknown numbers of women in these regions of the world are forced to acquire abortion services illegally. Thus, due to the varying legal status of abortion around the world, the availability and quality of the data cited by researchers interested in abortion represent the best available estimates, but the data are not definitive.

Table 1. Likelihood of Abortion

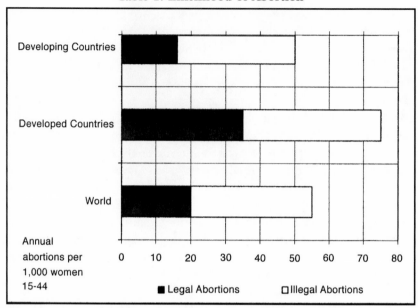

Global Distribution of Abortion

Globally the proportion of women obtaining abortions mirrors the percentage of women living in that region [Table 2 (AGI, 1999)]. Therefore, the majority of women obtaining abortions live in Asia (58 percent), Europe (17 percent), Africa (11 percent), Latin America and the Caribbean (9 percent), and the remainder of the developed world — Australia, Canada, Japan, New Zealand, and the United States (5 percent) respectively (AGI, 2003). In the United States, abortion is the most commonly performed gynecological procedure with an estimated 1.5 legal induced abortions performed each year (Atrash & Saftlas, 2000).

According to the AGI 2003 report, abortion rates vary enormously by country for the 65 countries covered in the study. Statistically, there was a greater frequency of variation of the number of induced abortions *within individual countries*, than by geographic region. Cultural factors such as socio-economic status, religious influence, and politics may explain to some extent why there is greater variability within individual countries than across geographic regions.

Table 2. Percentage of Abortions Worldwide

Percentage of Abortions Worldwide

Abortions in the Former Communist Bloc

In the Eastern European nations and some countries in Central Asia that formally composed the communist bloc, abortions were not only legal, but also not discouraged, and free (Stloukal, 1996; Caldwell & Caldwell, 2003). Women in communist and former communist countries; Cuba, Romania, and Vietnam have the highest reported abortion rates in the world with 73–83 per 1,000 (AGI, 2003). During the Cold War era, contraceptives for women in communist countries were virtually unavailable. At the same time, abortion services were legal, easily accessible, and provided free of charge. With the political, economic, and cultural changes that have affected these countries, contraceptives are now more readily available to women from both government and private sources (AGI, 2003). Other influential factors to consider include the global trend toward smaller family size and increase affluence of household units. Perhaps as a result of the combination of these factors, abortion rates in some of these countries have fallen by as much as 50 percent between 1990 and 1996 (AGI, 2003). Table 3 (Finer & Henshaw, 2006) shows the results of a study conducted in Russia between 1988 and 1998. The table illustrates the relationship between the falling rate of abortion in post-communist Russia and the correlation with the availability of contraception.

Table 3. Abortion Rates & Access to Contraceptives in Russia

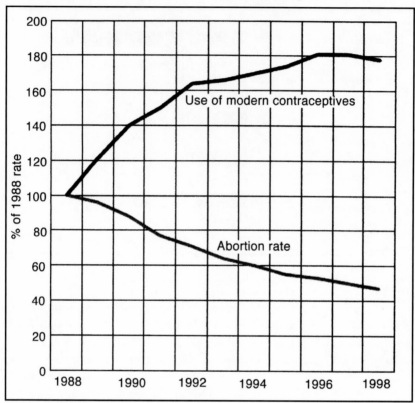

Statistics may tell us how many women worldwide have abortions, but they do not tell us why women choose to have abortions. The next section addresses some of the reasons why women choose abortion and provides a profile of who these women are.

Why Women Choose Abortion

Despite ethnic, economic, religious, and political differences, the reasons why women have abortions fall into seven broad categories. According to recent research (AGI, 2003, p. 17; Abortion Access Project, 2003) women indicate that they have abortions because of the following:

1. They want to stop childbearing;
   - I already have as many children as I want.
   - I do not want children.
   - The contraceptive method I used failed.

2. they want to postpone childbearing;
   - My youngest child is still very young.
   - I want more time between children.

3. socioeconomic conditions;
   - I can't afford to have a child now.
   - I want to finish my education or pursue my career.
   - I need to work fulltime to support myself and family.

4. relationship difficulties;
   - I am having problems with my partner.
   - I do not want to raise a child alone.
   - I should be married before I have a child.

5. age;
   - I am too young to have a child.
   - I am too old to have a child.
   - I don't want my parents to know that I am pregnant.

6. health; or
   - The pregnancy might be detrimental to my health.
   - The fetus may be deformed.
   - I am HIV positive.

7. they have been coerced.
   - I have been raped.
   - My partner or parent insists I have an abortion.

Although we tend to think that women having abortions and those not having abortions are two separate groups — those who are pro-choice or pro-life — in reality they are the same women at different points in their lives. In other words, the choice whether to have an abortion is more meaningfully understood by reflecting on women at different points in their lives and the associated desires, restraints, etc., rather than placing women into a dichotomy based on an oppositional categorization such as pro-choice or pro-life. The latter viewpoint is unhelpful because it does not allow women to occupy the multiple roles they juggle in everyday life. According to Jones,

Darroch and Henshaw's study, "Six in ten women who have an abortion are already a parent. Moreover, fifty-two percent of women having an abortion intend to have children or more children in the future" (2002, p. 230). In brief, women who choose to have an abortion are not doing so because they do not want to be parents, but because they have considered the factors influencing their lives at the time and have contemplated the circumstances that impact their ability to be good parents. This type of deliberation shows a high level of cognitive sophistication and the ability to think about the others outside of themselves.

Culture and Reproductive Choice

Most women around the world are at risk of becoming pregnant from early adolescence, when they first engage in sexual activity, and continue to be at risk for pregnancy until they reach menopause. Yet, many of the reasons why women do not, or are unable to, protect themselves from pregnancy is less about personal choice, than about cultural, religious, socioeconomic, and political circumstances. For example, in present day India, abortion is a legal right for all women, regardless of the cause of the pregnancy. Yet, like other laws in India forbidding the exchange of dowry[3] or pre-natal sex testing (India has a strong preference for males), the reason why abortion is legal in India seems to have very little to do with the Western notion of individual personal rights, and everything to do with over-population, limited natural resources, and westernized forms of development (Manivannan, 2008).

In many developing countries,[4] having a large family is common strategy for survival. Children's labor is an essential component of the household economy. In countries throughout Latin America, Africa, and Southeast Asia, young children haul water, gather firewood, and watch younger siblings. This enables adults to do more mentally or physically strenuous work for subsistence and cash income. Traditionally, while this work was mainly carried out in rural, agricultural-based communities, children's labor in urban centers is also important. Young children from rural villages are often sent to relatives or hired out to non-family members in urban areas to work as domestic servants, messengers, or shoe shine children (Hartmann, 1987).

Having a child in a developing country is a risky venture. There are few guarantees that the infant a woman gives birth to will live beyond its first birthday, let alone to adulthood. In the African country of Angola, the infant mortality rate is 185.4 per 1,000. The lowest mortality rate is in Singapore at 2.3 per 1,000 (World Fact Book, 2007). Diseases like mumps, polio, malaria, tuberculosis, intestinal parasites, and diarrhea claim lives of thousands of children every day. In the developing world, infant mortality rates continue to be extremely high, and therefore many families "hedge their bets" for the future by having multiple children in a short time span. Women may also choose to have large families for reasons of security. The majority of the world's population has limited access to public or private forms of insurance, retirement, and social security. Aging parents depend upon their children to help them in old age, when they are no longer able to provide for themselves.

Sub-Saharan African countries, for example, appear to be more resistant to adopting lower fertility rates than any other region in the world. The reasons behind the opposition are "cultural and have much to do with the religious belief system that operates to sustain high fertility but has also molded a society to bring rewards for high fertility" (Caldwell & Caldwell, 1987, p. 409). The emphasis on large families relates continuing heritage. In contrast to many Western societies where large families are often associated with lower socio-economic status, African families offer social and economic networks and rewards, such as elevated social status, for current and future generations.

Cultural norms, like socially chastising women who do not have large families, are often difficult to break. While these norms may have outlasted the rationale they had in the past, societies continue to embrace them. Thus, a culture can get stuck at a self-sustaining mode of behavior that is characterized by high rates of fertility. However, this does not mean that a culture or society is stagnant and unable to change. Some people cling to cultural traditions, while others do not. Inevitably some individuals will experiment, deviate from the norm, and refrain from joining the crowd. They are the nonconformists, and they assist with cultural change (Dasgupta, 1995).

Additionally, the relationship between women's status and reproductive choice is a prominent theme evident in most of the world's societies (Browner & Sargent, 1996). In cultures where a woman's worth is based upon the number and gender of children she produces, the choices surrounding abortion are different from those in a society where a woman's status and role in society are not based on whether she is a mother. Vielle, as cited in Browner and Sargent, writes that, in the Middle East, a woman is:

> Raised for marriage and procreation, [she] acquires her own social status only by fecundity.... The young woman [is inevitably] ... taken to be responsible for the sterility of the couple, [and] will do everything to change her state: pilgrimages, magic practices ... and so forth. If she does not succeed, she will have only diminished her status [1996, p. 222].

Traditionally, we see the highest birth rates in cultures where there is marked subordination of women (Hartmann, 1987) as opposed to societies where women have a greater range of social, economic, and political mobility. Norway, for example, is a country in which women have gained almost equal status with men in social, economic, and political arenas. Abortions were legalized in Norway in 1964 and further liberalized in 1978. Before 1964, abortion was allowed only for medical reasons and prior to legalization a woman who underwent an illegal abortion was subject to imprisonment (United Nations, 2008). The liberalization of abortion legislation in Norway is closely tied to the development of the women's liberation movement beginning in 1830. One important milestone for the legalization of abortion came on January 15, 1915, when Katti Anker Møller called for legalized abortion on demand saying that "the basis for all freedom is the governance over one's own body and everything that is in it. The opposite is the condition of a slave" (United Nations, 2008). Unlike Norway and other liberal societies, women who find themselves subject to male dominance within the household, the economic and political system, and suffer from the systematic exclusion from public life are presented with a narrow category of reproductive choices. In essence, this type of cultural environment leaves women in such societies with little or no reproductive choice (Hartmann, 1987).

Other examples from the Middle East further demonstrate the role of culture in the definition of womanhood. In the case of Israel, the emphasis on reproduction is tied to political, religious, and cultural autonomy.[5] According to Kahn (2000, p. 3):

> For Israeli Jews the imperative to reproduce has deep political and historical roots. Some feel they must have children to counter-balance what they believe to be a demographic threat ... others believe they must produce soldiers to defend the fledgling state. Some feel pressure to have children in order to replace the six million Jews killed in the holocaust. Many ... simply have traditional notions of family life that are very child-centered.

Haelyon (2006, p. 178) writes:

[T]hroughout Israeli-Jewish history, women were encouraged to reproduce. In 1950, Israel's first Prime Minister David Ben Gurion awarded 100-lira grants to "Heroine Mothers" of ten or more children. And in 1968, a national birth encouragement fund was established.

These examples show how political policy woven with historical events can mold the cultural construction of womanhood in one particular case. It is important to remember that by definition cultural constructions are arbitrary because they are created and maintained by individual cultures. Therefore, the cultural constructions of womanhood are not fixed forever; rather it is dynamic and constantly changing over time and through space (Kottak, 2002).

Contrast the above examples with one that many young women in North America may be familiar with — the HBO sitcom *Sex in the City*. While the show is fiction, according to author and creator Candace Bushnell, the female characters were based on a "chronicle of the true-life adventures of the "in" crowd" she works and socializes with in New York City (http://www.candacebushnell.com). So, while these characters represent one specific media example of contemporary American women, they are based on real American women's lived experiences. The show chronicled the professional and love life of Carrie Bradshaw, a thirty-something single female writer living in New York City. The sitcom, with its focus on Carrie and her close knit group of female friends, "explore[d] the meaning of women's sexual equality in the wake of the social and cultural achievements of second wave feminism" (Gerhard, 2005, p. 37). The popularity of the program was due in part to the "ideal" lives these female characters represented. Their status as women was defined by their cultural achievements in life: educational and job status, zip code, checking account balance, and the mobility they possessed as young attractive women. As in Norway, the "ideal" woman image has been linked in large part to the Women's Movement in the United States. If women liked, they could "work, talk, and have sex 'like men' while still maintaining all the privileges associated with being an attractive woman" (Gerhard, 2005, p. 37). These privileges included choosing to be or not to be a mother.

When Miranda, a single, high-powered partner in a law firm found out she was pregnant with her former boyfriend's child, she was horrified. She contemplated having an abortion and finally decided against it. She had not planned on having children as a single woman, and perhaps not even as a married woman. Charlotte, a character modeled on the pre-women's movement woman in the United States, yearned for the perfect wedding, marriage, and family with children. When she is unable to attain any of these goals, she begins to view herself as a failure as a woman and is jealous of what Miranda has and does not want, in the form of a child.

While I do not know any one woman who embodies all of the traits represented in each of these characters, I can say that I, like many other women I know, do have female friends who have faced similar circumstances. One classmate from my undergraduate alma mater was offered and accepted a prestigious government job straight out of college. The demands (long hours, limited social network largely populated by highly competitive married male colleagues, and frequent relocations to foreign countries) and rewards of the job (elevated social status for a politically visible position, a genuine love of her job, generous fringe benefits and perks, and a lucrative salary) made the decision to settle down and have family and child a distant thought. Now in her mid-forties she has attained a laudable professional career that is the envy of both men and women. However, the demands of her professional life have left little or no time for a family. When I spoke to her recently and asked if she ever thought of doing things differently, she offered no hesitation when answering no. For this particular woman, the social, economic, and political mobility she has achieved would have been hindered by the responsibility that comes with raising children. She sees no need for them in her life and does not regret not having children. This example is not unique, because according to the U.S. Census Bureau "44 percent of all women of childbearing age (15-to-44 years old) were childless. Seventy-one percent of these childless women participated in the labor force" (U.S. Census Bureau, 2003).

A second example of a real woman who embodies characteristics from the *Sex and the City* characters is drawn from an academic mentor. A highly acclaimed feminist scholar, researcher, and mentor found that in her early forties something was missing from her life. She had reached the pinnacle of her career and had accumulated all the security and benefits that one accrues over time. She was independently able to care for herself and a child economically and had a well established social network of family and friends to lend support when needed. She has not married the father of her child, yet she has raised an outstanding child to adulthood while maintaining an exceptional career. This woman's only regret was that "I didn't have the child earlier in life."

These examples, while not unique, show the influence the Women's Movement in the United States has had on the lives of these two women by having allowed them an opportunity to pursue an education, obtain gainful employment and thus define themselves as something other than mothers. Thus, we can see by contrasting these examples of a woman's gender role and subsequent status in the Middle East to that of a white, highly educated, and financially secure women in New York and elsewhere that the reproductive choices available and that status ascribed to being a mother are highly dependent on cultural, political, economic, and social norms of that particular society.

Who Are These Women?

On a global basis, abortion rates are highest among women between the ages of 20–24 and lowest among women under the age of 20 and over the age of 40 (AGI, 2003). This pattern simply reflects the biological pattern of reproduction and fertility among all women. Although previous examples demonstrate the strong influence of cultural, political, and historical influences on reproduction, from a global standpoint young women between the ages of 20–24 generally tend to be more sexually active and fertile than do women younger than 20 and older than 40. This again, is linked to the biology of women since as we age we become less fertile and therefore less likely to conceive and reproduce.

Worldwide, for every 1,000 women of childbearing age, 35 are estimated to have an induced abortion each year — 20 have legal abortions, and 15 illegal abortions (AGI, 2003). Whether a woman lives in a developed or a developing country, her average chance of having an abortion is much the same. However, a woman is more likely to have an abortion either at the beginning or the end of her reproductive lifecycle (AGI, 2003). This pattern mirrors some of the reasons women gave for obtaining an abortion — marital status, wanting to postpone starting a family, not wanting any more children, etc.

Reproductive Choices on the Homefront

While I was pregnant with my second child, I received a distressing email from a dear friend. She and her husband were five months into their second pregnancy. They had one child, age two at the time, and had carefully planned their second pregnancy so that the mother, whom I will refer to as Sarah, could spend time with the infant while taking a leave of absence from her work. Sarah and I had known each other from our graduate school days and for years talked about "trying not to get pregnant" so that we could complete our graduate degrees. As young female graduate students, we had several colleagues who became pregnant while still in school. We witnessed firsthand the challenges of being a student and parent. Neither of us wanted to spend more time in school and each of our friends who had children while in graduate school seemed to add years to their degree plans. Being mentored by second-wave feminist scholars, we were focused on completing our coursework and obtaining our degrees without the added challenges of raising children and supporting a family. However, after finishing our degrees the focus of our conversations shifted from avoiding pregnancy to "getting and staying pregnant." By staying pregnant I am referring to the fact that while neither Sarah nor I had any difficulty in conceiving, we both experienced multiple miscarriages and were well aware of the emotional and physical challenges often associated with "not staying pregnant."

Being "older" and highly educated parents over the age of thirty-five, Sarah and her husband decided to have all the genetic testing offered to them to assure that they would have a healthy child. The results, however, were not what they had expected. During the course of a high-level ultra-sound they discovered that the child they were so anxiously awaiting did indeed possess a serious genetic defect. The disorder was not one that the doctors were originally screening for, but it was detected nonetheless. Although Sarah and her husband thought they knew what they would do in such a situation, they discovered that the decision to keep or terminate the pregnancy was more complex than anticipated and influenced by a myriad of factors they had never considered. What followed were several weeks of agonizing decision-making for Sarah and her husband.

Sarah sought me out because I was the only one of her friends who she knew who had also dealt with difficult issues surrounding pregnancy and childbirth. Sarah and I both experienced health related situations that strongly influenced future reproduction.[6] Sarah and I proceeded to have several insightful and tearful conversations about the complex issues regarding abortion. As academics, Sarah and I were able to intellectualize the situation, thereby distancing ourselves to some extent, from the emotions surrounding abortion. Having spoken at length with Sarah, I know that the decision that she and her husband reached was influenced by a multitude of factors including age, religion, socio-economic status, education level, access to quality health care, and comprehensive health insurance.

Reproductive Choices in Rural Illinois

As an anthropologist, I wanted to test my assumption that culture — including all of the above mentioned factors — do influence women's perceptions of and decisions regarding reproductive health and abortion. In other words, would Sarah's experience be mirrored by other women facing similar challenges? Would women without access to comprehensive health insurance make different choices? Would the level of education influence a woman's choice to have or not have an abortion? Put differently, was Sarah's situation unique or were there factors that influence the choices a woman makes regarding reproductive health? Thus, situated in the larger national arena of women's reproductive health in the United States, I asked a group of rural Illinois women questions about reproductive health care and abortion. Using a combination of anonymous surveys and focus group interviews, the concluding part of this essay illustrates the cultural factors that influence the perceptions of reproductive health and abortion for rural women in western Illinois.

The Methodology

Several sources of data were incorporated into this case study, including the general body of peer reviewed anthropological and health care research on the topic. Data specific to the case study of rural Illinois women comes from a multitude of sources including the results of previous health care surveys of rural Illinois residents (Straub and McNamara, 2001), and publications and reports from Illinois health care agencies. This archival research served as the basis for the ethnographic research I conducted from 2002–2003.

For the ethnographic portion of the research, I administered a total of 102 anonymous questionnaires (Reproductive Health Questionnaire — RHQ) to women of childbearing age in Macomb, Illinois. A local women's health care facility whose clientele represented the socio-economic, religious, educational, and ethnic diversity found within this rural community served as the distribution point for the questionnaire. Facility staff distributed the questionnaires to women along with other paperwork. The questionnaire included an introduction explaining the purpose of the research and informed them that their participation was voluntary and anonymous and would not affect the services that they would receive.

In addition to the anonymous surveys, I facilitated two focus groups with female students at Western Illinois University. Flyers were placed in public areas notifying the entire student population of the research. Announcements were also made in anthropology, sociology, and women's studies classes. Women of all ages were invited to participate. The qualitative information solicited in the focus groups served to augment the quantitative data gathered through the questionnaires. A total of 14 women participated in the focus group discussions. The first focus group consisted of 5 women, all Caucasian between the ages of 18–23. The second focus group consisted of 9 women, 7 of whom were Caucasian, 1 Hispanic, and 1 African American. Ages for the women in this group ranged from 18–32.

The Findings

The four-page RHQ asked respondents several questions specific to the issue of reproductive health and abortion. When asked "Do you practice family planning?"[7] 53.8 percent of the respondents answered yes, with the remaining 46.2 percent answering no. This finding is in stark contrast to the findings of the AGI's 2006 report which indicates that "98% of sexually experienced American women have used a contraceptive method at some point in their lives" (p. 6). Research conducted by the Center for Disease Controls (CDC) indicates that contraceptive use is "virtually universal among women of reproductive age" (Mosher, Martinez, & Chandra, et. al, 2004, p. 1). With this information in hand, what variables could possibly explain the discrepancy between respondents in the RHQ research and the national studies? The answer may lie in the age and economic status of the RHQ respondents. According to the AGI (2006, p. 7):

> Women of color and those who are young, unmarried or poor have lower levels of contraceptive protection than do other women, leading to higher levels of unintended pregnancy in those groups.

This was indeed true of the women participating in the RHQ study. Fifty-two percent were between the ages of 18–25 with the remaining 16 percent between the ages of 26–35. The remaining respondents categorized themselves as over 40 years of age, yet still considered themselves to be of child-bearing age. Clearly the women responding to the RHQ represented a segment of the population that is generally younger than those responding to the AGI research.

Perhaps more influential were household income level and access to health insurance. Women participating in the RHQ study who indicated that they did not use contraceptives selected an average household income category of $15,000–$34,999 annually. Additionally an astounding number of households, 85 percent, indicated that they did not have access to health insurance. When combined, these factors tell us that the majority of women in rural McDonough County who responded to the RHQ are young, poor, and lack access to health insurance. These findings mirror those of Jones, et al. (2002) that suggests economically disadvantaged women may find it more difficult to obtain and use effective contraceptive methods than their more affluent counterparts. While contraceptives are available to economically disadvantaged women and those without access to health insurance, the barriers one needs to overcome to obtain these services are often challenging.

Conversely the women participating in the focus groups all indicated that they had health insurance[8] and 95 percent indicated that they used contraceptives. Increased access to education, higher standard of living, and health insurance were again factors influencing the decisions of these women. Ethnicity, however, did not seem to be a factor for either the focus group participants or the questionnaire respondents. The population of both McDonough County and Western Illinois University is relatively homogeneous with the majority of women participating in the RHQ research identifying themselves as Caucasian.

Despite the initial contradictory responses among the RHQ survey respondents to the previous question, their answers did mirror the findings of other researchers around the world who indicated that the majority of the world's population supports permitting abortions in some circumstances in countries ranging from Bangladesh (Amin, 2003) to France (Blayo & Blayo, 2003). When asked the following question on the RHQ:

> What is your opinion on abortion? Please ✓ the box that most closely fits your view.
>
> Women should have the right to decide if abortion is right for them ☐
> Against abortion ☐
> Depends on the circumstances surrounding the pregnancy ☐
> Undecided ☐

Thirty-three percent of the RHQ respondents indicated that women should have the right to decide if abortion is right for them. For the remaining respondents, five percent of the women indicated they were against abortion, while thirty-three percent indicated that their opinion on abortion depended on the circumstances surrounding the pregnancy. The remaining women, 28 percent, indicated that they were undecided about their opinion on abortion (See Table 4).

Table 4. Opinions on Abortion from the Rural Health Questionnaire

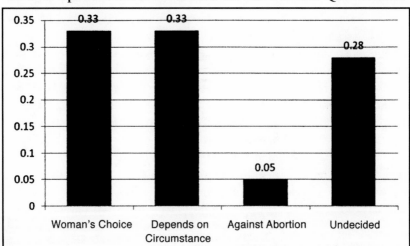

Focus group participants were posed the same question as the questionnaire respondents, yet they were given an opportunity to elaborate on their answers. Their responses help shed some light on the cultural context behind the above numbers. One participant said this about a woman's right to choose:

> My grandmother had my mom when she was 15. She (my grandmother) didn't have a choice about whether she wanted to have a child or not — abortion wasn't an option. In those days she had to quit school (high school), get married and raise her kid. I don't think she regrets having my mom, I know that she loves her, but I often think that she is sad about the life she couldn't have.

This comment reflects that limited options available to women at the time the respondent's grandmother was pregnant. In particular, this narrative supports the thesis of this essay that it is important to understand the cultural and temporal context a woman finds herself in when pregnant. As we see from the above account, this woman's decisions were influenced by the political reality and social expectations of the time. This leads us to question whether given a different temporal, cultural and political climate this particular woman's choices might have been different. Prior to the legalization of abortion in the United States, women had few alternatives if they found themselves with an unplanned pregnancy. One of the telling aspects of this particular story is that the respondent is a first generation college student who adamantly stated that she wanted to finish her degree. During the focus group discussion she often referred to the fact neither her grandmother nor mother were able to go to school beyond high school and the participant "didn't want to end up like they did," demonstrating an understanding of the relationship between educational attainment and standard of living. Clearly, completing her education is one way in which this particular woman feels she can have a better life than either her grandmother or mother. When asked whether she ever wanted to have children, the respondent replied "Yes! But only when I can provide for them."

Another focus group participant had a very different view on abortion:

> I'm a Christian and the Bible says not to take the life of another. I can't imagine killing my unborn baby or getting myself into the circumstances that would lead to that kind of situation. I mean if I was dumb enough to have sex before I got married, then shouldn't I suffer the consequences?

Among other things, this participant's comment illustrates the influence of religion on opinions about the conceptualization or understanding of conception and personhood, or how and when life begins. Anthropologists who study this topic have documented a wide variety of ideas of when life begins and ends from around the globe. When I posed the question "When do you think life begins?" to the focus group participants, their conversation dealt not only with this particular question, but also with the freedoms of the mother over that of an unborn fetus. Like most Americans, the focus group participants were unable to reach a consensus about when life begins. Several participants referred to what they learned in biology class where their professors emphasized that even scientists have no clear understanding of when life starts. Is it when the sperm fertilizes the egg or afterwards? Or could it even be before the sperm and egg meet, since these organisms are themselves alive? Others said, "...well if science can't decide maybe this is should be determined by religion." Yet within the group there was no universal religious understanding of the beginning of life either. The one and only Buddhist[9] participant said:

> I believe that life is a continuous circle. The form I have today may end tomorrow, but I really believe I will come back as something else. And before I had this body I was also here, but not in this form. So where does life begin and end?

Those participants who identified themselves as Christian[10] had a decidedly different viewpoint on the beginning of life. One participant said:

> Life begins when a sperm and egg meet. End of story. That makes abortion at any stage wrong because you are killing another human being.

From this discussion, participants returned to the question "are the rights of the mother or the unborn child more important?" As in the discussion about the beginning of life, participants were unable to come to a consensus. However, they did recognize that the inability to define the beginning of life results in a double definition of personhood that has long been at the center of the abortion debate in the United States. Based on the 1973 *Roe v. Wade* seven to two decision that ruled that a pregnant woman has the right to make the decision over the fate of the fetus, the in utero fetus is not yet a person (Tompkins, 1996). Yet the basis on which the ruling was made is highly influenced by culture. The Supreme Court ruled:

> [O]nly when it [the fetus] grows toward viability and reaches a point where it can survive on its own outside the uterus, ... does the fetus acquire personhood [Janzen 2002, p. 142].

Advances in medical technology have made it possible for infants born as young as 23 weeks gestational age (17 weeks premature) to survive outside the womb. Clearly, this definition is a precarious and ever-changing one that was not lost on the focus group participants.

When a fellow focus group participant posed the question to the group, "What if you were raped?" the discussants shifted their focus to the rights of the mother over the fetus, suggesting a shared understanding of person-hood based on the Western European concept of personal autonomy. Virtually all of the participants agreed that rape and incest were exceptional circumstances that warranted special consideration. In fact, from a global perspective the legality of abortion is influenced by rape and/or incest. According to Mundigo (2003), in 84 percent of developed or first world countries and 26 percent of developing or third world countries, abortion is legal under these circumstances.

As a feminist, I see the focus group discussions leading back to the more general question of the role of women in contemporary American society. When asked how they envisioned their future, 95 percent of all focus group respondents indicated that they wanted to have children at some point in time, yet not now. Their comments again mirror the data gathered by other researchers who indicate that a woman's decision to have an abortion or not often rests on whether she feels that she can care for the child at that time. The value of being a mother has clearly not vanished from our culture, but it is being reshaped by our changing understanding of what it means to be a woman in today's world.

Conclusion

Anthropologists are not the only ones who conduct research on abortion. However, what anthropology brings to the table is the ability to personalize the conversation by using women's voices and their subjective experiences as part of the analysis (Rylko-Bauer, 1996). In other words, the personal narratives collected through ethnographic research add meaning to the statistical data. Statistics are important tools because they can tell us how many women have abortions on an annual basis, but they cannot tell us why.

As we have seen in this essay, women have a wide variety of reasons why they may or may not have an abortion. And many of these reasons are influenced by culture. In other words, from an anthropological perspective it seems clear that a woman's decision about whether to have an abortion or not is based in large part on the multi-dimensional aspects of the culture she inhabits, e.g., the physical location of her residence, the political, economic, and social climate of the time and the biological time frame in which these particular choices are made. By this I mean, a woman who finds herself facing an unplanned pregnancy at 18, while still in high school and only beginning to think about how to support herself financially, may make a very different choice about an unplanned pregnancy than at age 31 with a well established career with financial and social stability.

From this brief overview about abortion around the world, we know that abortion remains one of our most socially divisive issues we face today. We also know that abortion has been practiced throughout history and by all cultures. The factors influencing a woman's access to a safe and legal abortion are constantly changing. The changing landscape surrounding abortion is largely out of control for those most directly influenced by it — namely women and children. While there are a few women who hold political positions of power around the world, the vast majority of women in the world are underrepresented in political life. In some countries in the Middle East, women are considered the property of men from cradle to grave. These cultural attitudes of gender superiority are reinforced through the creation of laws carried out by men.

Perhaps the argument about "abortion isn't about abortion" (Feldt, 2006, p. 241). Maybe the foundations of this debate are centered on the discussions of gender equality. While the public face of the women's movement has diminished and many young women are reluctant to call themselves feminist, I think that at the basis of the abortion debate is the ongoing struggle over gender equality. Other scholars like Beckwith (2005) agree when they write that if abortion didn't result in the termination of an unborn human, it is likely that the debate would diminish or perhaps even cease to take place. As in the focus groups, we find ourselves back to the question is the debate around abortion really about the medical procedure called abortion, or is the debate about the everyday cultural reality of being a woman?

From the examples in the essay, we have seen that regardless of whether a woman lives in rural Illinois, Eastern Europe, or Israel, her choices about abortion and reproductivity are influenced by factors which are often difficult to influence or control. These factors include the culturally constructed status of women in that particular society, politics, religion, access to health insurance, educational level, and many others. Women who have abortions are the very same women who either already have children or who will go on to be parents in the future. The debate in the United States around abortion is centered on the premise that the unborn fetus is unable to survive outside the womb, thereby denying the fetus the title of "personhood." Yet every day, technological advances in medicine push the gestation period and viability back from the standard 40 weeks. Our definition of the fetus and personhood is based on culture — and culture is ever changing. In April 2007 the Supreme Court, with two new Bush appointees, changed the legal landscape on abortion. By a five to four vote, the Supreme Court upheld a ban on a particular abortion procedure which abortion opponents call "partial birth" abortions, thereby opening the door to other challenges to abortion. Both sides of the Court — the majority and dissenting voices — represent that conflicting notions of whose interests count most in American society. Fifteen years ago, Justice Ruth Bader Ginsburg, a longtime women's rights advocate, noted that the Supreme Court recognized that a woman's ability to recognize her full potential is intimately related to controlling her reproductive life. A little less than one hundred years ago, women in the United States did not possess the right to vote. That changed. Culture changed. In 1973, women gained the right of reproductive freedom in the form of *Roe v. Wade*. In 2007, the Supreme Court changed the parameters of those reproductive rights. Is our culture changing the roles and expectations of women again, and if so what does the future look like? That is for us all to decide.

Notes

1. A wide variety of factors influence the legal status of abortion around the globe. It is helpful to understand the nuances between human rights, political rights, and moral grounds arguments.

Opinions formed from the interpretation of international human rights legal instruments which conclude that women have a right to decide independently in all matters related to reproduction, including the issue of abortion (Human Rights Watch 2008). Human Rights arguments conclude that women should be recognized as autonomous beings capable of making decisions independent of external influences.

Political rights arguements are influenced by religious, moral, and cultural sensibilities and vary widely around the globe. In the United States, pro-choice and pro-life groups both utilize the right to life, pursuit of liberty, the right to the security of person, and the right to reproductive health to bolster their arguments for and against laws pertaining to abortion.

Moral grounds positions must first be situated as part of the moral community. The definition must be made as to who belongs to the moral community. The question arises as to what sort of entity, as a member of this moral community, possesses the inalienable rights to life, liberty, and the pursuit of happiness? Thomas Jefferson originally attributed these rights to all *men*. However one must question whether or not he intended to attribute them *only* to men. Perhaps he ought to have attributed them to all human beings. If so, then we arrive at the point of defining what is a human being (Warren 1996).

2. I wish to thank the Illinois Institute for Rural Affairs for their support while conceptualizing and conducting this research. I also wish to thank all those who participated in and helped to facilitate this project.

3. Money or property brought by a bride to her husband at marriage.

4. A country whose per capita income is low by world standards.

5. Cultural autonomy is understood as "persons belonging to national or ethnic, religious and linguistic minorities have the right to enjoy their own culture, to profess and practise their own religion, and to use their own language, in private and in public, freely and without interference or any form of discrimination" (United Nations 1992).

6. I was pregnant twice before giving birth to my first child. One pregnancy was ended by a second trimester miscarriage, while the other was medically terminated as a result of a life threatening ectopic pregnancy. Both of the miscarriages resulted in some short term physical challenges, and some trepidation on the part of both me and my husband about conceiving again.

Having had a healthy third pregnancy, I assumed that I was out of the woods, so to speak, and that the birth of my first child would be "routine." My husband and I attended the childbirth classes and being academics had done a substantial amount of reading about all aspects of childbirth. However, the birth of our first child was a near medical disaster for both baby and mother. To make a long story short, I experience undiagnosed eclampsia and HELLP syndrome. Eclampsia is a life-threatening complication of pregnancy, which as in my case, is often undiagnosed. The symptoms are not uncommon with pregnancy — elevated blood pressure, weight gain, and fatigue. Eclampsia often follows pre-eclampsia. Full blown eclampsia may result in the presence of seizures or a coma. HELLP syndrome, is a syndrome featuring a combination of "H" for hemolysis (the breakdown of red blood cells), "EL" for elevated liver enzymes, and "LP" for low platelet count (an essential blood clotting element) and is a recognized complication of preeclampsia and eclampsia (toxemia) of pregnancy, occurring in 25 percent of pregnancies (Medical Terms Dictionary 2008). In short, my first child was born as the result of an emergency cesarean section and I ended up in the Intensive Care Unit for three days with liver failure. Fortunately both the baby and I were able to fully recover from this ordeal and are now healthy. Suffice it to say, I had sufficient insight into the parallels of pregnancy and childbirth to be a worthy sounding board for Sarah.

7. Family planning implies using some form (medical or natural) of contraception.

8. A requirement for university students

9. Reincarnation or rebirth in Buddhism is the belief that upon death the consciousness of a person becomes one of the contributing causes for the creation of a new group of *skandhas* or aggregates which may at some point again be what we consider a person or individual. The consciousness arising in the new person is neither identical to, nor different from, the old consciousness, but forms part of a causal continuum or stream with it (Collins 1982).

10. The majority of mainstream Christians reject the notion of reincarnation and consider the theory to challenge basic tenets of their beliefs such as the resurrection of the body of Christ.

References

Abortion Access Project. (2003). Retrieved June 19, 2003, *http://www.abortionaccess.org/*.

Alan Guttmacher Institute. (1999). Facts in Brief: Induced Abortion Worldwide. Retrieved July 13, 2007: *http://www.guttmacher.org/pubs/fb_0599.html*

Alan Guttmacher Institute. (2003). Sharing Responsibility: Women, Society, & Abortion Worldwide. Policy Paper.

Alan Guttmacher Institute. (2006). Abortion in Women's Lives: Monograph. Retrieved June 19, 2006: *www.guttmacher.org/pubs/2006/05/04/AiWL.pdf*.

Amin, S. (2003). Menstrual regulation in Bangladesh. In A.M. Basu (ed.) *The Sociocultural and Political Aspects of Abortion* (pp. 153–166). Westport, Connecticut: Praeger.

Atrash, H. K., and A. F. Saftlas (2000). Induced Abortion. In M. B. Goldman & M. C. Hatch (Eds.) *Women and Health* (pp. 160–170). San Diego: Academic Press.

Beckwith, F. J. (2005). Who and What Are We? (What the Abortion Debate Is Really About). Retrieved July 19, 2007: *http://www.trueu.org/Academics/LectureHall/A000000144.cfm*.

Blayo, C., and Y. Blayo (2003). The Social Pressure to Abort. In A.M. Basu (ed.) *The Sociocultural and Political Aspects of Abortion* (pp. 237–248). Westport, Connecticut: Praeger.

Browner, C. H. and C. F. Sargent (1996). *Anthropology and Human Reproduction.* In, C.F. Sargent and T. Johnson (eds.) *Medical Anthropology: A Handbook of Theory and Research,* 2nd edition, pp. 219–234. Westport, CT: Greenwood.

Bushnell, C. (2008). It's a Jungle Out There. Retrieved on April 21, 2008: *www.candacebushnell.com*.

Caldwell B.K. and J.C. Caldwell (2003). Below-Replacement Fertility in Asia: Determinants and Prospects in South Asia. *Journal of Population Research.* 20 (1):19–34.

Cohen, M. N. (1989). *Health and the Rise of Civilization.* New Haven and London: Yale University Press.

Collins, S. (1982). *Selfless Persons: Imagery and Thought in Theravada Buddhism.* Cambridge University Press: Cambridge, MA.

Dasgupta, P.S. (1995). Population, Poverty, and the Local Environment. *Scientific America.* 272(2):40–46.

Devereux, G. (1976). *A Study of Abortion in Primitive Societies.* New York: International Universities Press.

Feldt, G. (2006). Afterword. In Jacob (ed.) *Abortion Under Attack: Women on the Challenges Facing Choice* (pp. 241). Emeryville, California: Seal Press.

Finer, L.B., and S. K. Henshaw (2006). Perspectives on Sexual and Reproductive Health. New York, NY: Guttmacher Institute. 38(2), 90–96.

Gallen M., T. Narkavonkit, J. B. Tomaro, and M. Potts (1981). *Traditional Abortion Practices.* Research Triangle Park, NC: International Fertility Research Program.

Gerhard, J. (2005) Sex and the City: Carrie Bradshaw's Queer Postfeminism. *Feminist Media Studies.* Vol. 5, No. 1: 37–49.

Haas, L. (1994). Infanticide. In *Encyclopedia of Social History*, P. Stearns (ed.). (pp. 351–352). New York: Garland Publishing, Inc.

Haelyon, H. (2006). Longing for a Child: Perception of Motherhood Among Israeli-Jewish Women Undergoing *In Vitro* Fertilization Treatments. *National Journal of Jewish Women's Studies and Gender Issues.* 12: 177–206.

Hartmann, B. (1987). *Reproductive Rights and Wrongs: The Global Politics of Population Control and Contraceptive Choice*. New York: Harper & Row Publishers.

Human Rights Watch (2008). *Women's Rights:* Abortion. Retrieved June 26, 2008 from *http://www.hrw.org/women/abortion.html*.

Janzen, J. (2002). *The Social Fabric of Health*. New York: McGraw-Hill.

Jöchle, W. (1974). Menses-Inducing Drugs: Their Role in Antique, Medieval and Renaissance Gynecology and Birth Control. *Contraception*, 10(425).

Jones, R.K., J. E. Darroch, and S. K. Henshaw (2002). Patterns in the Socioeconomic Characteristics of Women Obtaining Abortions in 2000–2001. *Perspectives in Sexual and Reproductive Health*, 34(5), 226–235.

Kottak, C. (2002). *Cultural Anthropology, 9e*. New York: McGraw-Hill.

Manivannan, S. (2008) Beyond Pro-Life and Pro-Choice: Abortion in India. Retrieved May 7, 2008 from: *http://youngfeminists.wordpress.com/2008/02/07/beyond-pro-life-and-pro-choice-abortion-in-india-2/*.

Mankekar, K. (1973). *Abortion : A Social Dilemma*. Delhi: Vikas Publishing House Pvt. Lt.

McElroy, A., and P. Townsend. (2004). *Medical Anthropology in Ecological Perspective*, 4th Edition. Boulder, Colorado: Westview Press.

McFarlane, D. and K. Meier (2001). *The Politics of Fertility Control: Family Planning and Abortion Policies in the American States*. New York: Chatham House Publishers, Seven Bridges Press, LLC.

Medical Terms Dictionary (2008). Retrieved May 6, 2008: *http://www.emedicinehealth.com/*

Mosher, W. D., G. M. Martinez and A. Chandra et al. (2004). Use of Contraception and Use of Family Planning in the United States: 1982–2002. *Advance Data from Vital and Health Statistics*, No. 350.

Mundigo, A. (2003). The Challenge of Induced Abortion Research: Transdisciplinary Perspectives. In Basu (ed.) *The Sociocultural and Political Aspects of Abortion* (pp. 50–64). Westport, Connecticut: Praeger.

Newman, L. F. (1985). *Women's Medicine. A Cross-Cultural Study of Indigenous Fertility Regulation*. New Brunswick: Rutgers University Press.

Posner, R. (1992). Sex *and Reason*. Cambridge: Harvard University Press.

Riddle, J. M. (1992). *Contraception and Abortion from the Ancient World to the Renaissance*. Cambridge: Harvard University Press.

Rylko-Bauer, B. (1996). Abortion from a Crosscultural Perspective: An Introduction. *Social Science Medicine*, 42(4), 479–482.

Smith, E. A., and S. A. Smith (1994). Inuit Sex-Ratio Variation. *Current Anthropology* 35, 595–624.

Stloukal, L. (1996). Eastern Europe's Abortion Culture: Puzzles of Interpretation. Paper presented at the *International Union for the Scientific Study of Population Seminar on the Sociocultural and Political Context of Abortion*, Trivadndrum, India.

Straub, L. A., and P. McNamara (2001). Rural Illinois Women: Access to Health Care Services. Illinois Institute for Rural Affairs. *IIRA Reports*.

Taylor, T. (1996). *The Prehistory of Sex*. New York: Bantam Books.

Tompkins, N. (1996). *Roe v. Wade and the Fight Over Life and Liberty*. New York: Franklin Watts.

United Nations (2008). Abortion: Norway. Population Policy Data Bank maintained by the Population Division of the Department for Economic and Social Affairs of the

United Nations Secretariat. Retrieved April 21, 2008: www.un.org/esa/population/publications/abortion/doc/norway.doc

U.S. Census Bureau (2003). Percentage of Childless Women 40 to 44 Years Old Increases Since 1976, Census Bureau Reports. Retrieved May 7, 2008: *http://www.census.gov/Press-Release/www/releases/archives/fertility/001491.html*

Warren, M.A. (1996). On the Moral and Legal Status of Abortion. *In Biomedical Ethics. 4th ed.* T.A. Mappes and D. DeGrazia, eds. pp. (434–440). New York: McGraw-Hill, Inc.

World Factbook (2007). U.S. Census Bureau, International Database.

World Health Organization (1994). *Abortion: A Tabluation of Available Data on the Frequency and Mortality of Unsafe Abortion.* 2nd ed. Geneva: Maternal Health and Safe Motherhood Program, Division of Family Health, World Health Organization.

World Health Organization (1998). *Unsafe abortion: Global and Regional Estimates of Incidence of and Mortality Due to Unsafe Abortion.* 3rd ed., Geneva: World Health Organization.

Abortion, Polyphonic Narratives and Kantianism
Quality of Life Matters

SUSAN MARTINELLI-FERNANDEZ

Abstract

This paper explores various moral considerations within the context of individual decision-making about the permissibility of abortion. Arguing that a right to abortion does not capture the morality of a decision whether or not to preserve a pregnancy, I turn to the moral relevancy of quality of life issues. This is seen most clearly in pregnancies involving multiple embryos, when some embryos might have to be terminated in order that others may survive. A right to abortion seems meaningless in this context; instead, the focus is on considerations of the quality of life of all members of a pregnancy-relationship. I discuss the plausibility of a feminist Kantian perspective utilizing a conception of polyphonic narrative and Kantian notions of relational autonomy and respect.

Quality of life perspectives on pregnancy are nothing new in philosophical literature. However, such conversations seem to arise only when considering an alleged right to procreation. While ideas of how other people may be affected by the birth of another individual is at the heart of discussions about abortion in Japan and China, Western philosophers in the 20th Century have focused instead on the moral desirability of having children (Bayle, 1979; Hinson, 1979; O'Neill, 1979; Steinbock and McClamrock, 1994).

Commonly, the literature focuses on the wish to have and raise a child; that is, the desire for pregnancy and its completion. All discussion of a "right

Reprinted by permission from "Abortion, Polyphonic Narratives and Kantianism: Quality of Life Matters" in Teaching Ethics, *volume 6, number 1— Fall 2005.*

to abortion" seems meaningless in a context where the primary desire is to preserve a wanted pregnancy. This is particularly true in pregnancies involving multiple embryos. Here we see that the issue of abortion may emerge only because some embryos might have to be terminated in order that others may survive.

By reflecting upon the above, the primacy of quality of life considerations may emerge as paramount. It will be suggested that issues about quality of life are more morally relevant than rights based considerations, when considering whether to preserve a pregnancy. Further, quality of life actually falls under the wide concept of autonomy. In fact, one might understand part of this paper's present enterprise as a response to Marilyn Friedman's "second challenge for feminist relational accounts of autonomy ... to reconceptualize the notion of selfhood and individuality in a coherent manner" (219). Within a Kantian framework, quality of life is an end of all members of a pregnancy-relationship and, thus, must be respected. Finally, by adding the conception of polyphonic narrative to the Kantian framework, the plausibility of a feminist Kantian perspective, free of isolated individualism and reified abstraction is established.

Autonomy and Beneficence

Onora O'Neill distinguishes between a right to procreate and a right to become a parent. She claims that there is no unrestricted right to procreate, observing, "[B]egetters or bearers must have or make some feasible plan for their child to be adequately reared by themselves or by willing others" (1979, 25). O'Neill thereby isolates a problem that can serve as the basis of this paper's arguments for quality of life considerations; that is, How do we (correctly) identify persons upon whom the child can make claims? For present purposes, this paper demonstrates how this claim is disentangled from the notion of a "right," particularly a political right.

O'Neill argues that the claim that children ought to have their needs and interests satisfied is separate from determining the party that will satisfy them. She locates the moral salience here in the decision to have a child and the responsibility of decision-makers to consider the implications for the being that they want to bring into the world. The needs and interests (and the assignation of who will satisfy them) need to be seen as something required by not only "the baby," but by the unique human being who will be a child, teenager, and adult.

In pursuing the project of identifying persons upon whom the child can make claims, O'Neill distinguishes between liberty rights (rights concerning duties of non-interference) and claim rights (obligations that are owed to us and are assigned to particular people). Liberty rights can be understood as strict obligations and as a species of "perfect duties" and are legal requirements such as duties of justice.[1] Claim rights can be understood as broad obligations, a species of "imperfect duties," such as duties of beneficence. Duties of justice, understood as "perfect duties," are ethical requirements that help us discharge the first part of our Kantian duties, i.e., not to merely use each other. To anyone, regardless of our familiarity with that individual, we owe such duties. For example, physically abusing a parent is legally punishable not because the person is our relative (although morally abhorrent); rather, it is punishable because we are to refrain from physically harming anyone.

In contrast, duties of beneficence, are imperfect duties, i.e., obligations that arise only when we have a particular relationship within which specified persons can discharge these kids of obligations.[2] We may think less of a parent who does not put the needs of his child before his, but we cannot, in usual cases, prosecute such an individual. Likewise we might think that an adult child failing to call her parent regularly was repugnant, but there is no legal recourse to effect a different, more filial behavior.

One critical difference between the above two kinds of rights is that the latter are much more difficult to discharge and, therefore, satisfy. It is this point that O'Neill repeatedly returns to in her analysis of parental obligations to children. Rights that can't be discharged are impotent and, in a sense, self-defeating. What use is a "right" if, in reality, it can not be exercised?

However, how will the language of obligations get us any farther in this particular inquiry? It is a central thesis of this paper that it will. First, the language of obligation is present, as we have argued, in the notion of rights themselves. We acknowledge this in the correlation of rights and duties, understanding obligation as a type of duty. Second, the language of obligation can be located in a key term appealed to in philosophical and medical ethics literature that is often associated with rights, i.e., autonomy. We will require it in order to make the stronger claim about the strength of moral obligations: these must be understood as requiring a thicker sense of respect than that grounded in a strict rights' notion of duty.

Reflecting on the ground breaking work of John Hardwig in "What about the Family? The Role of Family Interests in Medical Treatment Decisions," and its influence on medical ethics literature, we can trace a trend from a patient-physician model that tends to focus on patients' rights and autonomy to a model that tends to emphasize the moral relevance of others' interests, particularly those of the patient's family (1990, 5–10; 1993, 20–27). Hardwig attempts to move medical ethics' discussions out of a rights-based perspective to one that acknowledges the moral force of reciprocal obligations between those individuals who are intimately part of a patient's life. He believes that rights-based discussions of medical treatment fail to recognize the obligatory force of such relationships. In Hardwig's view, the moral force of those relationships that the patient has must be considered since people other than the patient herself are affected by decisions made about patient treatment. His perspective is intended to make room for others who are impacted by the patient's decision and is not meant to ignore or replace patient decision-making. In fact, one might understand Hardwig's perspective as relational.

In the more traditional patient-physician and patient-centered rights perspective and even in Hardwig's alternative perspective, considerations of patient treatment and care based on autonomy are construed as markedly different from those that would be based on beneficence. In other words, people have a moral obligation to benefit others, even sometimes promoting their happiness. Here, we must be clear about whether one believes that happiness refers to a felicific calculus of hedonistic/psychological pleasure, i.e., pure felt pleasure. Alternatively, we can understand happiness as human flourishing, much like the Greek sense of "eudaimonia." Quality of life considerations and their connection to beneficence and, ultimately, autonomy are necessary parts of a conception of happiness understood as human flourishing as a moral being.

The purported dichotomy between autonomy and beneficence — and, in feminist literature, justice and care — references a similar problematic for both philosophical theory and medical ethics. The source of the problem stems from a misunderstanding of the idea of autonomy, particularly the Kantian one. Barbara Secker attempts to clarify the issue by suggesting a distinction between "Kant's concept of autonomy" and "the Kantian concept of autonomy." Arguing that both concepts may be troublesome when applied to bioethical issues, Secker offers "a more promising concept of patient autonomy." Unfortunately, this account, like many other attempts at refuting or revising the conception of Kantian autonomy rest upon a simplistic Kantian concept of autonomy rooted in Mappes's and DeGrazia's introductory remarks in *Biomedical Ethics* (1996) which perpetuates the dichotomy between autonomy and beneficence (1999, 43–66). However, in Kant, a full moral agent is one who discharges moral duties that come under the heading of justice and rights and who freely performs obligations that are understood as stemming from beneficence. The second formulation of Kant's Categorical Imperative also distinguishes between treating people as mere means and treating them as ends, understood as our rational capacity of setting goals. We discharge duties of justice when we avoid the former, and demonstrate our respect for persons when we act on our obligations grounded in beneficence. Thus, autonomy and beneficence are not mutually exclusive; rather, both are required for full Kantian moral agency.

In contrast, a thicker sense of respect is available when we actively take on the projects of others with whom we have entered into voluntary relationships. Ultimately, full Kantian moral agency requires us to do more than refraining from some activity that harms someone. O'Neill makes a similar clam and implies such a distinction about respect when she states "[M]aking another into a tool or instrument in my project is one way of failing to treat that other as a person; but only one way" (1989, 105). This paper builds upon O'Neill's discussions and suggests that there is a gradation of moral respect that rests on whether one is merely avoiding treating people as mere means or whether one is, in fact, actually promoting people's ends. As discussed more fully later, this will require actions that are "subject only to free self-constraint, not to the constraint of other men, and because they determine an end which is at the same time a duty" (Kant, *The Metaphysics of Morals, Metaphysical Principles of Virtue,* 395).

There are four kinds of respect, stemming from the performance of duties of justice and obligations of beneficence. The first kind of respect is based on our avoiding treating people as mere means. We can also understand this as the kind of respect that comes out of a rights-based ethical framework. This is the thinnest sense of respect. Some would argue that we show a lack of respect when we treat others as mere means. This may be true. However, it is a thin sense of respect that stems from discharging negative duties by following principles such as justice, for, in doing so, we are merely refraining from harming individuals and not actively promoting their ends. This distinction can be understood as the difference between external action (through the notions of right or "recht") and internal end-setting (through the notions of virtue and moral worth) (Kant, *MM, MPV* and *The Metaphysical Principles of Right—MPR*). Certain internal ends must be set to demonstrate respect. Merely performing an external action that is in conformity with the Categorical Imperative without setting the appropriate internal end may not command any notion of respect. Yet, even if there is some kind of respect resulting from the performance of such an action (if performed from duty), such respect is different in degree of moral approbation from those actions that arise out of more intimate kinds of relationships that provide the occasion for treating particular, identifiable individuals as the persons they are. Hence, "if we fail to respect or to share the other's ends, the failure is imputable to us" (O'Neill, 1989, 125). Thus, the responsibility to perform actions (which stem from beneficence) and the respect following the performance of these actions demand that a particular designated person has clearly set her own internal ends which include the ends of others, without coercion.

In contrast, the responsibility for performing external actions which are understood as duties of right (or juridical and perfect duties) are primarily understood as falling upon any individual and, as general kinds of duties, are not assigned to any particular person. The performance of these kinds of duties represents the exercise of external freedom. Although actions performed according to these kinds of duties are chosen, the duties themselves may be coerced. My keeping a promise in the form of a contract, for example, to any person can be enforceable by systems of justice (such as societal laws that enforce keeping a contract) and a motive underlying my promise keeping is threat of enforcement. If the external freedom of others is infringed upon, the use of force may be used against the agent so that she and her "use of freedom" are returned to a "lawlike state."[3] To treat someone as an end-in-her/himself is to recognize one's own ability and the ability of others to identify and freely take on distinctively human ends. Hence, the first kind of respect is so designated because the agent has performed only one kind of duty, which does not entail any free or uncoerced setting of ends.

Next, we have a second kind of respect that results from not hindering people's pursuit of their ends. Although respect in this sense stems from the obligatory force of voluntarily entered into relationships, it is still negative in the sense of not actively promoting such ends. While there is a recognition of the setting of a free and unforced end of another and one's self, the end (or ends) of the other has not been acted on — they have only not been interfered with. This kind of respect is less thin, but not as substantial as a third kind of respect, one which is generated by going beyond negative duties (respect in the first sense) and negative obligations (respect in the second sense) and actually benefiting the person *qua* person. Meeting this third kind of respect requires that an individual do all that she can to help others achieve their goal. This can also be understood as an imperfect duty of virtue, given that a positive end is set and being promoted. This third degree of respect has the agent act freely on her end of promoting the end (or ends) of others. It is subject only to free self-constraint, extending beyond external freedom (*MPV* 395–96).

Finally, there is a fourth sense of respect where new, mutually accepted and acted upon ends are generated. A caveat or, perhaps, a reminder is required. Each formulation of the Categorical Imperative entails the existence of all the other formulations. This means that the universalizabiltiy criterion and the kingdom of ends formulations are also present. The fourth sense of respect makes this quite clear — an individual sees herself legislating laws for herself as a fellow rational being and understands that her fellows do the same. The point of emphasizing the Formula of Humanity is to set out what the content of any law that is legislated or moral maxim is, *viz,* members of humanity understood as ends-in-themselves thus acknowledging their capacity to freely set ends (*Grounding,* 437; *MPV,* 392). In concert with the other member(s) of a freely entered into, specified relationship, the agent has revised her initial end of promoting the end of another and has set a new end that she and another have created and will act upon. Like her own initial end, the newly created end is one that has been freely entered into and cannot be coerced. This is the richest sense of respect and the hardest to achieve. These four gradations of respect each reflect a more morally mature and praiseworthy discharge of the requirements of the second formulation of the Categorical Imperative.

Thus, a more morally praiseworthy sense of respect arises out of the discharge of obligations of beneficence based on relationships that we voluntarily enter into (O'Neill, 1980, 285–94). Although it may not be immediately clear whether the fourth and final sense of respect is possible when any of the involved parties lacks full deliberative capacities, it will be one of the stronger senses of respect. In the present discussion, we would say that parents have obligations toward their own children. These obligation are different from the kinds of duties they owe children to whom they bear no biological relationship. As discussed in a previous example we might also say that adult children have obligations towards their aged parents. Although morally reprehensible, paying for medicine for one's aged father, for example, is not a legal requirement unless stipulated by some legal directive or agreement. In Kantian language, there is an obligation and, hence, an imperfect duty of benevolence to provide medications, if required to merely make the parent's life more comfortable.[4]

To recap, perfect duties are always required of us and imperfect duties are required of certain people who stand in relationship to each other in a particular way. A full Kantian moral agent, it has been argued, must discharge both kinds of duties. Hence, we find in a Kantian understanding of autonomy that morality requires performing the requirements of both autonomy and beneficence. Additionally we see that a relational understanding of moral obligation is actually embedded in the concept of autonomy itself. A final point of clarification will be required, however. In introductory remarks to *Relational Autonomy: Feminist Perspectives on Autonomy, Agency, and the Social Self,* Catriona Mackenzie and Natalie Stoljar argue that there is a distinction between the concept of autonomy and various conceptions of autonomy (2000). It is their central thesis that a feminist reinterpretation of autonomy yields a particular conception of autonomy, called relational autonomy. This paper rejects this view and has argued that autonomy itself has an important relational quality on a fair and reasonable reading of Kant's text. In fact, the Categorical Imperative itself presupposes a relational autonomy. First, there is the requirement to promote the ends of others, which is part of what it means to be a fully developed autonomous agent. Second, the relationship between the Formula of Humanity and the other formulations of the Categorical Imperative (especially the Formula of the Kingdom of Ends) further support the thesis that all members of a relationship treat each other as fully participating members of a community. This means that they share a common set of goals and values (understood as ends) as well as some ends, which are unique to each member. All members are to promote these ends.

Finally, four kinds of respect, based on a gradation of moral respect that rests on whether one is merely avoiding treating people as mere means or whether one is, in fact, actually promoting people's ends have been distinguished. Each kind of respect is dependent upon whether duties of justice or obligations of beneficence are performed as well as whether there is a sense of free and uncoerced setting of ends. The most morally robust form of respect results from not merely discharging duties that we would owe anyone; rather, this kind of respect rests on our meeting our obligations to those whom we are in a position to know best because we are in a particular relationship with them. In fact, it is our possession of a "detailed and intimate" knowledge of those people that means we can, in fact, fully discharge duties and obligations that autonomous Kantian moral agency requires (O'Neill, 1989, 252–77). Without such knowledge, it would be impossible to identify and to further people's ends at all.

The next section will focus on questions that arise when adjudicating selective termination. It will be a given assumption of this discussion that we cannot presume that the embryo is already a person, hence not having a moral right not to be terminated. Instead, the conversation of a couple, one not predicated on the presumption is imagined. Indeed, in this conversation, the notion of a "right to life" will not come up at all.

Abortion and Reproductive Technology

The introductory remarks have already suggested that cases where "selective termination" is the issue will be considered. One might readily suppose that the quality of life of the embryos selected to survive will come up only if there is some value attached to those selected for termination. For if there is no value attached to embryos about to be terminated, then morally we may terminate any number of them for the sake of some recognized value, such as optimizing the chances of birthing a normal healthy human infant.

Now suppose the pregnancy entails multiple embryos ranging from seven to two in number. Further assume that the people involved in deciding whether and how to preserve the pregnancy make their decision on the basis of consequentialist moral reasoning, with a desired outcome of preserving the pregnancy. The value of a given embryo depends in great part on the probability of its being born normal and healthy, which is directly related to the number of womb-partners it has. Even if the value of one of seven is low (based on probability of birth), the total value of all seven may be much lower than the value of one or two.[5] If this were the case, it would seem that the termination of all but one or two embryos is morally required. Yet, who are the relevant decision-makers who will determine this value? The physician, the begetters, or, some surrogate decision-maker for the embryos themselves?

Indeed, one might question the moral reasoning behind this appeal to a consequentialist standard of moral decision making.[6] One might argue that from a more general point of view the lives of all the embryos are equally valuable. There appears to be no basis to favor any one of the embryos over another. Furthermore, one will need to determine what other relevant factors may be present, such as the health of the woman, and the couple's desire for and ability to take care of more than one infant. These additional factors are a necessary part of quality of life considerations.

Perhaps a better route for this discussion is to move from calculating probability of birth to considering quality of life once born. Consider a distinctively feminist framework of a theory of care — Gilligan's theory of care — and its claim of the importance of moral obligations arising out of distinctive relationships. Both pro- and anti-abortion positions have employed this theory in support of their positions. Pro-abortion positions are usually bolstered by a more traditional analysis of what a person is and the rights that persons have (Jagger, 1979; Markowitz, 1990). Yet, this consideration is central to rights theory and is also often an object of feminist criticism. The anti-abortion positions are sometimes grounded in a holistic understanding of the interconnectedness of nature (Purdy, 1996; Rudy, 1996; Warren, 1997). Further, there is neither explicit or implicit reliance on nor appeal to the notion of rights. Human beings, *qua* persons, on this view are not creatures that are privileged over other living things. Hence, all claims to life are valuable and are equally worthy of preservation.

If this interpretation about Kantian moral obligations arising out of particular relationships and its emphasis on kinds of respect is correct, the Kantian account will be preferable to non–Kantian ones. First, it suggests how one might think about abortion issues in general, from a non–political rights view. Second, it acknowledges that the ends of all members of a relationship must be carefully considered. A woman facing the decision of whether to terminate a pregnancy must include a sense of what she owes to others with whom she shares or will share her life with. In matters of freely chosen pregnancies, perhaps most clearly seen in those involving technological interventions, it is hard to imagine that she has not made a determination of what the quality of her life will be. This determination surely includes the recognition of others whom she loves that make her life worth living and consideration for the quality of their lives as well.

In Kantian terms, a female begetter's moral deliberations about preserving or terminating a pregnancy must include consideration of the ends of the partner begetter, the unborn, existing young human beings, as well as other people including elderly dependent relatives. Respect for these ends are necessary, but not sufficient, constituents of the female begetter's inclusive end of quality of life.

This recognition of the need to acknowledge others' ends is a necessary part of the ethical deliberations of the fully autonomous agent given that she is required to discharge duties of justice and obligations of beneficence. Bearing her own moral scrutiny as an autonomous agent, she should assess the kind of respect that is possible to give to the members of the pregnancy relationship. She is morally required to respect each member of that relationship as fully as possible, for, it has been argued, she is in the unique position of having the ability, based on knowledge of the parties' ends, to do so. But, there are differences in the kind of respect that she can give, since the most morally mature kind of respect rests on our performing obligations to those whom we are in a position to know best.

Under the first kind of respect, based on refraining from treating people as mere means, a minimal respect might require the woman not just viewing her partner/begetter as merely a sperm donor and, thus, having no part in deliberations about preserving or terminating a problematic pregnancy. Not viewing the unborn entity in the pregnancy relationship merely as a means to maintain the partner-begetter's and the woman's relationship also reflects the thinnest sense of respect. From a rights-based view, someone who views herself as "pro-life" and chooses to not have an abortion on the sole basis that it is wrong to kill anyone reflects this first sense of respect. As a duty of justice based on the notion of "right," the action, while chosen, can be based on coercion. Further, there is no consideration of the unique relationship between the unborn and the female begetter. However, a woman who has made a conscious decision to bring "her" or "her and her partner's" child into the world has a particular kind of responsibility, and obligation, to that unborn. She does not have this kind of obligation to the unborn of other people since she is "in" a specific relationship with her own unborn.

One might argue that there may be no felt connectedness with the unborn. There are at least two possible responses. First, the relationship is based on being in the relationship and not on one's feeling(s) about the relationship. Second, the female begetter may have existing children who she "knows" better. This means that she will have obligations to additional interested parties in the relationship. Thus, she owes something more than the first kind of respect, hence discharging merely a duty of justice. The remaining and more morally salient kinds of respect demand considerations beyond avoiding merely using another and, in addition, acknowledging and acting upon the ends of others. In the case of a pro-life decision not to terminate, this decision must include consideration of the ends of the unborn.

Analogous to an assumption about the unborn having an interest in living which underlies Don Marquis's claim about the impermissibility of abortion, a Kantian moral agent could claim that there are ends of the unborn that must be respected. The most important of these ends is the opportunity to have a future including setting goals and achieving them. *A fortiori,* death would preclude such a future (Marquis, 1997). Yet, certain kinds of birth defects might also make such a future impossible; hence, the Kantian could argue for the permissibility of abortion.

However, a problem arises given that the unborn itself fails to be seen as a moral agent having such ends. This problem is, in part, perspectival: while the female begetter must consider the ends of all involved, from the deliberator's own point of view it is difficult to identify and then respect the ends of those who can not speak for themselves.

Imagine a woman who decides not to have an abortion. Her decision is based on the belief that killing in general is wrong and that terminating her own unborn is even worse. She may argue that she is in a particular relationship to the unborn and she owes the second kind of respect. This means that she is required to not get in the way of people's pursuit of their end; hence, termination is morally impermissible, since life is necessary in order for an end to be pursued. Although respect in this sense stems from the obligatory force of voluntarily entered into relationships, it is still negative in the sense of not actively promoting such ends.

Preserving the pregnancy is thus required for the second sense of respect. This kind of respect is less thin, but not as substantial as a third kind of respect, one which is generated by going beyond negative duties (respect in the first sense) and negative obligations (respect in the second sense) and actually benefiting the individual. However, without altering the example, it is not clear how she would be able to offer anything more than the second sense of respect. Presumably she would need more detailed knowledge of the unborn, its capacities, skills, more complex goals, etc., to achieve either the third sense of respect or the fourth sense of respect where new, mutually accepted and acted upon ends are generated.

Correcting Rights Theory: Kantianism, Feminism and Polyphonic Narratives

This essay has claimed that quality of life considerations are more important than rights-based considerations. However, it may be that what has actually been demonstrated is that emphasizing quality of life consideration can be understood as a corrective to rights-based theory. Further, a broader notion of autonomy might be required, for, as has been argued, autonomy and beneficence need not be interpreted in opposition or conflict with each other. Yet it has been a central thesis of this essay that the Kantian notion of autonomy is itself relational. To support this latter claim, this work has sought to demonstrate how the second formulation of the Categorical Imperative, The Formula of Humanity, can provide a framework for avoiding this seeming dichotomy. Obligations of beneficence are a species of duty required for full Kantian autonomous moral agency and, in fact, are embedded in the concept of autonomy itself, demonstrating that the Kantian concept of autonomy is indeed relational.

This essay has provided an account of a continuum of moral respect that might be useful in deliberations about various issues that sometimes arise for a female begetter, including preserving or terminating a pregnancy. Each of the four kinds of respect is determined by whether one is merely avoiding treating people as mere means or whether one is, in fact, actually promoting people's ends — ranging from the thinnest sense of respect that stems from only avoiding treating people as mere means and, thus, discharging negative duties of following principles such as justice, to the thickest sense of respect that results when we actively take on the projects of others and, together, form new projects with those whom we have entered into voluntary relationships. This continuum reflects how full Kantian autonomous moral agency requires us to do more than refraining from some activity that harms someone.

Notice that if a woman decides against termination on the sole grounds of a legal prohibition, there is no moral choiceworthiness to her action. Seen in this way, a woman's decision to preserve or terminate a pregnancy can never be seen as a moral one, if her ability to freely choose whether or not to have an abortion is either absolutely denied or restricted by law or some other coercive mechanism. Morality is about the ability to make a choice. Hence, I've focused on the point of a view of a woman, understood as a fully autonomous agent, making that choice; not from the point of view of a disinterested spectator assessing that choice. Indeed, the choice to become pregnant and bear a child is one that also entails (or at least should entail) the choice to become someone who is responsible for raising another human being. In discussions concerning whether the decision to become a mother can be understood to be autonomous, Diana T. Meyers writes "[I]f the value of motherhood is embedded in women's bodies, and if, therefore women's critical reflection about becoming mothers is usually superfluous, it must be shown that being a mother is an all but incontrovertible value comparable to life itself" (42–43).

As a Kantian, feminist, and reconstructionist, I would like to find a middle ground between notions of autonomy, freedom, care, otherregardingness, and respect for human as well as non-human nature. Within a Kantian framework, it has been demonstrated that quality of life is an end of all members of a pregnancy relationship and, thus, must be respected. Further, it has been argued that obligations of beneficence are a species of duty required for full Kantian autonomous moral agency. This means that obligations of beneficence and hence the idea of a "relational autonomy" are embedded in the concept of autonomy itself. By demonstrating how Kantian moral obligations actually arise out of particular relationships, typical objections of abstraction, impartiality and universality can be blocked.

Yet, this account is not without its problems, given the inability to go beyond a second sense of respect. Recall, because of the embryo's inability to participate in the pregnancy preservation conversations, the remaining more robust forms of respect cannot be acted upon.[7] Thus, how can we support the premise of the arguments thus far that the strength of the Kantian position is its ability to demand respect for all parties? If we take seriously the demands of autonomy (understood as relational) and the requirement of respect towards others that are embedded in the Categorical Imperative, more work needs to be done. Perhaps, a more robust analysis of the Formula of the Kingdom of Ends could be provided; yet, the relationship between members of this ideal construct are fully rational choosers and the unborn is (minimally) not a full member of this community. Or, turning to other works by Kant which address parent-child relationships might be fruitful. Yet, such accounts are few and lack direct discussion of the particular issue of this paper — members of a pregnancy relationship, one of which is unborn.

For now, asking, "Whose voice is missing?" is the next step, allowing us to take seriously why and how we account for the interested parties in a pregnancy relationship. This attention to voice, that is, considering who the relevant speakers are (or at least ought to be) and what their stories are, might strengthen the Kantian perspective and perhaps result in a distinctively feminist Kantian perspective. The importance of different voices is emphasized in the notion of a "polyphonic narrative," understood as a vehicle to construct an all inclusive feminist perspective that acknowledges more than two voices or two perspectives through which a distinct narrative, representing the interests of all participants, explicitly present or not, will be constructed (hooks, 228; Kristeva, 1986; Martinelli-Fernandez, 2000). Further, this conception must be understood as a necessary feature of a Kantian account, for it will allow us to give voice to, in addition to identifying, all interested parties as well as their particular interests in considering the desirability of preserving or terminating a pregnancy. There is no sense to be made of a self, independent of or from others. Our moral decision-making process does not occur from or in an ideal or hypothetical perspective; rather, it is a process that includes the particular concerns of others as well as ourselves.

Further this attention to voice strengthens the focus on what we owe to each other based on ties of love that connect us through our relational commitments. Feminist theories that incorporate care ethics are theoretically grounded in the idea of webs of relationships — relationships that are woven by women, lovingly spun as well as destroyed when the occasion warrants. In contrast, the rights' perspective has a language of bindingness that suggests coercion and slavery.

It is doubtful that the rights' perspective can or should be ignored, jettisoned, or rendered impotent. A woman must be free in the practical sense to make a decision. And, while that freedom seems to be so abstract in the words and mouths of philosophers, it is quire real when we make a decision that, in part, relies on the ability of others to help us act on that decision.

Politically, rights theories are necessary, for they do obligate others to agree to refrain from prohibiting us from making real, practical choices. Morally, however, these kinds of theories blind us from seeing all that is required to make those choices — in the case of determining whether to preserve a pregnancy, the members of that relationship, their quality of life considerations and our quality of life which is inextricably connected to theirs. Does this mean that a woman gives up her right to an abortion, based on others' explicit or implicit considerations of quality of life? Absolutely, not. Rather, she *chooses* whether or not to exercise this right. This choice is the expression of quality of life concerns for self and others and, hence, of relational autonomy — *viz.*, the free and uncoerced choice of an individual who understands, acts upon, and respects the well-being, life plans, and activities of herself and others, both near (e.g, family) and far (any fellow human being).[8]

Notes

1. MPV, 389–384.

2. The distinction between perfect and imperfect duties as well as their connection to Kant's notions of strict and broad obligations is notoriously complex. Contemporary Kantians have written extensively on the complexity and virtue of distinguishing between perfect and imperfect duties. For example, see Onora O'Neill, "A Simplified Account of Kant's Ethics," in "The Moral Perplexities of Famine Relief," in *Matters of Life and Death,* T. Regan (ed.), 1st edition (New York: Random House, 1980), 285–294; "Between Consenting Adults," (1985), in *Philosophy and Public Affairs,* 14(3): 252–77; and "Embodied Obligations," in *Towards Justice and Virtue,* (Cambridge: Cambridge University Press, 1996), 146–52. Barbara Herman, "On the Value of Acting from the Motive of Duty," in *the Practice of Moral Judgment* (Cambridge, MA: Harvard University Press, 1993), 1–22. Christine M. Korsgaard, *Creating the Kingdom of Ends* (New York: Cambridge University Press, 1996), pp. 18–24.

3. I thank an anonymous reviewer for making this point. Also, there are some promises that are not enforceable by legal coercion. See note 5.

4. A question may arise as to whether this may be a perfect duty, if the medication is required to sustain life. The case of providing medication for parents is complex — clearly, there is no threat of legal action if the medication is for a "better life." The beneficent action would be to make the parent's life more bearable if not happier. In addition, this may be seen as action that could be grounded in the duty of gratitude, another imperfect duty (MPV, 455). Such action stems from "a heartfelt benevolence on the part of the benefactor" (MPV, 455). The point here concerns legal enforceability with a contin-

ued focus on distinguishing between duties of justice and duties of beneficence (one kind of imperfect duty). Also, it would be remiss not to point out that the coercion of external action that distinguishes perfect duties may not always be legal. An anonymous reader suggests it is incorrect "to think that all perfect duties are legally coercible (the example of the obligation to provide medication being 'not a perfect duty'). This is incorrect according to the MM — some perfect duties are unenforceable by legal sanction (i.e., suicide) and some perfect duties ought not to be enforced." Yet, the threat of legal sanctions may keep an individual from performing an act of suicide if the agent assumes that the attempt could be unsuccessful; hence, a sense of legal coercion would be still present.

5. E-mail correspondence with H. William Davenport on 03/26/2004.

6. For an interesting discussion of consequentialist decision-making applied to issues concerning selective termination, see Walter Glannon's "The Morality of Selective Termination" in *Reproduction, Technology, and Rights,* edited by James M. Humber and Robert F. Almeder (Totowa, N.J.: Human Press, 1996).

7. Clearly, this problem is not unique to this particular issue. Indeed, it occurs whenever there is a situation in which participants are not fully formed moral agents, such as children or the elderly. Often, requirements of paternalism in the best sense seem to replace obligations of beneficence.

8. I have avoided a discussion of duties (perfect and imperfect) to oneself purposely so that the focus is on the relational quality of autonomy and on the duty of beneficence to others.

References

Bayles, M. (1979). Limits to a Right to Procreate. In O. O'Neill and W. Ruddick (Eds.) *Having Children: Philosophical and Legal Reflections on Parenthood* (pp. 13–24). New York: Oxford University Press.

Christman, J. (1995). Feminism and Autonomy. In D. E. Bushnell (Ed.) *Nagging Questions: Feminist Ethics in Everyday Life* (pp. 17–39). Lanham, Maryland: Rowman and Littlefield.

Friedman, M. (2000). Feminism in Ethics: Conceptions of autonomy. In M. Fricker and J. Hornsby (Eds.) *The Cambridge Companion to Feminist Philosophy* (pp. 205–224). Cambridge: Cambridge University Press.

Glannon, W. (1996). The Morality of Selective Termination. In J. Humber and R. Almeder (Eds.) *Reproduction, Technology, and Rights.* Totowa, NJ: Human Press.

Hardwig, J. (1993). The Problem of Proxies with Interests of Their Own: Toward a Better Theory of Proxy Decision. *Journal of Clinical Ethics,* 4(1), 20–27.

_____. (1990). What About the Family? The Role of Family Interests in Medical Treatment Decisions. *Hastings Center Report,* 20(2), 5–10.

Herman, B. (1993). On the Value of Acting from the Motive of Duty. In *The Practice of Moral Judgment* (pp. 1–22). Cambridge, MA: Harvard University Press.

hooks, b. (1990). *Yearning: Race, Gender and Cultural Politics.* Boston, MA: South End Press.

Jagger, A. (1994). Abortion and a Woman's Right to Decide. In R. Baker and F. Elliston (Eds.) *Philosophy and Sex* (pp. 324–337). Buffalo, NY: Prometheus Press.

Kant, I. (1785). *Grounding for the Metaphysics of Morals.* Trans. by James Ellington in *Immanuel Kant: Ethical Philosophy.* (Indianapolis, Indiana: Hackett Publishing Co., Inc., 1983).

Kant, I. "The Metaphysical Principles of Right" and "The Metaphysical Principles of Virtue" in *The Metaphysics of Morals.* (1797). Trans. by James Ellington in *Immanuel Kant: Ethical Philosophy.* (Indianapolis, Indiana: Hackett Publishing Co., Inc., 1983).

Korsgaard, C. (1996). *Creating the Kingdom of Ends.* New York: Cambridge University Press.

Kristeva, J. (1986). Word, Dialogue, and Novel. In T. Moi (Ed.) *The Kristeva Reader* (pp. 34–61). New York: Columbia University Press.

Mackenzie, C., and N. Stoljar (Eds.). (2000). *Relational Autonomy: Feminist Perspectives on Autonomy, Agency, and the Social Self.* Oxford: Oxford University Press.

Mappes, T. A., and D. DeGrazia (Eds.). (1996). *Biomedical Ethics,* 4th edition. New York: McGraw-Hill, Inc.

Markowitz, S. (1990). Abortion and Feminism. In *Social Theory and Practice* 16 (Spring). pp. 1–17 (Florida State University, Department of Philosophy).

Marquis, D. (1997). An Argument that Abortion is Wrong. In H. LaFollette (Ed.) *Ethics in Practice* (p. 91). Oxford: Blackwell Publishers.

Martinelli-Fernandez, S. (2002). Kant, Lies, and Business Ethics. *Teaching Ethics: A Journal of the Society for Ethics Across the Curriculum,* 2(2), 41–52.

_____. (2000). Social (re)construction: A Humean Voice on Moral Education, Social constructions and Feminism. In A. J. Jacobson (Ed.) *Feminist Interpretations of David Hume* (pp. 184–217). University Park: Pennsylvania State Press.

Meyers, D. T. (2005). *Gender in the Mirror: Cultural Imagery and Women's Agency.* Oxford: Oxford University Press.

O'Neill, O. (1979). Begetting, Bearing, and Rearing. In O. O'Neill and W. Ruddick (Eds.) *Having Children: Philosophical and Legal Reflections on Parenthood* (pp. 25–38). New York: Oxford University Press.

_____. (1980). A Simplified Account of Kant's Ethics. In T. Reagan (Ed.) The Moral Perplexities of Famine Relief in *Matters of Life and Death,* 1st Edition (pp. 285–294). New York: Random House.

_____. (1987). Between Consenting Adults. In *Constructions of Reason: Exploration of Kant's Practical Philosophy.* (Cambridge: Cambridge University Press). pp. 105–125. Originally published in 1985. "Between Consenting Adults" in *Philosophy and Public Affairs,* 14(3): 252–277.

_____. (1996). *Towards Justice and Virtue.* Cambridge: Cambridge University Press.

Purdy, L. (1996). *Reproducing Persons: Issues in Feminist Bioethics.* Ithaca, New York: Cornell University Press.

Rudy, K. (1996). *Beyond Pro-Life and Pro-Choice: Moral Diversity in the Abortion Debate.* Boston, MA: Beacon Press.

Secker, B. (1999). The Appearance of Kant's Deontology in Contemporary Kantianism: Concepts of Patient Autonomy in Bioethics. *Journal of Medicine and Philosophy.* 24(1), 43–66.

Steinbock, B., and R. McClamrock (1994). When Is Birth Unfair to the Child? *Hastings Center Report.* 24(6), 15–21.

Warren, M. A. (1997). *Moral Status: Obligations to Persons and Other Living Things.* Oxford: Oxford University Press.

Staying Within an "Understanding Distance"

One Feminist's Scientific and Theological Reflections on Pregnancy and Abortion

ALTHEA K. ALTON

Abstract

Scientific and theological viewpoints on abortion are often at odds with one another. A common result is that scientists and theologians are reluctant to engage in productive dialogue on the issues. In this essay, I share my reflections as a feminist, developmental biologist, and seminary-trained theologian. I examine concepts of authority, mind/body dualism, self, personhood and soul from a feminist perspective. I summarize major scientific views on the question of "when life begins," evaluate each view scientifically, and share my theological reflections. Based on these evaluations and reflections, I propose a theology of creation that views life as both fully embodied and a continuum. Such an understanding may help others to hold the viewpoints of science and religion in tension, to the end that they inform one another. This provides a unique framework to evaluate issues of pregnancy and abortion so that those with various scientific and theological perspectives may reengage in productive dialogue.

As a feminist biologist, a seminary-trained theologian, a person who has actually done experiments in reproductive biotechnologies in the mouse (Alton, 1981), and a former pastor, I have a unique perspective on abortion that I bring to this essay. I bring my scientific knowledge, my theological training and reflection, my feminist perspective and my experience as a pastor to the conversation on abortion. It is a conversation in which these different ways of knowing and understanding the world have often been at odds with one another. Instead of remaining within an "understanding distance" of one another, parties to the conversation often choose to leave the table. I cannot, obviously, walk out on myself. I have had to remain at the table and let my various understandings of the issue inform one another. I hope my reflections will be of interest to all who seek a better understanding of the issues.

The incredible progress in scientific information and biological technology in the last century has resulted in the concentration of authority in an elite group of individuals with specialized knowledge and standing in this field. These technologies are on the cutting-edge of science, and are not accessible for study to many of those outside the ivory towers of academia, the campuses of well-funded research-1 institutions, federal agencies, and successful biotechnology corporations. As a result, only the most ambitious, the most aggressive, the most intelligent, and the least encumbered with excess baggage are successful in the field. This often translates to white, male, wealthy, Ivy-league educated individuals with M.D.s, Ph.D.s, M.B.A.s, and J.D.s. Progress in the field is rapid, research is expensive, funding is scarce, and competition is intense. If a woman readjusts her priorities even slightly, in order to have children for instance, she soon finds herself far behind the competition.

Even when women attain sufficient education, experience, and stature to be counted as one of the elite, it is difficult for them to remain in the field. Moreover, as tenured professor and accomplished surgeon Frances K. Conley, M.D., found, intelligence, skills, dedication, and hard work were insufficient as she struggled to advance at Stanford University's School of Medicine. "In addition, I would need to wage a life-long battle to overcome imprinted cultural expectations, especially those defining a woman's limits and be willing to persist in the face of misogynistic antagonism" (Conley, 1998, p. 10). In her book *Faculty Diversity: Problems and Solutions,* national diversity consultant Jo Ann Moody, Ph.D, J.D., points out that:

> Even women who have become members of the distinguished American Academy of Sciences and other elite groups can face harmful assumptions and instrumental exploitation, both of which slow down their career advancement. For example, at MIT in 1996, sixteen of the seventeen tenured women faculty in science documented that they (in comparison with their 194 tenured male colleagues) received less lab space, lower research funding from the institution, and fewer promotions to leadership

roles, such as department chair — despite their equal qualifications with male faculty [Moody, 2004, p. 84].

Within the sciences, biomedicine in particular, has gained a special status. Paul Starr notes that practitioners of biomedicine

> come into direct and intimate contact with people in their daily lives; they are present at the critical transitional moments of existence. They serve as intermediaries between science and private experience, interpreting personal troubles in the abstract language of scientific knowledge]Starr, 1982, p. 142].

Practitioners of reproductive biomedicine come into direct and intimate contact with women at particularly critical and often vulnerable times in their lives.

Although U.S. law clearly supports the concept that, in most circumstances, decisions on medical treatment rests with the individual person, many people feel inadequate to make an informed judgment about the treatment of their bodies. As a result, the right to make a judgment about the treatment of our bodies is often abdicated to those in positions of medical "authority." This same tendency often results in an acceptance of health policies created or supported by those who claim this authority. We need a better understanding of our bodies before we can make informed decisions about them. This is particularly true in the issue of abortion which involves both the body of the embryo/fetus and the body and life of the mother with which it exists only in inseparable biological relationship.

Why have women been so willing to yield power over our bodies? Feminist and gerontologist Sally Parker Thomason traces the roots of our willingness back to Descartes and the idea of mind/body dualism as well as to modern Western philosophy's reliance on the power of human reason to explain the physical universe. Quoting Descartes' thesis that, "There is a great difference between mind and body, inasmuch as body by nature is always divisible and the mind is entirely indivisible," Thomason argues that mind/body dualism had profound implications for the development of medical science.

> The belief that the physical body, completely separate from the numinous mind and spirit, is a divisible, mechanical object that must be reductively examined to be understood became the fundamental premise, the epistemological foundation of modern medicine [Thomason, 2006, p. 62].

Theological and religious beliefs have also reinforced the understanding of mind and soul as separate from the physical body. One of the earliest schisms in the Christian church, for instance, was caused by the position taken by some bishops that Mary was the mother of Jesus' human nature but not of his divine nature (Christ). In this view, Mary served only as a vessel through which Christ passed. Although this position was formally rejected at the Third Ecumenical Council in 431 C.E., this idea persists in some Christian doctrines. Paradoxically, the Christian doctrine of salvation depends on the understanding that God was made incarnate (embodied) in Jesus and that it was Jesus, the Christ, fully human and fully divine, who died on the cross in atonement for the sins of humanity.

Many of us remain uncomfortable with the more recent and holistic view that we do not simply have a body, we are our bodies. We experience our body as self. Our perception, experience, and understanding of the world cannot be separated from our bodies. The body is a dynamic entity, always in interaction with any and all the input it receives from the world. The stimuli we receive in the form of visual cues, smells, tastes, emotions, pheromones, sounds, touch, stress, and day length, all act on the brain's pituitary gland which in turn organizes the body's response. The pineal gland, which Descartes called the "seat of the soul," is found deep within the brain and yet it reacts to cycles of light and dark to regulate our circadian (daily), monthly, and seasonal rhythms. The body's interactivity is particularly important in women, where the monthly rhythmicity of hormones affects receptivity and generativity (Borysenko, 1997).

When considering our positions on abortion it becomes even more uncomfortable because we are asked to not only separate our bodies and our selves but to further separate ourselves from another "body" and another "self." Thus, a major issue in the abortion debate is now "when does a new life begin?" and, furthermore, "does one separate this new body from new mind and soul?" Dealing with these questions is difficult because, from a biological perspective, both the egg and the sperm are living cells; thus life, from one generation to the next, can be viewed as a continuum.

In this essay, I summarize the basic scientific facts about early development that help elucidate the question of when life begins. Then, to address the separation of mind/body and evaluate the role of the soul, I reflect theologically on the critical issues involved. Throughout the essay, I use scientifically and medically accepted terms for the stages of human life.

125

Specifically, *sperm* and *egg* unite during *fertilization* to produce a single-celled embryo referred to as a *zygote*. The *zygote* develops as an *embryo* which after nine weeks is called a *fetus* and at birth is called a baby. I have chosen to use these terms because they are descriptive rather than evaluative. The terms were coined and defined by embryologists long before the beginnings of the abortion debate. Many critics of abortion use the term baby to refer to the fetus because they object to the connotation of "fetus" as containing less value than a baby. My intent is to present scientific facts as well as my theological reflections and evaluative understandings of the facts. It is critical, therefore, that I use descriptive rather than evaluative terms and that my readers understand my use of these terms.

Is there a consensus among scientific viewpoints about when life begins? No, there is not consensus among scientists as to when life begins. In strictly scientific terms, sperm and egg are living cells and so one cannot argue scientifically that life starts from scratch each generation. Perhaps a question that science may better address is "when in the process of human development does an organism reach sufficient individualization to be considered a separate organism?" (Gilbert, Tyler, & Zackin, 2005, p. 40). Are sperm and egg separate living organisms? While to many, the obvious answer might be an unequivocal no, the answer is not that simple.

In several animal species, eggs can and do develop parthenogenetically, that is, develop into the next generation with no input from sperm. Several species, such as the fruit fly (*Drosophila mangabaeri*), the grasshopper (*Pyncnoscelus surinamensis*), and the lizard (*Cnemidophorus uniparens*), exhibit exclusively parthenogenetic development and all of these species consist of entirely female individuals (Gilbert, 2006, p. 632). In mice, egg cells can be chemically or mechanically activated to divide and form embryos with spinal cords, muscles, skeletons, and other organs including beating hearts (Kaufmann, 1997, pp. 53–55). In marmoset monkeys, parthenogenetic embryos can develop and successfully implant in the uterus (Marshall, Wilton, & Moore, 1998, pp. 1491–97). Much of our understanding of both normal and abnormal human development and human disease has been derived from model systems such as the mouse and various primates such as the marmoset and the chimpanzee.

In their book *Bioethics and the New Embryology*, Gilbert et al., present an excellent summary of current scientific views on when life begins (2005). Gilbert is also the author of *Developmental Biology* (2006), the most widely used textbook in the field of developmental biology. Gilbert et al. posit that there are at least four stages of human development that different scientists have labeled as the point at where human life begins:

1. Fertilization (the acquisition of a novel genome)
2. Gastrulation (the acquisition of an individual physical identity)
3. EEG activation (the acquisition of the human-specific electroencephalogram, or brainwave, pattern)
4. The time of, or surrounding, birth (the acquisition of independent breathing and viability outside the mother)

I use this framework to structure the remainder of this portion of the essay.

Does Human Life Begin at Fertilization?

The first viewpoint, which life begins at fertilization (often referred to in humans as conception), is known as the "genetic" view of human life. The fusion of sperm and egg typically combines, in a new cell called a zygote or embryo, the genes from male and female parents to form a new "genome" with unique properties and sets into motion a long and complex series of biological processes. This zygote, with its unique genome, has the "potential" to develop into a human being. According to the "argument from potential," some theologians and ethicists hold that the zygote is indeed a living human person (Reichlin, 1997). While the zygote certainly has the potential to develop into a fetus or a newborn, biomedical statistics show that even without including induced abortions, between 50–60 percent of all human embryos conceived do not survive until birth and most of these embryos are "miscarried" before the eighth week of pregnancy (Cummings, 2006, p. 142). I believe that while the entity created by fertilization is indeed, by scientific definition, a human embryo which has the potential to be born and develop into a human adult, whether or not this fact is the *sine qua non* of personhood is a question that cannot and should not be answered by science. Indeed, as noted above, parthenogenetic development in other primates can proceed as far as implantation in the womb without the need for fertilization. In other words, not only is science unable to claim that the creation of a new genome resulting from fertilization is the *sine qua non* of personhood but it cannot even claim that fertilization is the *sine qua non* of development of the new individual organism.

Does Human Life Begin with the Acquisition of an Individual Physical Identity?

In this "embryologic" view, gastrulation, the beginning of the actual differentiation of the embryo into specific cell types is when human personhood begins. During normal human development, this occurs about 14 days after fertilization. It is the first point in development where the embryo can no longer divide to form twins and because it can only give rise to a single person, many scientists consider this the point at which the embryo becomes a person (Gilbert et al., p. 43). This viewpoint is endorsed theologically by Gilbert (2006), Ford (1988), and McCormick (1991) among others. It is this embryonic viewpoint that is consistent with the use of embryonic stem cells in biomedical research as adopted by the National Institutes of Health Human Embryo Research Panel. This view has also been used by some theologians to argue that "ensoulment" does not happen before day 12–14, since each twin is a distinctly different individual with its own unique soul (Shannon & Wolter, 1990). Just as many believe that a metaphysical event occurs as the soul departs the body at death, ensoulment is the metaphysical event where the soul enters the body. After the soul has departed the body at death, there is no personhood and, likewise, prior to ensoulment there is no personhood. The argument based on twinning is that while human embryonic cells can divide to form a twin embryo, unique souls cannot divide and therefore ensoulment cannot occur before the last day that twinning can happen.

Does Life Begin with the Acquisition of the Human EEG (Brainwave) Pattern?

In the United States, as in other countries where the technology to monitor vital signs are readily available, death, or the absence of life has been defined as the end of the human brainwave pattern. Thus, while a person may have a heartbeat, and be breathing with or without medical assistance, the absence of human brainwaves is legally considered to be the equivalent of death. Following this line of reasoning, the "neurological" view of life posits that life begins between 24–27 weeks of development with acquisition of the human brainwave pattern (Morowitz & Trefil, 1992). While the human nervous system begins to develop during the early part of the first trimester and cerebral nerve cells proliferate and differentiate throughout the entire second trimester, the actual connections between these nerve cells do not occur in significant numbers until the seventh month of human pregnancy. It is these synaptical connections between nerve cells that allow communication and the subsequent coordination of neural activity characteristic of active, conscious, cerebral brain function. If we accept the idea that conscious awareness defines personhood, then the "neurological" view provides a reasonable point to consider as the beginning of human life.

I remind the reader, once more, that the scientific evidence provided by mammalian model systems indicates that a level of brain activity necessary to sustain a beating heart exists in unfertilized parthenogenetic "embryos." While we cannot know, with any certainty, to what extent parthenogenetic development can occur in human embryos, evidence from non-human primates such as marmoset monkeys (Marshall et al., 1998) and rhesus monkeys (Mitalipova et al., 2001) indicates that parthenogenetic development in humans is certainly a possibility. Indeed about 1 in 1500 human pregnancies is the result of the presence of a hydatidiform mole and ultimately results in miscarriage. A hydatidiform mole is a growth that resembles a mass of placental tissue which usually originates from a normal sperm fertilizing an egg which is missing its nucleus. The fertilized egg proceeds to divide and may then implant in the womb even though no embryonic tissue is present (Gilbert, 2006, p. 212). The origin of a hydatidiform mole is thus the opposite of a parthenogenetic embryo and when considered with the evidence of parthenogenetic development in non-human primates, supports the possibility of partial parthenogenetic development in humans. Nonetheless, complete parthenogenetic development has never been documented in mammals.

Does Human Life Begin at Birth?

The view that a fetus acquires personhood when it can survive on its own is not new to either science or society. The view that life begins with the first breath is the most Biblical of all the views presented thus far. Genesis 2:7 of both the Hebrew Tanakh and Christian Bible states that "the Lord God formed the man [sic] from the dust of the ground and breathed into his nostrils the breath of life and the man became a living being"(NIV, 1984; TNHK, 1985). Biomedical technology has probably influenced the development and understanding of this view more than it has any other. Sufficient development of the respiratory system to allow the fetus to survive outside the womb is the limiting factor to viability. Fetal lungs are sufficiently mature for survival outside the womb at minimally 28 weeks of development (Stoelhorst et al., 2005, p. 396; Markestad et al., 2005, p. 1289). Although fetal lungs may be structurally mature at this point, their ability to function effectively outside the womb depends upon the presence of sufficient levels of surfactant bathing the surface of respiratory cells through which gas exchange occurs. Lung surfactant allows the cells to "capture" oxygen from the air by lowering the surface tension of the thin walled lung cells to near zero. Without surfactant, these cells tend to collapse under the pressure of air. When an infant takes its first breath, this air pressure closes a flap in the heart which thereafter separates oxygen depleted blood circulation to the lungs and oxygen rich blood circulation to the body. When this happens, the infant can now breath independently, and the umbilical cord to the mother can be cut. Physiologically useful levels of surfactant are not generally present until week 34 of human pregnancy (Gilbert, 2006, p. 515) and "normal" levels are not reached until week 37, just 3 weeks before the fetus reaches "full term." Infants born prematurely often have difficulty breathing, a condition known as respiratory distress syndrome. Prior to current biomedical advances, infants born prematurely were often referred to as "blue babies," indicating insufficient levels of oxygen in their blood and incomplete separation of oxygen depleted blood (blue) from oxygen rich (red) blood in the heart.

Even with advanced medical intervention there are obvious limits to viability of the fetus. While medical technology to induce production of surfactant by the antenatal administration of corticosteroids, and/or direct postnatal administration of surfactant into the lungs of premature infants has been practiced in Neonatal Intensive Care Units (NICU) since 1991, there has been little change in the limits of viability (23 weeks of gestation = 17 weeks premature) in the decade and a half since (Stoelhorst et al., 2005, p. 396; Markestad et al., 2005, p. 1289). Furthermore, those infants that survive have severe complications such as respiratory distress syndrome, patent ductus arteriosus[1], septicemia, and cerebral palsy among others, and in some studies complications such as respiratory distress syndrome and septicemia show a clear increase in incidence (Markestad et al., 2005, p. 1289). While there is no clear consensus among scientists as to when life begins, there is ample data that, given the state of our medical technology and knowledge, the limits of fetal viability continue to be at about 22–23 weeks of gestation. This is before the establishment of the human brainwave pattern which, as noted in the previous section, occurs from week 24–27 of gestation.

Moreover, from a biological perspective, when life begins is not really the most important issue since, with regards to reproduction, life is a continuum. The sperm and egg are living cells which have the potential to develop and be born. Fertilization, in humans more commonly referred to as conception, accomplishes two separate things: the combination of maternal and paternal genes forming a unique embryonic genome and the activation of the egg metabolism to trigger it to start development. The formation of a unique genome via fertilization is not a requirement for embryonic development nor is its simple presence sufficient for development.

The observable traits or characteristics of an individual are indeed potentially determined by our genes or DNA, but it is incorrect to simply equate genes with observable traits. Thus it is inaccurate to talk about the gene(s) for cancer, or the genes for intelligence, or the genes for dark skin. Science itself has taught and reinforced this inaccuracy by its use of metaphors. We are taught, for example, that DNA is the "blueprint" of life. Our genes or DNA in fact are not the blueprint for anything because that is not how genetic information is encoded or processed. For example, the human brain contains about 100,000,000,000 (10^{11}) largely identical neurons which make 1,000,000,000,000,000 (10^{15}) totally unique neuronal connections (Coveny & Highfield, 1995). Does the DNA provide a blueprint for these 10^{15} unique connections? It clearly does not. The human genome has been totally sequenced and is known to consist of approximately 3.1 billion base pairs. The average human gene is approximately 27,000 base pairs and thus even if the entire human genome were devoted solely to specifying neural connections it could only specify 115,000 unique connections. Clearly there is insufficient storage capacity in the human genome by at least ten orders of magnitude to provide a blueprint for each neuronal connection in the human brain!

In fact DNA does not provide blueprints for human traits or characteristics but rather the information encoded in the linear sequence of the DNA controls the processes of development that always occur in an environmental context. It is the interaction of genetic information with environmental variables throughout the process of development that result in our human characteristics. Essential human characteristics emerge from genetically influenced dynamic processes whose outcome depends upon environmental context.

What is the environmental context for human development? While many developmental processes depend upon cell to cell interactions within the proximate environment of the developing embryo/fetus, human development occurs within the larger environmental context of a pregnant woman's body. The extent of the environmental influence of a woman's body on a developing fetus is dramatically illustrated by such tragedies as the effect of chemicals such as thalidomide[2] or alcohol, the effect of viruses such as rubella (German measles) or HIV, and even the effect of malnutrition or specific dietary deficiencies on fetal development.[3] In fact, we can only guess at the true extent of the effects of environmental context on embryonic and fetal development. As noted earlier, discounting induced abortions, only 50–60 per cent of all conceptions result in live births and many pregnancies are lost before eight weeks of development at which time many of these pregnancies have not even been detected. These figures led John Opitz, a professor of pediatric medicine and human genetics, to testify to the President's Council on Bioethics that our society is apparently not prepared to value the fetus as a person.

> If the embryo loss that accompanies natural procreation were the moral equivalent of infant death, then pregnancy would have to be regarded as a public health crisis of epidemic proportions: Alleviating natural embryo loss would be a more urgent moral cause than abortion, in vitro fertilization, and stem cell research combined [cited in Gilbert, 2006].

Many opponents of abortion have viewed a woman as a mere incubator or vessel for the growth of an embryo/fetus. As illustrated above, this view is clearly inconsistent with our knowledge of developmental genetics. A pregnant woman's body, as the environmental context for the genetically influenced developmental processes required for embryonic/fetal development, is an active and critical participant in the process of human development. The view that the womb is nothing more than a vessel is not only an abrogation of a woman's selfhood and personhood but is also scientifically unjustified. Human beings can survive with an artificial heart but fetuses cannot develop in an artificial womb. Even the most sophisticated reproductive technologies require the contributions of a living surrogate mother in order for development to proceed as far as implantation and beyond. This surrogate mother is precisely a surrogate *mother* and not a vessel because her body provides the environmental context necessary for the development of a viable human being. The mere presence of a unique human genome is not sufficient for the development of a living being.

If the development of a living being requires the active participation of a woman's body, then the critical question is not simply "When in the process of human development does an organism reach sufficient individualization to be considered a separate life," but also "Is the pregnant woman willing and able?" A woman's participation in the developmental process makes incredible demands on her body; her body is not a simple vessel, incubator, nor even a passive participant. By providing the environmental context for development, she is committed to providing oxygen, nourishment, protection, waste disposal, and indeed the very ground for the developing embryo or fetus and all of this at great physiological and metabolic and emotional cost to her own body. The demands of pregnancy can cause anemia, malnourishment, loss of bone density, hypertension, diabetes, and many other threats to her physical, mental, and emotional health. The developing embryo/fetus is not a gentle presence within a pregnant woman's body. In fact, developmental biologists describe implantation, the first major contact between a developing embryo and a woman's womb, as follows

> The endometrial cells lining the inside of the uterus "catch" the blastocyst [preimplantation embryo] on a mat that the endometrial cells secrete. This mat contains a sticky concoction of proteins that bind specifically to other proteins that are present on the embryo's trophoblast, thus anchoring the embryo to the uterus. Once this "anchor" is in place, the trophoblast secretes another set of enzymes that digest the endometrial protein mat, enabling the blastocyst to bury itself within the uterine wall.
>
> At this point a complicated dialogue between the [embryo's] trophoblast cells and the uterus begins. First the trophoblast cell's "invade" the uterine tissue, secreting a hormone called human chroionic gonadotropin, or hCG. (This is the hormone that is measured in pregnancy tests.) Human chorionic gonadotropin instructs the mother's ovaries to make another hormone, progesterone.... Under the influence of progesterone, the uterus makes new

blood vessels and starts to form a new region, the decidua. The decidua will become the maternal portion of the placenta. The decidual region then tells the trophoblast cells of the embryo to become the chorion. Together the decidua and the chorion form the placenta. Thus the placenta is a single organ formed from two different organisms, the embryo and the mother [Gilbert, 2006, pp. 18–19].

From this description, it is clear that the mother's uterus is not a simple vessel to contain the embryo but rather that a woman's body is an active participant in development from at least the point of implantation.

Mary Mahowald (1994, p. 225) points out that only in the past few decades have fetuses been considered apart from the women in whom they are developing and says that this view constitutes the fallacy of considering an object as if it exists without a context. Discussing fetal tissue transplantation from the perspective of feminist ethics, she warns that fetuses should not be considered separate from the pregnant woman (Mahowald, 1994, p. 232). I would add that, as illustrated here, it is a fallacy from the viewpoint of developmental genetics as well.

A Theology of Creation

Genesis 1:1 of the First Testament of the Christian Bible begins

[1]In the beginning when God created the heavens and the earth, [2]the earth was a formless void and darkness covered the face of the deep, while a wind from God swept over the face of the waters. [3]Then God said, "Let there be light"; and there was light. [4]And God saw that the light was good; and God separated the light from the darkness. [5]God called the light Day, and the darkness he called Night. And there was evening and there was morning, the first day [NRSV, 1984].

As a scientist, I obviously do not take these verses literally but they do inform my theology. I believe that, in the beginning, God saw potential. God took this potential and actualized it and continues to actualize it in God's creation. The complex processes by which creation is being actualized are the subject of humanity's ongoing scientific inquiry. In a similar manner, I see an individual human life as being "conceived" in the mind of God long before the biological process of fertilization. God sees the potential for a human life and begins actualizing it. I understand each unfertilized egg and each sperm to have the potential to become a human being but this does not mean that the potential for life will be realized in each one of them.

The single-celled fertilized egg known as the zygote is developmentally totipotent. It can divide and its progeny cells have the capacity to develop into any type of cell in the human body if presented by its environment with the appropriate developmental cues at the correct time. As development continues, cells become physically different from each other and also become progressively restricted in their potency. Thus while the original zygote is totipotent, cells become progressively restricted in their developmental potential in inverse proportion to the progressive physical actualization of their potential. In other words, any given cell will eventually have only a single potential actualized. This biological process of development parallels closely my theological understanding of the creation of a human being. The fertilized egg, a single-celled human embryo has the full potential to become a human being but this does not mean that each one will. If God conceives of the actualization of this embryo's potential and if in fact continues to create in partnership with the woman who has the capacity to provide the womb for this potential human's source of being, the uterus that will provide the nurturing environment needed for the actualization of this potential, then a new human life will emerge.

As noted previously, a woman's participation in the process of creation makes incredible demands on her body. By providing the womb for nurturing God's creation, she is committing her body's resources to providing oxygen, nourishment, protection, waste disposal, and indeed the very ground of being for the developing embryo or fetus. Pregnancy and gestation are processes that only a woman can undertake and only at great physiological, metabolic, emotional, and spiritual cost. This raises another very important issue: that of self-hood.

Western philosophical and theological tradition, particularly that of the Enlightenment, developed the two major ideas of dualism. The first, based largely on the narrative of Genesis 1 and 2, posits that humans are "higher" than all the rest of creation which we are to subdue and dominate. This fallacy has led to our current environmental crises. The second is that of mind/body dualism, the idea that the mind is somehow separate from, and superior to, the body. The mind was also believed to be the seat of the soul and thus soul or spirit is also separated from body. As I have argued previously, we are our bodies. Mind and soul exist only in inextricable relationship with the body. To believe in the incarnation of God in Jesus Christ; to believe in the Trinity, Father/Mother, Son and Holy Spirit, demands the proclamation of a theology of embodiment (Moltmann-Wendel, 1994) Indeed the New Testament meaning of the word salvation, as witnessed in the healing acts of Jesus and his disciples, is, "to make whole." Feminist theologian Elisabeth Moltmann-Wendel describes salvation thus:

> Salvation, healing, therefore does not just affect what is within human beings, their souls. Salvation concerns the whole person, since according to the New Testament the salvation of the soul is not yet salvation. The message of Jesus relates to human beings in their totality, in their bodies, in which the soul dwells and gives them life. The message of Jesus seeks to change conditions and behavior which make people blind, deaf, bowed down, paralyzed and possessed. It wants people to see, walk, hear and be liberated from all alien determination, including that of the body [Moltmann-Wendel, 1994, p. 37].

One of the earliest schisms in the Christian Church arose because of the question of whether Mary was *Theotokus* (God-bearer) or only *Christotokus* (Christ-bearer, referring to Jesus the man). The disagreement about whether Mary was the bearer of God (by the Holy Spirit) or the bearer of Jesus Christ (the man) had serious implications about both the divinity and humanity of Christ. One of the serious heresies of the early church was Nestorianism which posited that Mary was the mother of Jesus's human nature but not of his divine nature. Nestorius believed that Mary should be designated as Christotokus and theodochos (recipient-of-God) as if Mary was simply a holding-place, a vessel or a channel through which the Son of God passed. This is in direct conflict with the Christian doctrine of Incarnation which requires that Jesus Christ, both fully divine and fully human died on the cross. If the crucified Christ was not both fully divine and fully human (incarnate) this posed a serious threat to Christian soteriology or understanding of salvation. The Third Ecumenical Council in Ephesus in 431 C.E. affirmed Mary's role as Theotokus and anathemized Nestorianism (McKim, 1988, p. 34).

Moltmann-Wendel provides two very different cultural interpretations of the "body as vessel." "In a matriarchal context the great vessel produces its own seed. It is parthenogenetic and uses the male only as an opener and to disseminate the seed." This is a powerful metaphor and, as I have already documented above, parthenogenetic development is possible in many organisms, and that in some organisms it is the norm. Activation or "opening" of the egg, which is the first of two functions of the sperm at fertilization, can be accomplished by mechanical (pricking the egg) or chemical (changing salt concentration of its surroundings). In contrast, Moltmann-Wendel continues:

> [I]n the later patriarchal understanding it [the woman's body] is only the place through which the seed passes and in which it is nourished. This patriarchal interpretation stamps the present notion which already occurs in Plato, in the apostle Paul, in Judaism, Christianity and Islam and keeps recurring in different contexts down to modern times: art, philosophy, theology, medicine [Moltmann-Wendell, 1994, p. 80].

While Moltmann-Wendel does not deny that much of the female imagery in the Bible consists of vessels to be filled, she finds a more affirming self-understanding for women in the story of the Samaritan Woman at the well (John 4).

> a woman who wants to draw water from the well with her jar meets Jesus, and in conversation with this woman Jesus develops an unusual image of human beings. Stimulated by this situation of the woman and referring to old female symbols (well= *pege*= goddess of the spring), he speaks of human beings as a spring. "The water that I give to men will become in them a spring of water welling up to eternal life." The woman, source of life, independent, natural, creative and spiritual life!
>
> And then, as the story goes on we are told that the woman leaves her jar, the jar, the vessel, her symbol as a woman, and runs off to tell her fellow-countrymen what she experienced. She leaves behind her old female symbol, the jar, the vessel, because she may be something different: a source from which ever new, independent and living things can proceed [Moltmann-Wendell, p. 83].

One further facet of Moltmann-Wendel's theology of embodiment which I find compelling is her understanding of the relationship of body to space. While our bodies are not simple vessels waiting to be filled, we do have unused free spaces within our bodies which we can "fill with our breath and our spirit and through which we can give expression to our vision of a whole life" (Moltmann-Wendell, p. 98). Beyond the space inside our bodies, our bodies need space to develop. All bodies claim public space and like all social phenomena of space "whenever someone occupies space at the expense of another a hierarchy arises, a gradation of power which curtails living space and thus life" (Moltmann-Wendell, p. 99).

Conclusion

I have tried to illustrate both the scientific and theological complexities of some of the issues related to abortion. I don't see abortion as a matter of Pro-Life versus Pro-Choice. I believe that any decision to abort a fetus is a painful and an agonizing one. I don't support it as a means of birth control but if birth control has failed, I can see situations where it may be the most loving solution. I don't believe that the God of my faith would "conceive" of a child that would be actualized out of the potential presented by an act of rape and incest. I see a woman as an active partner with God in the creation process and therefore I have difficulty with the concept of keeping a brain-dead woman alive by extraordinary means for the sole purpose of continuing gestation. I believe that a theology of embodiment is not only consistent with, but a necessary and natural extension of the Christian Doctrines of the Trinity and the Incarnation; therefore, I think we need to seriously reflect on Moltmann-Wendel's assertion that "whenever someone occupies space at the expense of another a hierarchy arises, a gradation of power which curtails living space and thus life."

In this essay I have considered the questions of "when does a new life begin" and, "does one separate this new body from new mind and soul" from both theological and scientific perspectives. Clearly there is no consensus among scientists or among theologians, let alone between the two groups, nor do I believe one should be reached. The values and standards of science and theology are vastly different. Nonetheless, I believe the dialogue must continue as we struggle to understand the different issues surrounding abortion.

Notes

1. *Patent ductus arteriosus* is a condition where the duct in the heart which allows blood in the fetus to bypass the non-functional fetal lungs fails to close shortly after birth. The result is that some of the blood continues to bypass the neonate's lungs as it flows through the heart and thus preventing the blood from obtaining oxygen.

2. Thalidomide was prescribed as a mild sedative in the early 1960's for women suffering from severe morning sickness. While thalidomide had no apparent effect beyond mild sedation in adults, it caused a host of severe birth defects the most well known of which is phocomelia — the lack of proper limb development.

3. Folic acid deficiency is associated with spina bifida, failure of the spinal cord to develop completely, which causes many debilitating and life-threatening conditions.

References

Alton, A. K. (1981). The Histological, Cellular and Molecular Correlates of the T[Hairpin] Maternal Effect in the Mouse. Ph.D. Dissertation. Cornell University Graduate School of Medical Sciences.

Borysenko, J. (1997). *A Woman's Book of Life: The Biology, Psychology and Spirituality of the Feminine Life Cycle.* New York: Riverhead Books.

Conley, F. (1998). *Walking Out on the Boys.* New York: Farrar, Strauss and Giroux.

Coveney, P. and R. R. Highfield (1995). *Frontiers of Complexity: The Search for Order in a Chaotic World.* New York: Fawcett Columbine.

Cummings, M. R. (2006). *Human Heredity: Principles and Issues,* 7th ed. Belmont, CA: Thomson, Brooks/Cole.

Ford, N. M. (1988). When Does Human Life Begin? Science, Government, Church. *Pacifica,* 1, 298–327.

Gilbert, S. F. (2006). *Developmental Biology,* 6th ed. Sunderland, MA: Sinauer Associates.

Gilbert, S. F., A. L. Tyler and E. J. Zackin (2005). *Bioethics and the New Embryology: Springboards for Debate.* Sunderland, MA: Sinauer and Associates.

Jewish Publication Society (1985). Tanakl = [Tanakh] = a New Translation of the Holy Scrptures According to the Traditional Hebrew Text. Philadelphia: Jewish Publication Society.

Kaufmann, M. H. S., S. C. Barton and S. A. H. Surani (1977). Normal Post Implantation Development of Mouse Parthenogenesis Embryos to the Forelimb Bud Stage. *Nature,* 265, 53–55.

Mahowald, M. B. (1994). Fetal Tissue Transplantation and Women. In F. Beller and R.Weir (Eds.), *The Beginning of Human Life* (pp. 225–32). Dordrecht, The Netherlands: Kluwer Academic.

Markestad, T., P. I. Kaaresen, A. Rønnestad, H. Reigstad, K. Lossius, S. Medbø, G. Zanussi, I. E. Engelund, R. Skjaerven and L. M. Irgens (2005). Early Death, Morbidity, and Need of Treatment Among Extremely Premature Infants. *Pediatrics,* 115, 1289–98.

Marshall, V. S., L. J. Wilton and H. D. M. Moore (1998). Parthenogenetic Activation of Marmoset (*Callithrix jacchus*) Oocytes and the Development of Marmoset Parthenogenones *In Vitro* and *In Vivo. Biol. Reproduction,* 59, 1491–1497.

McCormick, R. (1991). Who or What is the Preembryo? *Kennedy Inst. Ethics J.,* 1(1), 1–15.

McKim, D. K. (1998). *Theological Turning Points: Major Issues in Christian Thought.* Atlanta: John Knox.

Moody, J. A. (2004). *Faculty Diversity: Problems and Solutions.* New York: Routledge Falmer.

Moltmann-Wendel, E. (1994). *I Am My Body: A Theology of Embodiment.* New York: Continuum.

Morowitz, H. J. and J. S. Trefil (1992). *The Facts of Life: Science and the Abortion Controversy.* New York: Oxford University.

New International Version, International Bible Society. (1984).

Reichlin, M. (1997). The Argument from Potential: a Reappraisal. *Bioethics,* 11(1), 1–23.

Renfree, M. B. (1982). Implantation and Placentation. In C. Austin and R. Short (Eds.), *Reproduction in Mammals 2. Embryonic and Fetal Development* (pp. 26–29). Cambridge: Cambridge University Press.

Shannon, T. A. and A. B. Wolter (1990). Reflections on the Moral Status of the Pre-Embryo. *Theological Studies*, 51, 603–626.

Shoukhrat M. Mitalipov, K. D. Nusser and D. P. Wolf (2001). Parthenogenetic Activation of Rhesus Monkey Oocytes and Reconstructed Embryos. *Biology of Reproduction*, 65, 253–259.

Starr, P. (1982). *The Social Transformation of American Medicine*. New York: Basic Books.

Stoelhorst G. M., M. Rijken, S.E. Martens, R. Brand, A. L. den Ouden, J.M. Wit and S. Veen (2005). Changes in Neonatology: Comparison of Two Cohorts of Very Preterm Infants (gestational age <32 weeks): the Project On Preterm and Small for Gestational Age Infants 1983 and the Leiden Follow-Up Project on Prematurity 1996–1997. *Pediatrics*, 5, 396–405.

Thomason, S. P. (2006). *The Living Spirit of the Crone: Turning Aging Inside Out*. Minneapolis: Fortress.

Orphans, Abortions, and the Public Fetus in *The Cider House Rules*

LORI BAKER-SPERRY

Abstract

The degree to which the popular text turned film The Cider House Rules *reflects the current social ethos surrounding abortion and reproduction in the United States is examined in light of the text's use in a college classroom. Grounded textual analysis allows for the identification of six meta-themes in the text: pro-choice as status quo, sin and penitence, pro-life perspective, the public fetus, how the individual scenario sways opinion, and the business of abortion. The text ultimately illuminates the complexity of the abortion in the U.S. today.*

As a feminist with one foot firmly in both the second and third waves (one by training, one by age), I understand issues of reproduction and control of sexuality to be fundamental to the feminist agenda and to the individual woman's life opportunities. At least, I understand these things theoretically. More close to the heart, I have avoided addressing issues central to reproduction as I have always found myself in the center of a vortex of emotion and social belief, none of which clearly pointed in a direction, and in no way has the "abortion question" ever been settled in my mind.

Although reproduction and sexuality have been peripheral areas of exploration, abortion and abortion rights have never been a specific topic of my research, nor have I openly professed to take a personal or professional stand on the issue. I unquestionably appreciate the historical time period in which I live, where the number of children I have is a result of planning and intervention and not a result of a husband's generosity or the decision to "wait and see" what comes "naturally." As a Christian feminist (raised on the belief that abortion is a sin), and a wife and mother, I struggled when it came to the question of choice, reaping the benefits of a social life where family planning and control of sexuality were normative expectations (fought for, in part, by the abortion rights activists of the last two centuries), understanding that there were times where "abortion might be necessary," but with a strong sense toward preserving human life and difficulty accepting pregnancy as anything but life, albeit parasitic. As a teacher, I have not been surprised to find that my student's views often mirror my (silent) ones: many are ambivalent about and disconcerted by abortion.

With two children of my own, I understood, theoretically, that my life exists within the context of a social ethos where choices were available to me (such as the choice to limit the size of my family). The reality that reproductive rights did not evolve in a vacuum, and that the abortion rights movement and the family planning movement were clearly joined and, originally, meant to achieve the same end did not escape me, and therein lie the hypocrisy of the vortex of emotion and belief that often surrounds abortion.

The Personal and the Professional, or How an Intellectual Argument Masks a Personal Quandary

Simultaneously, a sociologist and discourse analyst by training, I have taught John Irving's novel *The Cider House Rules* in my Introduction to Women's Studies course for the last five years. This text is a fascinating fictional account of an orphanage where women travel to either "have an orphan or an abortion (Irving, 1985, p.74)." As I have used this text in class, I have come to realize that the story itself contains most of the major elements of the current reproductive/abortion discussion and that it serves as an excellent tool for students as they explore the fundamental issues of sexuality, reproduction, subordination, and male domination and control of female sexuality.

In class, I argue that *The Cider House Rules* closely mimics the abortion debate today, and addresses the tensions between the larger theoretical, political perspectives surrounding abortion (the meta-issues) and the practical and personal issues, often less clear in the public abortion debate, in ways that are nuanced and insightful. Strikingly situated as a means to outline not only the current issues surrounding the abortion debate, the text highlights the lived experiences of women within a patriarchal society, and in so doing also clarifies the practical implications of abortion. In class, those involved in the interaction between reader and text (myself and my students), may find that they struggle with the professional/intellectual nature of the role of teacher or student and the more personal and individual elements that exist in our real lives. The theoretical issue of abortion, then, is sometimes in conflict with the reality of studying abortion for the individual.

Theoretically, *The Cider House Rules* tells a story about who is in control of the construction of the abortion debate, and, more basically, who is in control of the practice of abortion. Author John Irving, the grandson of an esteemed surgeon, writes a novel about two men, one an obstetrician, the other his prodigy, who wrestle with the morality of available abortion through their individual decisions about whether or not to perform abortions and under what conditions. The depiction of abortion in the story, reflective of current social views espousing multiple perspectives, allows students to find their place in the text, while at the same time not requiring that the reader align with a specific abortion perspective (in fact, the opposite seems to occur with my students — they begin to open to different perspectives through the development of the characters in the story). This relationship between the student and textual narratives represents layers of the personal that may be accessed in conjunction with the text.

The Cider House Rules is one of those rare texts where most readers may find their perspective represented, where both firmly liberal and conservative viewers identify with characters and can enjoy the experience. I would also argue that *The Cider House Rules*, although fictional, allows for growth as well, as many students will attest to shifting perspectives, particularly to more inclusive ways of understanding the issues as portrayed through the novel and through in-class discussion and information.

One striking element within *The Cider House Rules* is the extent to which female autonomy is subordinated in the text. Students may find it more comfortable to consider abortion when the story contains only male main characters and is written by a male author as the argument is not viewed as a personal gripe, but instead a "social issue." This, initially, displaces women in the abortion question, often taking ultimate responsibility out of their hands. We do critically evaluate this relationship in class, and students often problematize male power of the abortion question. Overall, using *The*

Cider House Rules in the classroom is an effective teaching tool. It is a powerful moment when the students realize the story of abortion, as described in a novel cited as a new classic (McIntosh, 1999), is written by and about men.

For all of my success with this novel in the classroom (in that the text allows the reader to deeply delve into the issue of abortion, with meaningful discussion and, I believe, reflection), *The Cider House Rules* is at times harsh and even sordid, containing descriptions of botched abortions and bestial pornography. As such, it serves as not only a fictional representation of the current abortion/reproduction ethos but also of my experience with this journey — particularly with this essay, which was a long time in coming. In the text of *The Cider House Rules*, a young girl, left dead from a botched abortion, with a note pinned to her chest, is Dr. Larch's initial impetus to address the "abortion problem" and begin to perform (illegally) abortions himself. His own knowledge of the girl meant that he could not easily extricate himself from her situation nor should he hide from the responsibility of the larger issue — the note, addressed to him, read simply "shit or get off the pot." This has been my mantra these long months working on the many reformations of this paper. I have tried to get off the pot many times! But, like Larch, and then Homer, I have found myself complicit. The issue is professional and personal and I, too, have found it impossible to walk away from. Therefore, I turn to this text each semester as a very intriguing way of addressing the concerns of reproduction and women's experience.

The following is a synopsis of what I do with this text in my courses. I follow a model which identifies the meta-themes within the text, suggests that within those themes perspectives have profound practical implications, and that the personal is never far from the abortion question, it may only be silent. In this way, we utilize the text *The Cider House Rules* to explore much more than simply the act of abortion, but the cultural and gendered social constructions that support and define the institution of abortion.

Current Abortion Ethos and The Cider House Rules

In March 2007, *The New York Times* ran an article reporting on some rather puzzling findings about generation Nexters — they might be doing some relatively new political morphing in terms of positions on hot button issues. For example, while 50 percent indicated that they were amenable to same-sex marriage (a 15 percent increase from the 1980s), only one-third favor legalized abortion, about 50 percent are opposed, and 15 percent believed it should be illegal (Hulbert, 2007). This is conservative compared to the general population. The fundamental question — 'what might this trend mean?' resonates throughout studies, stories, tales, and narratives of attitudes towards abortion and birth control as well as political polls.

One of the simultaneously fascinating elements of the generation Nexters is the degree to which the media and internet world merge as means with which to grapple with the social questions of import. If "text is culture steeped in" (Valerius, 2005), then one measure of the sentiment towards abortion and reproductive rights today, as well as one way to evaluate the abortion perspective holistically, is to evaluate what we produce in the form of social stories about abortion and reproduction in light of the research collected, like the recent data reported in *The New York Times*. The story of abortion and reproductive rights in the United States is not limited to the tales told by this most recent generation to be sampled, nor is the current abortion ethos limited to the political process of vying for candidacy, as it has often been characterized in popular mainstream news. It is not limited to the tales of back-alley abortions or to current discussion placing abortion on a continuum of birth control options. These are fragments of the larger social story — which, taken singly, limit understanding of the complexity of the issues at hand. The larger questions are more inclusive: What is the story of abortion and reproductive rights that most cohesively resonates today? Who has constructed the debate and what are the "rules?" Whose rules are they?

In the current social environment, abortion is an issue that is explored in a number of venues; for example, popular film and literature. Many scholars have traced manifestations of social meaning and value through such vehicles (Gledhill, 1997; Hall, 1997), and some have gone so far as to explore the social litmus of abortion and reproduction as socially reflected and created in image and text (Valerius, 2005). The purpose of this paper is to examine the degree to which the popular text, *The Cider House Rules*, reflects the current cultural ethos surrounding abortion and reproduction in the United States.

The Cider House Rules: *Litmus of Opinion*

When considering the social climate and the ways these and other related issues are addressed in literature and film, one might expect to find some attempt to re-tell our social story in *The Cider House Rules*. To this extent, an exploration of similarities between the current ethos and the textual representation is necessary, as well as a discussion of the differences. Some differences, however, are only so on the surface. For example, abortion is currently legal in the U.S. In *The Cider House Rules*, abortion is illegal. At St. Clouds, however, Dr. Larch, an obstetrician and abortionist, performs abortions illegally for all women who come with the request. Larch is quickly ensconced as the "expert," a doctor who is esteemed by the nurses on his staff, admired by the orphans, and loved by the novel's main character, Homer Wells. The status quo in the main of the text, therefore, is that abortion is performed at St. Clouds as Larch readily performs abortions and is actively striving to train Homer in his philosophy. Homer Wells, his prodigy, questions the morality of abortion and, represents, more generally, a common pro-life position in his resistance to perform abortions. Homer summarily states that he does not have a problem with Larch performing the abortions, but he refuses to perform them himself, preferring to deliver babies instead. Homer does eventually agree to perform an abortion, but the differences in the ways that this fact is divulged and manifested in text and on screen are of importance, and are representative of both the differences in perspectives on abortion given particular "facts" as well as assumptions about readership vs. viewership.

Other characters also serve to flesh out the abortion debate. After leaving the orphanage (seemingly to escape further pressure from Larch to learn to perform abortion), Homer works as an apple-picker in an orchard where he is taken in by the owning family. Homer, although welcome by those in the "Big House," works alongside the migrant workers who come each year during picking season. Mr. Rose, the leader of the migrant group, represents a particular perspective on the nature of "rules," and the issue of rules for Irving is one that is interwoven with the abortion question, as is captured in the title *The Cider House Rules*. Mr. Rose argues:

> Who *live* here in this cider house, Peaches? Who grind them apples, who press that cider, who clean up the mess, and who just plain *live* here ... just breathin' in the vinegar? Somebody who *don't* live here made them rules.

Them rules ain't for us. *We* the ones who make up them rules. We makin' our *own* rules, every day. Ain't that right, Homer? [Irving, 1999, p. 127–128].

One might imagine that a popular film or book would be wise to address abortion in ways that were important to individuals today. In addressing such a hot-button issue, authors and filmmakers might also be particularly wary of portraying too clearly partisan a position to a mainstream audience. This is, in fact, a concern for Irving and, particularly, the film producers of *The Cider House Rules* (1999). Favorable public response and social acceptance are understood goals of a novel or film (in that, one might suppose, few set out to fail in the mass market or box office), and the social temperature must be an assumed check. One way that a novel or film might succeed in resonating with its audience is to clearly connect to the social environment into which it is introduced. For example, the 1968 film *Rosemary's Baby* dealt with a related issue, the "sentimental ideal of motherhood" (Valerius, 2005, p. 123) which Valerius argues is a focus of concern in the 1960s. "Rosemary trusts in modern medicine to navigate her safely through pregnancy" (p. 123) which serves as an indication of class privilege and access to medical care, practical and personal realities, as much as it does the importance of evermore strongly contested ideal of motherhood (a theoretical meta-issue). Similarly, *The Cider House Rules* "articulates this charged public debate" (Valerius, 2005, p.119), and serves to replicates the current social environment in fictional form first through the novel and then, even more carefully elucidated for a general audience, through the recent (1999) feature film. Novels and movies tell social stories about their subjects or subject matter and the social story clarified in *The Cider House Rules* is one that is consistent with the political and moral debate surrounding reproduction and abortion in the U.S. today (Irving, 1999, p.28). In this way, the cultural climate is both reflected and reified in telling the story.

Currently, abortion is situated within a continuum of reproduction (from natural conception to family planning/birth control, including abortion) and is discussed in terms of reproductive rights. Constructing abortion in this way is indicative of the social norms, and is political in its controversial and contested nature as well. Such "politics of abortion" (fetal rights vs. right to choose) and the current and ever growing dependency on an institutionalized medical model of health care (as well the subsequent inaccessibility of even rudimentary care for large groups of poor and working-class women) serve to obscure the otherwise "objective" biological processes on which a strong portion of the debate claims to rest (when does life begin?). Similarly, the acceptance of underlying "midwifery" or "alternative" practices that either supplement or replace, in certain cases and in certain areas, institutionalized medicine in the case of reproduction also influences the perspectives surrounding the practice of abortion. Finally, the overarching social fear of female control of sex and reproduction (sexual independence) contributes to the process of defining the practice of abortion.

Although the infamous court cases *Roe v. Wade* and *Doe v. Bolton* ruled that to allow restrictive abortion laws was unconstitutional, thereby legalizing abortion, abortion is a complex social and medical issue still strongly debated for numerous reasons (Cates, Grimes, & Schultz, 2003, p. 25). Of the 1.3 million women obtaining abortion per year, many choose to terminate because the pregnancy was unplanned (Finer, Frohwirth, Dauphinee, Singh, & Moore, 2005). Today, much of the debate polarizes the rights of the pregnant woman vs. the rights of the unborn, and "... the topic of abortion remains one of the most controversial areas of public policy" (Cates et al, 2003, p. 27). The purpose of this paper is to explore the relationship between the construction of the abortion/reproduction debate in a highly popular novel turned film and the current social ethos of abortion and reproduction today.

Methods

The use of the methodological tenets of grounded theory (Glaser & Strauss, 1967; Strauss & Corbin, 1998) allows for a detailed and thematic exploration of the text where the findings and theoretical assumptions reflexively develop as a result of the process of data collection and analysis. The identification of themes occurs in a fluid manner, with an emphasis on the textual context in which the themes are embedded. It is the primary intent that theory be generated from the identification of these strong themes. Further, theory develops "as additional data are carefully weighed against the existing formulation" and as a tool for "clarity and rich understanding of a particular area of investigation" (Glaser, 1978, p. 2) and is developed and strengthened through interaction with the text. This is performed by constantly comparing the emerging themes and the original data.

Working within the theoretical framework of grounded theory, textual analysis is also utilized, which emphasizes the practice of "asking" the text systematic, rhetorical, and analytical questions, the result providing guiding questions that may be addressed within each meta-theme. So, for example, we might "ask" the text "what are the circumstances surrounding acquired abortion in the text?" or "in what ways are decisions about abortion impacted by the social situation of women in the text?" The questions asked are developed from pre-existing theoretical perspectives or expectations concerning the subject as well as those developed from close reading of the text itself. Textual analysis also provides a methodological support for a more theoretical perspective of grounding the theory in the data. In this way, data collected on the previous questions is informed by not only what a review of the literature might suggest needs to be asked, but also what the text itself provides in terms of insight. Holsti (1969) originally clarifies this relationship as one that systematically and objectively supports textual meta-themes and makes inference (develops new theory) from these themes, simultaneously. Van Dijk (1998) identifies the strong themes and connections between the themes and the larger social world as the product of the data collection in a theoretically grounded textual analysis.

Several meta-themes related to abortion and reproduction clearly emerged from the discourse analysis of the novel *The Cider House Rules*. Based upon a review of current academic literature and of the political media coverage of the abortion debate in the U.S., the findings of the textual analysis very quickly documented the strong comparison between the textual representation and the current social environment surrounding abortion today.

Each meta-theme developed from a close reading and analysis of John Irving's *Cider House Rules* has been described in relation to the current cultural ethos surrounding abortion and the understanding that may be gleaned from the debate represented in this form. Furthermore, considerations of changes between text and film, where applicable, are addressed, particularly when such changes serve to gauge the (anticipated) audience reaction/degree of palatability in terms of the issues and their representation.

The identified meta-themes are as follows: (1) Pro-Choice as status quo and the Abortionist's Rules; (2) Cultural association with Sin and Penitence/No one is innocent; (3) Pro-Life perspective: "I disapprove of it — it's not for me"; (4) The public fetus and the Autonomous Life; (5) A Continuum of Women and How the Individual Scenario Sways Opinion; and (6)

The Business of Abortion and the Rules of the Cider House. Each theme is explored fully in the following pages, both in isolation and in relation to the other themes in the larger text.

Findings: Emergent Themes in the Text
The Cider House Rules

> ...When absolutely helpless women tell me that they simply can't have an abortion, that they simply must got through with having another — and yet another — orphan: do I interfere? Do I? ...I give them what they want: an orphan or an abortion," Larch said.
> "Well, I'm an orphan," said Homer Wells.
> "Do I insist that we all have the same ideas? I do not," Dr. Larch said.
> "You wish it," said Homer Wells.
> "The women who come to me are not helped by *wishes*," said Wilbur Larch [Irving, 1985, p. 187].

Meta Theme #1: Pro-Choice as Status Quo
and the Abortionist's Rules

The first meta-theme, ***pro-choice as status quo***, is, at its core, a perspective that is representative of the current status of abortion law in the U.S. Although set in pre–*Roe v. Wade* U.S., the center of activity in *The Cider House Rules* is a dismal orphanage in St. Cloud where Dr. Larch, the resident obstetrician and abortionist, delivers babies and performs abortion upon demand. In fact, Larch's character construction embodies much of the current abortion law sentiment, where, instead a pre–*Roe v. Wade* therapeutic abortion board, an adult woman currently does not have to argue her case or be deemed worthy for a first trimester abortion.

In the film commentary, *My Movie Business*[1] (1999), Irving states that he chose Maine as the backdrop for *The Cider House Rules* as Maine was the first state to decree abortion illegal. Prior to formal anti-abortion mandates in the U.S., abortion was permitted until quickening (until the fetus made movement which could be differentiated from the mother's). This usually occurs at the end of the first trimester, and therefore, abortion was permitted and practiced in the first trimester in the United States, in colonial times. This placed the abortion decision, and its manifestations, firmly in the hands of women in the early history of the country. In other words, what later becomes the "business" of abortion was a woman's business, both through midwifery and in a personal, autonomous sense, and not a function of the male medical model (Irving, 1985). Of course, the rules of "business" shift depending upon the powers that be, depending upon whether the power to decide is in the hands of the physician or is the woman's. These rules are also dependent upon the legal and normative ethos of abortion, and reflects as well as impacts the social situation of women.

Larch, although he refused to judge the women who came to him, was caring and looked to their comfort. Larch is concerned with the process, with easing the pain and anxiety, and is, above all, a champion of the women who come to him. He is a doctor, impersonal, yet he has a personal stake and motivation for this work. His nurses love him, and see him as a "hero."

Larch's sense of responsibility is a consistent thread throughout the text. In his urgings to Homer, he pleads "How can you feel free to choose not to help people who are not free to get other help?" (Irving, 1985, p. 518). His concern that the women who come to him will be forced to go elsewhere, to someone who does not know how to perform a safe abortion, or to someone who will shame them and kill their spirit, pushes him to spur Homer (his reticent pupil) towards performing abortions as well. "This is what doing nothing gets you, Homer. It means that someone else is going to do the job — some moron who doesn't know how!" (Irving, 1985, p. 162).

Lest Larch seem entirely non-judgmental, his character construction is extremely disapproving of a social world which contributes to the existence of an orphanage, the men involved (often invisibly), and of unidentifiable "others" who he fears may not set the rules his way, making his decisions, doing it "right." One of the overarching moral lessons in *The Cider House Rules* is that rules are constructed. When rules and personal interest collide, some choose to write their own rules. The consequences of doing so are weighed, but "doing nothing" is also fraught with negative repercussions. As with pregnancy, something happens whether you intervene or not ... an orphan, an abortion, or a child.

Meta Theme #2: Cultural Association with Sin and Penitence/No One Is Innocent

Abortion has historically been associated with inappropriate sexual activity, destitution, and immorality (Valerius, 2005) although the demographics today do not support such stereotypical assumptions about who seeks abortion and why, *The Cider House Rules* does depict the "sometimes deadly reality created by a conservative sexual morality in combination with the criminalization of abortion, where infanticide, suicide, and dangerous back alley abortions were the last resort of desperate women" (Valerius, 2005, p. 123). The continuum of women who request abortion depict a much larger range of reasons and social access in *Cider House Rules*, as well. The women who come to St. Clouds are not cast in terms of ideal motherhood, but the cult of expectation may be strengthened in its relief. In many ways, *The Cider House Rules* reinforces the idea of natural motherhood (in that women get pregnant and then are, automatically, mothers very naturally and quite often) while at the same time illuminating the ideal of motherhood crystallized in its negative: the women who will not be mothers, or at least not mothers now or not again.

Of course, in an orphanage, there is an inherent guilt reminiscent of current perspectives associated with available options such as adoption. Furthermore, the orphanage's very existence indicates a sordid necessity:

> Spring in St. Cloud's meant trouble: drinking trouble, brawling trouble, whoring and raping trouble ... in the spring, the seeds for an orphanage were planted and overplanted" and "would an orphanage bloom in an *innocent* town?" [Irving, 1985, p. 4].

Larch's position, representative of the current pro-choice position and legalized abortion, rests on his belief that he is not fit to judge another's situation based upon his own sordid experiences with sex and reproduction when he himself had dressed in the light of a prostitute's daughter's cigar. He later saw both women dead of botched abortions, in part because he would not offer assistance (Irving, 1985). He did not believe that anyone who had seen what he had would ever force a woman to deliver an unwanted child. His belief that the individual situation need not be known to be understood and trusted as one necessitating intervention is paramount to the current belief that the individual rights of the woman are sacrosanct. The construction of Larch's character as an obstetrician first and a man second also characterizes the initial abortion debate as it is initially one discussed in medical or clinical terms and then in terms of individual people or experiences, at least in the public pro-choice discourse.

"Sometimes," said Dr. Larch, "the woman knows very early in her pregnancy that this child is unwanted." "An orphan, from the start," said Homer Wells. "You might say," said Wilbur Larch. "So she kills it," said Homer Wells. "You might say," said Wilbur Larch. "You might also say that she stops it before it becomes a child — she just stops it. In the first three or four months, the fetus — or the embryo (I don't say, then, 'the child') — it does not quite have a life of its own. It lives off the mother. It hasn't developed" [Irving, 1985, p. 73].

Larch's knowledge of the world most clearly stems from his knowledge of obstetrics, and he relates to the world through that lens. He also strongly relates with the issues of sex and reproduction through his personal experiences as a young man. He first acknowledges his own guilt and responsibility to the "problem" of unwanted children, not through his contribution to an orphanage, but through his initial interaction with a prostitute which results in a sexually transmitted disease, eventually leaving him sterile and an ether addict who practices sexual abstinence. He states clearly that, given his past experience, "He could quite comfortably abstain from having sex for the rest of his life, but how could he ever condemn another person for having sex?" (Irving, 1985, p. 52).

Interestingly, those who Larch holds most responsible are not likely the women themselves, but the men he believes should have helped them, including his early self. The current pro-life (anti-abortion) position, depicted in Homer's character, also addresses the issue of blame, albeit with a bit of understanding and some hedging. Homer did not blame Larch for performing abortions per se, and the text leads the reader to believe that Homer understood some of Larch's motivation. In fact, "Homer felt there was nothing as simple as anyone's fault involved: it was not Larch's fault — Larch did what he believed in" (Irving, 1985, p.169). Larch was a mentor and teacher to Homer, but most of all he was the closest thing to a father the orphan had known. Homer, however does not absolve Larch from responsibility, nor does he reserve blame only for the (often missing) men, as he holds the mothers accountable as well — he believes abortion to be a woman shirking personal responsibility. There is a strong relationship and bond of trust between the two men, but, on the issue of performing abortions, there is a mutual disapproval of the other's perspective, and mutual frustration. The strongest internal struggle with the question of abortion is, as well, embodied in the character of Homer Wells who, becomes involved in the practice of abortion through his training, whether he performs abortions or not. For these men, no one is innocent, not themselves and certainly not each other.

Meta Theme #3: Pro-Life Perspective: "I disapprove of it — it's not for me."

> ... that quick and not-quick stuff: it didn't work for Homer Wells. You can *call* it a fetus, or an embryo, or the products of conception, thought Homer Wells, but whatever you call it, it's alive. And whatever you do to it, Homer thought — and whatever you call what you do — you're killing it. Let Larch call it whatever he wants, thought Homer Wells. It's his choice — if it's a fetus, to him, that's fine. It's a baby to me, thought Homer Wells. If Larch has a choice, I have a choice, too [Irving, 1985, p. 169].

Much of the internal dialogue of the text (and also much of the dialogue contained in the film that is attributable to Homer's character) fairly accurately represents common mainstream pro-life sentiment today. Homer argues that he will *never* perform an abortion, although he refuses to admit to disapproving of Larch ... he says instead, that he disapproves of *it*, and indicates that the practice of performing an abortion is not for him (Irving, 1985, p. 172). As a part of Homer's obstetrical training, Larch attempts to teach him the procedure, and Homer states that he does not even want to *witness* the performing of an abortion. Larch tells him he must watch, that he must learn to perform the procedure, whether he ever actually does perform a real abortion. He must know how, as a part of his training. He must not be ignorant to the reality of the situation. Larch will not allow Homer to look away. Homer's written response to Larch is firm:

1. I am not a doctor
2. I believe the fetus has a soul
3. I am sorry [Irving, 1985, p. 545].

Homer's refusal to participate emanates from his personal experience as a child growing up in an orphanage where he witnesses the women coming, some obviously pregnant, some not. He sees the babies who are left behind, and, as he grows and trains to assist Larch, he comes to know that many women come to St. Cloud's to abort as well. He could have been either an orphan, as he was, or an abortion. He indicates that he is grateful that he was born, and that is the basis for his personal stance. Homer's characterization is steeped in the language of the rights of the child and the chances of the unborn, as well as the moral responsibility for personal actions, that also resonates with a current mainstream pro-life, anti-abortion stance.

Homer states that he has no problem with Larch performing abortions, although he does refuse to perform them himself. His disobedience towards his mentor's authority bespeaks a disapproval and a "problem" with the practice, however, his refusal to clearly disapprove and speak against Larch resonates with current, pacifistic pro-life movements that serve to resist the current legalized abortion in theory and personal practice, but who do not politically move to undermine or resist the status quo (such as moving to overturn *Roe v. Wade*) for fear of negative perception or out of an avoidance of volatility. The abortion debate has strong advocates for and against the more temperate beliefs which may be silenced for fear of the sheer passion of a strong, counter argument. This is reflected in the relationship between Homer and Larch. Further discussion below attests to ways that *The Cider House Rules* serves to illuminate the relationship between legalized first-trimester abortion and the personalization of the abortion issue; particularly in terms of the construction of the most needy or desperate women who turn to Larch or Homer for abortions.

To Homer's initial refusal, Larch responds that Homer does indeed know how to perform the procedure, and that he *chooses* not do so. Larch, frustrated, demands to know how he, Homer, can possess both the social and clinical knowledge and not feel obligated. In Larch's mind Homer's knowing obligates him (Irving, 1985). Therein lies a very interesting element. As with many social problems, knowledge spurs social action, and so we often choose to know little-so as not to be obligated to act on our knowledge. We may read Homer's early attempts as clear evidence that he does not agree with abortion practice, and that he simply does not wish to go up against Larch so strongly. But, we might also understand his earliest refusal as a wish to remain ignorant to the reality of the demand for abortion, to the situations which bring women to Larch, and to the difficulty in the decision about whether or not to perform the procedure. In layperson's terms, to, politically, make abortion legally available and accessible.

In the mainstream Catholic journal, *Commonweal* (2000), the review of the film's treatment of abortion is critical but relatively benign. "Abortion, whatever one thinks of it morally, remains a violent act, and ... yet the movie coyly undermines the idea that there can be any strict accounting for, or any "rules, ... no one is really responsible" (p. 126). *Commonweal* condemned abortion, but the stronger criticism was of the myriad of stories used to cause the reader to empathize with Larch or those in the story that might be making questionable choices in unforgiving or impossible situations. Unforgiving language, such as "whatever you call what you do — you're killing it," (Irving, 1985, p. 169) underlines the ultimate responsibility of each character for their individual situations, a very different message than the one Irving seems to be creating. The language of *Commonweal* mirrors that of Homer Wells in part, in its clarity of the moral line and its call to responsibility of those involved and defense of the unborn as a person. The review strongly criticizes the construction of Dr. Larch as a hero who argues that blame for abortion cannot be assigned. Their answer is also similar in bent to Homer's: *Commonweal* (2000) responds with "There is no avoiding moral dilemmas in which all the choices may seem unsatisfactory. But how we approach such decisions will in large part determine whether we do harm or good" (p. 126). This is similar in many ways to Homer's position of "waiting and seeing" in its hesitancy to take a particular stand or to align with a set of perspectives.

As the review alludes, by the book's end, Homer does perform an abortion for Rose Rose, the victim of incest and rape. It is his knowledge of her desperate situation that prompts him to agree to perform an abortion, and to take on the mantle of his mentor, Dr. Larch. This is one important point upon which the film and text diverge, however. In the novel, a fifteen year relationship between Homer and Candy, the female lead character, ensues, hidden from Wally, Candy's husband and Homer's friend. Homer is personalized and his stance on abortion, though it does not change outwardly, shifts for personal reasons. In the text, Homer agrees to an abortion, should it be necessary, before he actually does perform one for Rose Rose. He agrees to perform an abortion if Candy, his lover, would ever need one. This is the only way that their relationship might continue, as Candy cannot be "caught" pregnant. Eliminating much of the personalization that pages of text allows, which a much shortened film version does not, does Candy (and other women of the text as well) a strong injustice. The film, however, does not choose to show this less moralistic side of Homer Wells and instead sacrifices Candy's character (Irving, 1999) to carry the shame and guilt of abortion and much of a secret affair alone. She absorbs the angst of the abortion question, while Homer remains morally upright, his personal transgressions hidden from the camera (Wally, Candy's future husband, does "the right thing" in going with Candy to St. Cloud's when she has an abortion. A guileless young man, he seems too young and irresponsible to know what he is doing). Candy, however, is much more seductive and knowing, particularly as she enters into a relationship with Homer Wells who is very knowledgeable of medical reproduction, but naïve of sexual relationships.

The ultimate anti-choice disapproval comes in the form of the stationmaster (played in the film by the author himself). In the text, the stationmaster's view of the women who come to St. Cloud's is one of silent condemnation, with no understanding and a heaping dose of judgment. In fact, judgment clouds most of the stationmaster's thinking, and he is characterized as a demented, off-center and lonely man, who was a strong purveyor of "crackpot mail-order religion" (Irving, 1999, p. 131). The stationmaster represents an extremely radical pro-life perspective, with strong elements of judgmental, erratic emotions close to the surface and where violence, in the name of right, is only a few breaths away. The abortion clinic bomber is characterized in fiction and in the media as no less stable or irrational than the stationmaster. In the author's memoirs, Irving explains that the "obdurate disapproval" of the stationmaster (Irving, 1999, p. 133) is fearful and reactionary, characterized much like the anti-abortionists in Susan Faludi's *Backlash* (1992), where activists were both zealous and dangerous.

Meta Theme #4: The Public Fetus and the Autonomous Life

One of the subtexts underlying the abortion question culturally, as well as in the text, *The Cider House Rules,* is the extent to which motherhood is a necessary, God-granted part of a woman's life. It is negligent to ignore the religious impact on the abortion debate, even as a motivator for volatile anti-abortion activists. The thread of the cultural mainstream in the United States is woven with Judeo-Christian values. And, although anti-abortion sentiment takes many forms, both pacifistic and violent, and religious traditions are not entirely consistent, on the abortion issue many Christian traditions agree (Tone, 1997): abortion is morally wrong. Mother Teresa's words at the 1994 National Prayer Breakfast (1994) have been reproduced in the mainstream media for a worldwide audience: "The greatest destroyer of peace today is abortion, because it is a war against the child ... and if we accept that a mother can kill even her own child, how can we tell other people not to kill one another?" The history of the abortion debate has also been greatly influenced by social understanding of biological processes. The two merge, at any given point, in threads of the debate. In *The Cider House Rules*, Larch performs both "the Lord's Work and the Devil's Work" (in fact, "The Lord's Work" is the title of chapter two). This was Larch's way of conveying to the nurses whether it was a delivery or an abortion, and was also his sarcastic way of saying it was all "the Lord's Work." Larch is accused of playing God, of making his own rules, and of taking life and death upon himself. Larch's view of God is one of understanding, or at least of a God that is less judgmental than characterizations of a God of hellfire and brimstone. "A fussy or critical God, thought Wilber Larch, would strike us all dead" (Irving, 1985, p.52). To be most clear: to Larch, God was in man and man must choose to act.

Choosing to act for Larch means regulating sexuality. The abortion debate in the U.S. has never been free from its association with the birth control movement. It is estimated that, by the mid–1960s, over six million women were using the birth control pill (Tone, 1997). The introduction of birth control and the widespread availability does two things, single-handedly: the number of unwanted pregnancies are reduced and the construction of abortion as birth control waivers. "Birth control" comes to be understood, in the mainstream, as legalized contraception, and abortion rhetoric begins to construct abortion as something outside of the birth control spectrum, even upon *Roe v. Wade*. Early speak outs calling for legalized abortion called for safe and supportive services for women. *Roe v. Wade* demonstrated the deregulation of abortion during the first trimester. In fact, it is only at viability that the state demands a more inclusive understanding of personhood. Until that point, abortion regulations revolve around the safety of the pregnant woman.

Such a ruling, however, is often in conflict with popular constructions of the fetus as an autonomous, independent entity. This concept, termed "the public fetus" (Valerius, 2005) has been perpetuated in many ways, including visual prompts that project an image of the fetus as a singular subject, independent from the female, literally floating alone. Other images cast the pregnant woman as merely a vessel with much of her personhood stripped. The person is the fetus in many of the constructions perpetuated by, in particular, many anti-abortion groups today. Valerius argues that anti-abortion groups perpetuate this image of the "public fetus," depicting the unborn as supported by medical knowledge and morality. This public fetus renders the female body merely the environment in which the fetus exists, creating an independent "fetal subject" (Valerius, 2005, p. 131). Casting the pregnant body as vessel, the current pro-life stance often depicts the unborn in ways that may be viewed as separate from the female body (Liggins, 2000; Valerius, 2005).

The concept of fetus separate from pregnant woman, or of fetus as non-parasitic (not dependent upon the pregnant woman), pervades the visual literature even at stages significantly prior to developmental viability of the fetus. The pregnant woman seeking abortion is often perceived in the reverse, as a host or as an entity in an equation seeking self control at the mercy of another. These conflicting images crest and crash in the constructed images of abortion today and they also do so in the text, *The Cider House Rules*. In fact, one might argue that Homer Wells and the children at the orphanage are an extension of the image of the fetus severed from the pregnant woman: they are the ultimate children without mothers. They are, literally, the non-aborted "products of conception."[2] After numerous unsuccessful attempts to place Homer in a foster home, Larch writes "I have made an orphan; his name is Homer Wells and he will belong to St. Cloud's forever" (Irving, 1985, p. 23).

> The women seeking abortion at St. Cloud, trudging to the orphanage alone, left alone. They were kept from the sound of the delivering women as the sound of the newborn babies "upset the women having abortions" [Irving, 1985, p. 79].

In Irving's literary construction of abortion ethos, the orphanage is the backdrop for the quintessential public, autonomous fetus and the women themselves, who come to St. Clouds, are also symbolic hosts, who sever the relationship before they become mothers to these children.

Perpetuating an image of the public fetus raises the fetus to individual status, in much the same way that the pregnant woman seeking an abortion creates a space for defining her own self as person with the right to claim control. Both perspectives threaten the opposing perspective. "Pro-life discourse suppresses fetal dependence on pregnant women and conceals its own productive role in materializing a fetal subject when it claims to mimetically represent real, material fetuses (Valerius, 2005, p. 130)." To emphasize a perspective that diminishes the physical role of the female in pregnancy, raising the fetus to individual, non-dependent standing is problematic, for fear that the perception can, at any time, slip when reminded of the reality of the parasitic relationship. Valerius argues that a realistic understanding that the fetus is a dependent entity, united with another entity which is not dependent, is necessary in order to have any authentic public discussion of what the legal or ethical rights of the fetus might be. *The Cider House Rules* combats this tendency by carefully constructing the characters of the women, juxtaposed with Homer as walking, public fetus.

The text is it's most graphic and anti-abortion in the textual description of the products of conception. When Homer Wells finds the remains of an aborted fetus, he runs to Larch's office, literally carrying the products of the abortion "business." Akin to posters of severed fetuses, the descriptions of the products of conception are disturbing and shocking:

> One day, walking back from the incinerator ... it weighed less than a pound, it was maybe eight inches long, and that shadow on its almost translucent head was the first phase of hair ... those were almost eyebrows on its scrunched face, it had eyelashes, too.... Homer ran with it, straight to Dr. Larch.... "I found something," Homer Wells said [Irving, 1985, p. 69–70].

The positions on abortion are made clear by juxtaposing them in the relationship between Larch and Homer. Homer argues that he is not sure when or how, but he only knows that it is a child to him, and he knows this from his experiences. Larch, talking past Homer's position (which occurs often in the text, as in the current abortion debate), makes it a matter of rights, responsibility, and ability to dictate another's decision as he states that he cannot judge another for a sin associated with sex, when he himself is not guiltless. To him, it is not yet a child, but she is a woman who has rights, which should be protected. To Homer it is the self, also a product of "business" — the orphan business.

Meta Theme #5: A Continuum of Women and How the Individual Scenario Sways Opinion

Americans' support for abortion rights in a general sense has remained at a slim majority for the last decade but shifts radically in favor or against when individual circumstances are raised [Hanna, 2003].

When asked "are you in favor of legal abortion" or "should abortion be legal," 55 percent of the U.S. population consistently respond supporting legalized abortion with governmental control, as with *Roe v. Wade* (Shaw, 2003). This slim majority has remained steady over the last decade, regardless of the sometimes heated debate surrounding abortion, or political or medical changes such as RU486, the "abortion pill" (mifepristone). Scholars argue that the consistency of these responses indicate that the public is fairly comfortable overall with the current situation, even given the 45 percent that did not respond in support of legalized abortion (Shaw, 2003). The way that you frame the survey question can also impact the response rate. Shaw (2003) argues that with manipulation through word choice, you can encourage 85 percent support in favor of legalized abortion, or 25 percent. While the majority of the population wants abortion to be legal, they often view abortion as a significant decision and a moral dilemma.

Oftentimes, the reasons that a woman would desire an abortion strongly impact the overall perception or judgment of "worthiness" as does the timeliness of the procured abortion (first trimester vs. second). Shaw (2003) found that if you ask respondents if they feel that abortion is wrong, many will indicate that they do. But, the majority of the respondents still feel that it should be legal because illegality means that those abortions deemed "acceptable" by the majority would also be subject to sanction. People may tolerate what they view to be morally wrong in theory if they feel it may be necessary in some cases. Some then concede that the practice be legal, in that the slim majority has held its ground for a time, when they believe abortion to be, fundamentally, morally wrong. This is Homer's position. Such a hands-off idea, says Shaw, gives abortion rights advocates hope for long-term success, despite the recent Senate legislation banning so-called "partial-birth" abortions, which most of the public likewise opposes.

What becomes extremely salient, then, in the abortion question is the issue of "some cases" in which abortion may be warranted, even in the eyes of those who are anti-abortion. In *The Cider House Rules*, multiple stories of women seeking abortion, with different situations and motivations flesh out the abortion issue and provide examples of the situational nature of judgments about abortion. Interwoven throughout the framework of two men and their positions on performing abortion, live the women who do not wish to be or simply *cannot* be pregnant. When Homer initially refuses to perform an abortion for Rose Rose, he repeats his position on abortion, but Candy provides the justification for his involvement:

> "I know I can do it. It's just that, to me, it is a living human being. I can't describe to you what it feels like — just to hold the curette for example. When living tissue is touched, it responds — somehow," Homer said, but Candy cut him off.
> "It may help you to know who the father is," she said. "It's Mister Rose. Her father is the father..." [Irving, 1985, p. 567].

Solinger (2001) argues that for the everyday public to empathize with an unknown woman, and to feel animosity towards the situation which produced the pregnancy and the surrounding conditions, the woman must be characterized as a "good woman," i.e. one who is able to care for herself and take control of her future situation. "Strong examples" (Solinger, 2001, p. 26) must be used to make the case for either side, and garner emotional support from both sides of the debate, and these strong examples must embody and signify shared social values. Therefore, key images and constructs become very important, such as whiteness or social class. But stories of rape, particularly of very young women coerced by older men or by male family members, strike a deep cord and provoke sympathy and protective response, as well. For example, in *The Cider House Rules*, a male character is asked what he knows of abortion:

> "I know it's a sin," Meany Hyde said, "and I know Grace Lynch has had one once — and in her case, I sympathize with her — if you know what I mean." Grace's husband, Vernon, beat her [Irving, 1985, p. 152].

Ultimately, of all of the women who consider abortion in *The Cider House Rules*, it is Rose Rose, the young victim of incest by her father, which rouses Homer to perform an abortion.[3] Stereotypically characterized as the young, black daughter of a migrant worker, she is illiterate, powerless to stop her father's sexual demands, and despondent when she finds herself impregnated by him. Homer, who has grown to know her by working in the orchard, fears that she will hurt herself in an attempt to self-abort. It is her story which most closely resonates with abortion law prior to *Roe v. Wade*, and which still resonates with the most commonly accepted reasons for sanctioning abortion today, the physical or mental health of the mother, fetal abnormality, or, as is particularly the case with Rose Rose, rape or incest.

The numerous social reasons (Finer et al., 1985) that might cause women to hesitate to parent a child are illustrated in *The Cider House Rules*, such as financial insecurity (Rose Rose), lack of a partner (both Mrs. and Miss Eames, as well as multiple women who come alone to St. Clouds), or a volatile marital relationship (as with Grace Lynch's husband). Many women in *The Cider House Rules* have frightening or fatal experiences at the hands of abortion "butchers" such as "Mrs. Santa Claus" who performs abortions in an urban clinic. Two women, Mrs. Eames and her daughter, who seek Mrs. Claus for an abortion, die from complications (Larch knew both of these women; they are the impetus for his work as an abortionist). Mrs. Claus condemns Larch for his earlier lack of action, and forces him to open his eyes to the social injustice that a young woman may face. "About a third of them get it from their fathers, or their brothers. Rape ... Incest. You understand?" (Irving, 1985, p. 57). The message is clear in the text: you can have your own perspective, but you cannot be ignorant to the social ethos of abortion. And once you know, it is much more difficult to ignore.

The deserving and undeserving woman are interestingly juxtaposed in *The Cider House Rules* in the form of two women in particular: Candy and Melony, one who seeks abortion and one who does not. One is privileged, beautiful, and supported by a loving fiancé and family, the other is an orphan, big and brash who is used for her body and whose body, upon her death in the end of the text, is returned to St. Clouds, to be used for medical research. Candy, a beautiful, promising, young woman engaged to be married and on her way to college finds that she is pregnant but is not yet ready for motherhood and marriage. Her fiancé, Wally, is willing to marry her, or to support her decision to abort. She represents *the* woman who Homer believes should be having children. This is quite different from the portrayal of all other women who seek abortion in *The Cider House Rules*. Candy alone has social status, beauty, youth, and a loving partner. This makes her a winsome and "acceptable" character, but it also creates a dilemma ... why can she not simply accept Wally's marriage proposal and have the child? She is the example of the woman who chooses her own life course over unplanned motherhood. She is not the strong case that wins favor of pro-life advocates. She wants an abortion because it is not the right time for her to have a child. In other ways, as well, she is characterized as acting with her own interests at the forefront: for example, she has an affair with Homer while married to Wally and she agrees to tell everyone that their child together is an orphan they simply could not leave behind when visiting St. Clouds. Her choices illuminate the reality for many women who are, first and foremost, human, and who have dreams and aspirations that they choose to follow. Candy is, quite literally, the "girl next door" who seeks abortion.

Melony, however, is an orphan who, like Homer, was never successfully adopted. Introduced to sex at a young age, she is an example of the ways in which society uses women's bodies and exploits their sexuality. Melony, who does not procure an abortion in the text, is Homer's first sexual experience (she bribes Homer with sexual favors in exchange for her case files — she wants to know the name of her mother, indicating that she wants to find her and kill her). Melony is the antithesis to the "good woman." She is big, volatile, and dominating. She is involved in a lesbian relationship after she leaves the orphanage and pushes Homer throughout the novel. She serves as an example of the missed opportunities women face. She was not selected, as was Homer, to walk in Larch's footsteps. She was, instead, meant for a different road. She is, quite simply, one of the most fascinating characters in the text. Even in the face of promiscuity, deviousness, and pent-up rage, she is the character that ultimately brings Homer up short with her painful disappointment in his life choices. Because of Melony's deep-seated sense of justice, Homer realizes that he must go back to St. Cloud's to take Larch's place.

When we take into consideration the ability of the situation to influence our judgments of a woman's abortion decision, the characterization of each player is of utmost importance, as is the textual construction of the situation that surrounds the decision to abort. Which character/s ultimately prevail in *The Cider House Rules*? Homer, with his love for his fellow orphans and his desire to protect what he views as innocent life? Melony, as an example of a woman society threw away from birth? Candy, who is golden? Or is it Rose Rose, who experiences extreme pain and grief at her father's hand? Maybe Mr. Rose, who, although he is an abuser and rapist, earns the begrudging respect of the fellow migrant workers and even of Homer himself? Maybe it is ultimately Larch's story which is most moving, which most clearly outlines the issues at hand? With whom do we empathize and why? And, why do male characters ultimately shape the perspective on abortion rights for women in this text? Was Irving so naïve as to not realize that the abortion decisions are driven and shaped by men as he has written it? Probably not. In fact, this may be his most appropriate comparison to the current abortion ethos in this text.

Meta Theme #6: The Business of Abortion
and the Rules of the Cider House

What is their business? The hero business ... Homer Wells made up his mind; he would be a hero [Irving, 1985, p. 562].

The Cider House Rules is really about a man's world with abortion as its topic of interest. Abortion is the business and the products of business are literally the products of conception. The main characters are white, privileged in their opportunities, and in control of their personal choices as well as the personal choices of many others in which they come in contact. Homer is straight, and Larch, if not heterosexual, is cast as asexual (Larch determines never to have sex again when first sex, with a prostitute hired by his father, is traumatic; the film, however, alludes to a mild romantic relationship between Dr. Larch and Nurse Angela). Abortion service is but one way that these men exert control over their own worlds and others,' even fatherless or as orphans. "It turns out that abortion, and even rape and father-daughter incest, are about a man's right to choose" (Booth, 2002, p. 293) and Irving identifies abortion as "an afterthought" (Booth, 2002, p. 293) of the interaction among men. Supposedly, the key motivating factor in the text is the search for a father-figure for Homer and the grooming of an heir for Larch. But, the representation of the availability of abortion as lying solely in the hands of men is a point in the text that cannot be underestimated. Comparatively, men in the U.S. hold positions of power: political, medical, etc., and have significant control over the availability of abortion services. In Irving's words, the rules are Larch's, and, comparatively, in a patriarchal society, much of the abortion question today is answered by men and male perspective.

"What business you in?" is the question Mr. Rose asks of Homer, and it becomes symbolic of the overall search for identity in the form of occupation and in the concept of "creating rules" by which the business of everyday life is lived. It is the ultimate "man question." Dr. Larch insists that, one must "be of use," and must attend to business in a helpful and purposeful way. They are to go about *the business* of *making their own rules*. In this sense, there is not an appropriate way to ask the women in the text what "their business" might be ... they are not, surely, in the baby-making business, or in the abortion business, or in the business of making decisions on either subject for others. In fact, they serve as examples of the ways that women are limited in the very ability to make the decision for their own personal selves, limited in the making of the "business" of their lives. In this way, female reproductive capacity has, historically, been an impediment to the very question "what business you in?" for women and has shaped the way that women have been viewed as citizens, workers, and human beings. It is men who have, historically, had a business to tend, even marginalized men and men of color.

Mr. Rose is in the cider making business, but we know, as do all of the other workers and, eventually, Homer and Candy, that he is in the business of making his own rules, as well, within the hierarchy of men. The rules that he lives his life by do not only influence his life, however, but those dependent upon him. The text leads us to assume that this tendency to create counter rules is a function of an unjust society. On this level, Mr. Rose is a sympathetic character. However, his daughter, Rose Rose, eventually exerts her own independence and takes control of the abusive dynamic that exists within the set of rules Mr. Rose has constructed in the cider house. But, we do not see in Irving's text what may occur when Rose Rose sets to make her own rules, to take her own control of her destiny autonomously outside of someone else's dictate (although connections may be made to Melony's character). Rose Rose does make a choice in leaving, fleeing after stabbing her father in self-defense, but it is within the constraints of what is made possible for her.

Candy faces coercion that limits her choices, as well, as her choices are restrained. This may explain why she remains an active part of the story for so long. Melony is unstoppable ... forcing her business into the midst, although to no avail, as she dies angry and frustrated, despondent and unsatisfied. Melony may also serve as a reminder that resisting male rule does not end happily — she is the product of rage against the social rules that do not value a female with determination, physicality, or overt sexuality. Understanding that the control of the abortion decision is largely a male decision; in that access, availability, perspective, and the construction of the abortion question is, historically and currently, in male hands, one might wonder how we can socially talk of the morality or immorality of choice when choice itself is a control issue? It is sometimes "moral" to have a child (Homer is the father of Candy's child, Angel. Homer would not allow his child to be aborted, although he did tell everyone, including Angel, that he was an orphan),[4] sometimes immoral to have a child or to be pregnant (as in the case of Rose Rose and the many unwed mothers who came to St. Clouds), to abort (many examples provided in *The Cider House Rules*). The judgment may shift depending upon the situation or individual woman or group of women, because the value of that group or individual, but the bottom line is that many women are at the mercy of whether or not their abortions are "acceptable."

Conclusion: What Are the Lessons of The Cider House Rules?

In *The Cider House Rules*, rules are rooted in the business of men's and women's lives. "Who makes the rules?" is possibly the most important question of the novel, alongside the emphasis on the products of the business of abortion and reproduction (the mutually inclusive public fetus and the pregnant woman). We find that, in *The Cider House Rules*, Larch's rules really stand (Irving, 1999, p. 33). How do Larch's rules translate into current practice? Irving comments that "Politically speaking, if I were to make a list of people who should see *The Cider House Rules*, two groups would go to the top of the list: politicians who call themselves pro-life (meaning anti-abortion) and twelve-year-old girls" (Irving, 1999, p. 162).

A common element throughout the novel *The Cider House Rules* is the idea of "waiting and seeing." This does not work well for pregnancy, particularly if the pregnancy is not wanted, and it really equates in many cases to doing little or nothing. Doing nothing is the opposite of following Larch's rules. In many ways Larch's urging to remove judgment and make abortion available is the status quo today, however much "waiting and seeing" (i.e. doing nothing) may be occurring. Put a slightly different way, the tension between Larch's perspective and Homer's "waiting and seeing" may be equated to the mainstream sentiment towards abortion today. The lack of real impetus to eliminate legalized abortion, consistently, particularly in the face of evidence that personalizing the stories often results in stronger support for a pro-choice perspective, signifies the overall comfortability in holding judgment on women (and therefore normatively punishing women for not following the rules of morality) but, at the same time, not really wanting to see the overt consequences that are much more far-reaching than the woman herself, or even the pregnancy if choice is eliminated. Not really taking a stand, not really wanting to know or to get involved, that is the equivalent to "waiting and seeing" that kept Homer in a fifteen year relationship and kept him from making any real decisions either way for a very long time.

Larch responded, alternatively, to the admonition to "shit or get off the pot" (Irving, 1985, p. 50). His impatience with those who did not see his way is akin to the frustration of over a century of birth control and abortion rights activists who argue that it is the social structure and social condition of woman that contributes to the problem of abortion, not the inadequacy of individual women. The limitations that women face, such as poverty, violence, and poor health care, are not only individual elements of the abortion situation, but are the reason for abortion. Larch's character clearly conveys that the culprit is not illicit sex but the mistreatment of women. *The Cider House Rules* eloquently explores the connections between the social problem that is abortion and the connections between the use of women and of women's bodies in a patriarchal society.

Furthermore, the relationship between birth control and abortion is possibly the *most significant* related issue to be addressed today; and is very clearly stated in *The Cider House Rules*. Pregnancy occurs. Irving clearly traces the connections between education about birth control, the birth rate, the abortion rate in St. Cloud's, noting that as the first goes up the second and third go down. "It would take Larch years to educate the population regarding birth control — the ratio would endure for some time: one abortion for every three births. Over the years, it would go to one in four, then to one in five" (Irving, 1985, p. 68). Today, when we focus on the right to life or the right to choice, or we discuss abstinence vs. sex education in schools, it becomes clear that possibly the most frightening element of the abortion question is our lack of real, clear, and accessible information about sex, sexuality, and birth control. This is particularly salient for young people, as is always clear from my students' reactions to this text. Currently, the options are a relatively short list: abstinence, childbirth, abortion, adoption…. The debate is often constructed by multiple perspectives as clear; the text *The Cider House Rules* makes it very complex. As complex as is currently evident in our social climate of abortion and abortion experience once we allow ourselves to consider individual elements.

Notes

1. There are many differences between the text of *The Cider House Rules* and its film reproduction. The decisions surrounding many of these differences are documented and explored in Irving's commentary, *My Movie Business* (1999).

2. I wish to enthusiastically thank editor and mentor Susan A. Martinelli-Fernandez for her assistance with the organization of this paper and for her insight into the concept of the public fetus as represented in the text.

3. Homer, however does initially agree to an earlier abortion if it ever need be performed. In order to continue their secret love affair, Homer must agree to perform an abortion for Candy if she were to become pregnant. Homer agrees, although Candy does not become pregnant after this agreement is struck, and therefore, Rose Rose is Homer's first abortion performed. The film does not portray this element; in the film, Rose Rose is the first abortion Homer agrees to perform.

4. "Our baby is adopted?" Candy asked. "So we have a baby who thinks it is an orphan?"

"No," Homer said. "We have our own baby, and it knows it's all ours. We just *say* it's adopted — just for Olive's sake, and just for a while. "That's lying," Candy said (Irving, 1985, p. 408).

References

Booth, A. (2002). Neo-Victorian Self-Help, or Cider House Rules. *American Literary History*, 14.2, 284–310.

Cates, W., D. Grimes and K. Schultz (2003). The Public Health Impact of Legal Abortion: 30 years Later. *Perspectives on Sexual and Reproductive Health*, 35, 25–28.

Code of Canon Law (2006). IntraText Edition LT, *Èulogos*.

Commonweal (2000). Hard Cider: *The Cider House Rules* as Meditation on Abortion, 5, 126–7.

Costa, M. (1991). *Abortion: A Reference Handbook*. California: ABC-CLIO.

Faludi, S. (1992). *Backlash: The Undeclared War Against Women*. New York: Anchor.

Finer, L., L. Frohwirth, L. Dauphinee, S. Singh and A. Moore (2005). Reasons U.S. Women Have Abortions: Quantitative and Qualitative Perspectives. *Perspectives on Sexual and Reproductive Health*, 37 (3), 110–118.

Glaser, B. (1978). *Theoretical Sensitivity*. California: Sociology Press.

Glaser, B. and A. Strauss (1967). *The Discovery of Grounded Theory: Strategies for Qualitative Research*. Chicago: Aldine Publishing Company.

Gledhill, C. (1997). The Case of the Soap Opera. In *Cultural Representations and Signifying Practices*. California: Sage Publication.

Hall, S. (1997). (Ed.). *Cultural Representations and Signifying Practices*. California: Sage.

Hanna, J. (2003). Public Opinion on Abortion Remains Constant Over Decade, According to Study by Illinois Weslyan University professor. *Ascribe Newswire*, 1.

Holsti, O. (1969). *Content Analysis for the Social Sciences and Humanities*. Massachusetts: Addison-Wesley Publishing Co.

Hulbert, A. (2007). Beyond the Pleasure Principle. *The New York Times*.

Irving, J. (1985). *The Cider House Rules*. New York: Ballantine Books.

Irving, J. (1999). *My Movie Business*. New York: Random House.

Liggings, E. (2000). 'With a Dead Child in her Lap': Bad Mothers and Infant Mortality in George Egerton's discords. *Literature and History*, 9(2), 17–34.

Margolis, M. (2000). *True to Her Nature*. Illinois: Waveland Press.

McIntosh, S. (1999). *The Cider House Rules: The Making of the Movie*. [Documentary].

Mother Theresa. (February 3, 1994). Speech at the National Prayer Breakfast.

Shaw, G. (2003). Trends: Abortion. *Public Opinion Quarterly*, 67, 407–429.

Smith, A. (2005). Beyond Pro-Choice Versus Pro-Life: Women of Color and Reproductive Justice. *NWSA Journal*, 17(1), 119–140.

Solinger, R. (2001). *Beggars and Choosers: How the Politics of Choice Shapes Adoption, Abortion and Welfare in the United States*. New York: Hill and Wang.

Strauss, A. and J. Corbin (1998). *Basics of Qualitative Research*. California: Sage Publications.

Tone, A. (Ed.). (1997). *Controlling Reproduction: An American History*. Delaware: Scholarly Resources, Inc.

Valerius, K. (2005). Rosemary's Baby, Gothic Pregnancy, and Fetal Subjects. *College Literature*, 32.3, 116–135.

van Dijk, T. (1998). *Ideology: A Multidisciplinary Approach*. London: Sage Publications.

Abortion and Mental Health

Gayla Elliott

Abstract

Controversy surrounds the question of whether or not abortion negatively affects mental health. Although research shows that abortion alone does not impair mental health, some factors related to the abortion experience, such as pre-existing mental/emotional distress, lack of emotional support during and after abortion, coercion, age, poverty, conflicting values, and concealment, can create problems for abortion patients. Society has a powerful impact, within religious, political, and social structures, on how women experience unwanted pregnancy and what choices that are available to them. A case study from a local women's crisis center illustrates factors that can complicate the abortion experience and lead to psychological distress after abortion. A feminist, person-centered approach to counseling provides an effective model for counselors helping women who do report psychological suffering after abortion. Interventions suggested for post-abortion counseling are eclectic, multi-cultural, and non-judgmental. Because of women's compromised status in society, their voices about reproductive freedom are often lost in religious and political rhetoric. Understanding what issues complicate abortion, why certain women choose abortion, and how these factors can create a negative emotional response in women is crucial to providing adequate mental health services to those in need.

This essay presents an anecdotal case study to illustrate examples of how and why abortion can be psychologically problematic for some women. Although research has found no serious threat to a woman's short-term or long-term mental health after abortion (Adler et al., 1990; Bradshaw & Slade, 2003; Lemkau, 1991), related factors such as social stigma, lack of support, and conflicting internal feelings about abortion can create significant distress when these factors are present before, during, or after an abortion (Rubin & Russo, 2004). Most women do not find the need to seek mental health counseling after abortion (Adler et al., 1990; Major et al., 2000). When they do, counselors and therapists need to understand what factors typically create a distressing abortion experience. Understanding these factors will enable mental health professionals to provide services that are relevant and sensitive to women's post-abortion needs.

A feminist approach to counseling requires examining the context of cultural and social dynamics that influence women's lives (Stoppard, 2000). Although there are many feminist theories, for the purpose of this essay a feminist approach means the counselor brings basic feminist principles into the treatment process (Brown, 2004). Some of these principles include treating the client as an equal, assuming the client (not the counselor) is the expert about her own life, and creating a trusting, non-judgmental and collaborative therapeutic relationship. The feminist counselor also strives to raise the client's awareness about how sociocultural circumstances (e.g. the imbalance of power that is inherent in a Western, white-male-dominated society) have negatively impacted her. Feminist counselors are nonpathologizing in that they are reluctant to use diagnostic labels and refrain from doing so unless necessary for medical or insurance purposes (McCloskey & Fraser, 1997). Educating women about the social structures that keep them marginalized can build feminist consciousness, which, in turn, decreases self-blame and helps empower them. In other words, the focus is on what is wrong with a society that tolerates women's diminished social status and abuse toward women, not what is wrong with the woman. Finally, a feminist counselor's goal is to honor and empower women to make their own decisions based on their own perceptions, desires, and the complex, idiosyncratic consequences of any choices they make. A heightened feminist consciousness can help women make informed choices. Counseling techniques modeled in this essay are not necessarily feminist techniques. The way in which they are used, and the climate of the therapeutic environment are what are essentially feminist in nature (Brown, 2004).

Feminist approaches to counseling women through abortion and post-abortion help women understand the many sociocultural factors that can create, complicate, or exacerbate the emotional impact of abortion. Making the choice to end a pregnancy, difficult as that choice may be, becomes more complex and potentially more stressful because it is an issue that has a history of controversy within the political, religious, and economic elements of society. Women often experience a lack of power and control over circum-

172

stances that affect their health, reproductive choices, and their destinies, because their choices are limited by society through such things as social policy, abortion laws, medical access, or religious influences. This lack of power and control contributes to overall mental health and well being when women find themselves in the uncomfortable situation of unplanned or unwanted pregnancy. Exploring the effects of abortion on women's mental health warrants a close examination of the factors that influence how we view abortion in this society, and how those views impact a woman's experience. The following case study can help provide examples of challenges encountered by one woman who did suffer psychological and emotional pain from her experiences surrounding an abortion.

Case Study

28-year-old Amy (not her real name) had been receiving counseling from me through the local crisis center for about six months. She had arrived there because of violence in her relationship with an emotionally unstable boyfriend. His verbal/mental abuse had once again escalated into physical violence that knocked out two of Amy's teeth. This event was a wake-up call for Amy, motivating her to call our hotline for help.

It is not uncommon for adult victims of domestic violence to discover, through counseling, that the abuse in their lives started in childhood. Over the course of a few months, Amy and I explored the impact that child sexual abuse, neglect, verbal abuse and physical abuse from the past had on her current life. Together we had created a place for her to express her difficult emotions — emotions that had never before been safe for her to express due to risk of further harm. Amy was in the process of learning how the cycle of abuse had perpetuated throughout her life. She was discovering that she had some choice in whether or not to remain engaged in abusive relationships. She was learning to create safe boundaries for herself. She was on the road to recovery.

One day I sensed that Amy had more to tell me. She was edgy. Tearful. She was avoiding eye contact. She told me she was ashamed and was afraid to tell me what was on her mind. I wondered what we had missed. Was there more sexual abuse? Were there more memories from her childhood? More abuse in her current relationship that she had not yet disclosed?

Amy began to weep, and I quietly waited for her to gain her composure so *she could speak. Finally she told me that at 15 years of age she had become sexually active and subsequently pregnant. Amy was not aware that she was pregnant at first, because she did not recognize the physical signs. But her mother was aware and scheduled an abortion for Amy without her knowledge. Amy was told only that she was being taken to a doctor for a medical procedure. It was not until after the abortion that she understood what had happened.*

Telling this story triggered a flood of tears unlike any I had seen from Amy up until this point in her counseling. The pain and grief, the shame and fear were palpable. My calm presence and non-judgmental stance in the therapeutic relationship enabled her to speak about what had haunted her since her adolescence.

Women's Crisis Work

As a counselor at a domestic violence and rape crisis center, my job entails listening to women like Amy, one-on-one, an hour at a time, for many hours each day. These women speak to me about the most personal, private, and sometimes most traumatic stories of their lives. The center where I work provides free services to victims of domestic violence and sexual assault. Although not considered a glamorous job in our society, I feel honored to be in that place, hearing women's voices, listening to their pain, holding the space for their tears and rage, and celebrating with them when they recover their strength and power.

Crisis centers like this one typically have specialized training for staff so that the philosophy of the agency is communicated through the counseling, education and advocacy provided. The philosophy is secular and not aligned with a political party. The mission is to recognize the seriousness and severity of crimes against women and to work toward social change by raising awareness and creating a social system that is more responsive. Other goals of women's crisis centers are to provide safety (through developing safety plans and sheltering), enable clients to gain legal assistance, educating and escorting them through the steps necessary to gain court orders of protection against batterers, and advocating and referring to other social service agencies in order to meet the many needs of battered women or survivors of rape (McCloskey & Fraser, 1997).

Crisis center training manuals stress that the counselor's role is to encourage all women to make choices that are in line with their own individual values and beliefs, choices that will protect and empower them. Some of the goals of counseling are to dispel myths about sexual assault and domestic violence, alleviate guilt and self-blame that victims often feel, and encourage clients to take proactive steps in their lives while learning to honor and respect themselves. Education provides information that helps women understand cultural norms that hinder women's strength, power and control. Empowering women and restoring control over their lives are the ultimate goals of the crisis center agency.

This place is where I developed a person-centered, feminist style of counseling while also using cognitive-behavioral approaches that work well with trauma victims. By person-centered I am referring to the approach developed by Carl Rogers (1965) who claimed that clients benefit from experiencing their counselors as warm, empathic, authentic, nonjudgmental, and unconditionally accepting. Rogers felt that the counselor should be viewed as someone whose role is to help and who does not wield any particular power (Rogers, 1965). This philosophy fits in well with the feminist counseling ideal of an egalitarian relationship in which the counselor and client are seen as equal partners (McCloskey & Fraser, 1997). As described earlier, the feminist approach adds the culturally sensitive piece, acknowledging that all experiences happen within a social context and are therefore influenced by that context (Brown, 2004). Because I felt a need to provide more than warm, emotionally supportive, and feminist-driven counseling, I sought out training to implement some simple yet powerful cognitive-behavioral approaches specifically designed for survivors of trauma. These techniques were designed to help victims of abuse or disaster directly face the emotional impact of their experiences, express their feelings freely, and create more powerful internal constructs of self as survivor rather than victim (Smucker & Dancu, 1999).

Although mostly short-term crisis intervention and follow-up services are provided at the crisis center, there is the opportunity for clients to continue counseling for longer periods of time, depending on their choice and need. Sometimes when a woman seeks counseling services for one particular issue, such as rape or domestic violence, the safety of the counseling environment creates a climate conducive to allowing for other disclosures. Such was the case with Amy, who originally sought out services because of domestic violence, but during that process felt it was time to share her story of abortion.

Amy originally came to the agency to receive advocacy and counseling for issues related to domestic violence. She had very little experience with counseling and was not sure what to expect. Initially she wanted help in understanding the cycle of abuse, which was repeating itself in her life and specifically, now, in her intimate relationship. As she shared stories from her past abuse and described the dynamics of her current relationship, she was aware that I was listening intently, interested in her story, nonjudgmental, and open to hearing her perspective. I did not tell her what to do, imply blame, or offer any professional advice, but I did point out where I heard her blaming herself for events that were not her fault. Amy learned that in our relationship I would support her in her choices, allow her to express feelings freely, and provide resources such as books and crisis center literature, so she could educate herself about domestic violence. She began asking me to help her find words and behaviors that would be effective in setting safer boundaries for herself in her interpersonal relationships, which she then actively employed. As she experienced success in this area, she developed mastery in asserting herself and learning to say "no" to abuse. The counseling relationship was built on confidentiality, trust, respect and education. These elements had rarely (if ever) been part of any relationship Amy had experienced. The quality of our relationship most likely made it safe for her to share her story of abortion for the first time in her life.

Does Abortion Compromise Mental Health?

A key question explored in this essay is whether or not abortion is a traumatic event that requires a counseling intervention. Most women do not experience trauma or compromised mental health after abortion (Adler et al., 1990), so why present a essay on abortion and mental health? This question is quite complex because so many issues surrounding abortion make the experience potentially disruptive to women's mental health or emotional well-being. Furthermore, the distress experienced by women who have had an abortion is likely to have originated in events and conditions that existed before they became pregnant (Russo & Dabul, 1997). Examining the psychosocial issues surrounding abortion is important in order to identify exactly which factors cause distress and under what circumstances.

Most well designed research supports the position that abortion in and of itself is most often not a traumatic event in a woman's life. In a study by

Nancy Adler et al. (1990), 76 percent of women reported relief as the most predominant emotion they experienced following the termination of an unwanted pregnancy. Major et al. (2000) concurs with this position and found that the majority of women (80 percent) who choose abortion within the first trimester suffer no long-term psychological distress and feel satisfied with their choice. Additional research has supported these findings (Bradshaw & Slade, 2003; Rubin & Russo, 2004).

If little or no distress is present, is there a need for post-abortion counseling? Although the majority of women report no significant emotional distress, a percentage of women do report negative psychological experiences after abortion (Adler et al., 1990). Research studying the emotional impact of abortion on women revealed that about 20 percent of post-abortion women suffer from clinical depression, which is the same rate of depression as the national average of all women during child-bearing years (Major et al., 2000). The women who suffer negative emotional consequences most likely struggle with issues that have complicated the abortion experience for them (Adler et al., 1990). Many factors in a woman's life can contribute to her vulnerability to psychological distress following an abortion.

Controversy and Limited Research

One of the factors that contributes to the distress some women feel is that the issue of abortion receives sharply focused attention and heated debate from the political and religious realms of society (Cozzarelli et al., 2000; Major, 2003; Rubin & Russo, 2004). How our culture conceptualizes abortion stems from attitudes originating from political, economic, medical, and moral systems. These systems influence how the culture views abortion and whether or not it is a matter of human rights, a question of ethical morality, or a medical danger to women's physical or mental health.

Extensive research explores the psychological impact of abortion, much of which has been fueled by pro-life or pro-choice advocates who are driven to support their point of view (Rubin & Russo, 2004). For example, research suggesting that abortion causes mental/emotional harm in women is valuable to those who want to influence others to join the pro-life (anti-abortion) movement and affect legislation controlling abortion. In the late 1980's pro-life advocates identified a condition called Post Abortion Syndrome (PAS). They claimed that abortion causes a psychological response mirroring symptoms found in Post Traumatic Stress Disorder (PTSD) (Almeling & Tews, 1999; Major, 2003). Information retrieved from the National Abortion Federation's (NAF) website (*www.prochoice.org*) states that in 1989, after thorough examination of rigorous scientific studies, PAS was ultimately rejected by the American Psychological Association (APA) as a bona fide diagnostic category (Almeling & Tews, 1999). The bottom line was that the cause of psychological distress could not be attributed to abortion through any valid research method. Since then, more empirical studies have found the incidence of depression or traumatic stress to be no greater in post-abortion women than women in the general population (Adler et al., 1990; Major et al., 2000; Russo & Dabul, 2004).

Psychological Distress Pre-Abortion

Pre-existing mental health issues can predict a more difficult response to abortion (Russo & Dabul, 1997). A negative impact on psychological well being following abortion often correlates with compromised mental health of the woman before or during the pregnancy. For instance, the stress accompanying unplanned pregnancy often requires difficult decision-making and re-evaluation of personal ethical judgments that can cause significant emotional upheaval (Major, Richards, Cooper, Cozzarelli, & Aubek, 1998; Russo & Zierk, 1992).

Studies show that when women report high self-esteem before abortion, they are more likely to have positive feelings after terminating an unplanned or unwanted pregnancy (Major et al., 1998). Good self-esteem generally means that an individual feels confident, operates from a positive identity, and trusts her own judgment. When a woman is solid in her convictions, trusts her own judgment, and exercises the power and freedom to make decisions about reproduction that are in her best interest, she is less likely to experience adverse effects from abortion (Adler et al., 1990; Cozzarelli, Sumer, & Major, 1998; Major et al., 1998; Russo & Zierk, 1992).

Women who struggle with depression, anxiety, feelings of inferiority, or experience a lack of control, generally have a harder time dealing with any kind of difficult challenge (Major et al., 1998; Teichman et. al., 1993). A study by Russo & Denious (2001) found that the incidence of domestic violence was higher in the lives of abortion patients. Women who have suffered violence in their lives are conditioned to feel a sense of powerlessness, which may have a negative effect on their ability to make decisions based on their own opinions and appraisals. Feelings of powerlessness stemming from exposure to domestic violence can contribute to symptoms of anxiety and depression. The stress involved in coping with a difficult life event, such as abortion, will be more challenging for a woman who suffers from compromised mental health resulting from living in an oppressive domestic environment. Here we see this history of psychological and emotional distress illustrated in Amy's early life:

As a child, Amy suffered from physical and emotional abuse, experienced sexual assault, and was neglected by her parents. Alcoholism was prominent in the home. As a very young girl, Amy was responsible for the care of her two younger brothers, one of whom was disabled. She learned from an early age that her wants and needs were not a priority in the family. She was given responsibilities that were inappropriate for a youngster. Abuse in her life created fear and shame. By the time she was a teen she had experienced a great amount of trauma with no intervention and minimal support from adults. Amy reported that when she was 15, she suffered from anxiety and depressive symptoms. Looking to meet her needs for love and attention, she became sexually active and then accidentally pregnant.

Lack of Emotional Support

Literature on the subject of post-abortion distress suggests that a lack of emotional support from the woman's partner, family members, or friends can increase her risk of emotional distress (Major et al., 1998; Rubin & Russo, 2004). If the choice to end a pregnancy risks a woman's close relationships, she has a more difficult time weighing the consequences of that choice, and may have a more difficult post-abortion experience if she is isolated or ostracized. When women feel secure in their close relationships and understand that they are unconditionally supported in their choices by loved ones, the choice to end a pregnancy is less difficult and the period after abortion is conducive to healing. The presence of emotional support helps women feel safe to verbalize thoughts and feelings after their abortion experience, decreasing the likelihood of internalizing those more problematic feelings (Adler et al., 1990; Cozzarelli et al., 1998; Major & Gramzow, 1999). Amy's story gives an example of this phenomenon by the complete lack of emotional support she received at the time of her abortion and afterward:

As Amy recounted her memories of the abortion experience within our counseling sessions, she recalled that her boyfriend was 18 years old at the time. She believes now that he knew she was pregnant, but just like her mother he kept silent. Since he did not acknowledge her pregnancy, he did not offer any emotional support.

Amy remembers her mother driving her to the clinic, telling Amy she had scheduled her for a "procedure." On the way home, Amy was lying in the back of her mother's car, crying and feeling some pain. She remembers her mother parking the car at a bar to go have a cocktail, leaving Amy to "sleep it off" in the back of the car. Amy was not sleeping. She was awake and experiencing confusion, physical discomfort and emotional turmoil, all alone.

Coercion

In the crisis center where I work, our mission is to restore power and control to those who have lost sovereignty over body, mind and spirit. At the heart of the women's crisis movement is an attempt to recognize that all domestic violence and sexual assaults are a result of one person using aggression to overpower another. Intimidation, controlling behaviors, verbal abuse, degrading and humiliating acts, physical violence, destruction of property, and rape are examples of abuse that victimize others, most often women. In order to heal from the trauma of abuse, victims must restore power and control in their lives.

Research suggests that abortion is potentially harmful to mental health when the decision to end a pregnancy has been strongly influenced by something or someone other than the pregnant woman (Lemkau, 1991; Russo & Denious, 2001). When the choice is forced on women, or there are no healthy choices available, women can experience a sense of powerlessness. For example, if an adolescent is forced by her boyfriend or parents to end a pregnancy, she is more likely to feel victimized by the event because she does not feel a sense of control over her body. She loses the ability to choose her own destiny. In another scenario, a controlling husband may demand that his wife end her pregnancy because he refuses to allow another child into the family. In these situations, the decisions over whether or not to give birth are highly influenced by external voices threatening a woman's safety, her sense of belonging, her economic security, her close relationships, and perhaps many other factors that put her general well being at risk. This limits her choices, decreases her feelings of power and control over her body and her life, and can reinforce feelings of helplessness and self-doubt, key characteristics of many emotional difficulties women face. We return to our case study to see how this factor played out in Amy's life:

Amy was not aware of her pregnancy at the early stages because she did not recognize the physical signs. Her mother was observant and recognized the symptoms of pregnancy such as a missed menstrual period, bloating, and weight gain. Amy's mother withheld the information, choosing not to tell Amy that she was pregnant. This failure to inform Amy ultimately empowered her mother to take control of the situation by scheduling an abortion. Amy experienced the abortion without a clear idea of what was happening to her. She was not consulted at all, her thoughts and feelings were not taken into account, her right to know her own body was not honored, and the decision to abort was made before Amy had knowledge that she was even pregnant. In Amy's case, coercion was evident in the way Amy's mother handled the decision about her daughter's pregnancy.

Age

Age is a factor that can affect human experiences because it guides physical and emotional maturity. Developmental milestones and transitions help form personality and mark progress throughout the lifespan. Events perceived as both positive and negative that happen throughout each life stage sculpt identity and self-perception. These events can take on different meaning depending on the individual's age. For example, does an adolescent experience abortion the same way an adult does? Quinton, Major, and Richards (2001) examined this question and in their research found that minors do not experience any more negative emotions (particularly depression) during and after abortion than women 18 years and older. Similar results, discovered by Adler, Ozer, and Tschann (2003) found that both post-abortion minors and adults scored within normal bounds on psychological measures. Factors that did make the abortion experience more difficult for teens were higher conflict with parents, an avoidant style of coping, and lower self-efficacy (Quinton, Major, & Richards, 2001).

Amy was 15 years old when she experienced abortion. Certainly issues related to her age, because of her status as a minor, contributed to her distress. She was going through a difficult transition of adolescence, marked by abuse and neglect in her home. Amy had troubled relationships with her parents. She did not feel a sense of power in her life, especially when she became pregnant. She was coerced by her mother into getting an abortion and this lack of control over her situation had long lasting effects on her overall sense of self-esteem and self-efficacy. As discussed earlier, negative emotional experiences of abortion can be related to low self-esteem and feelings of powerlessness.

Financial Stress

Economic factors can also influence a woman to end a pregnancy when she is financially unable to support a child. Her fear of raising children in poverty may be a strong deciding factor to abort (Jagannathan, 2006). When a woman chooses out of fear, she is not really experiencing freedom of choice. Instead, she is trying to avoid the possibility of creating a situation in which she fails to provide for her child. In this sense, the lack of economic resources is a strong influence over her choice, and may be the deciding factor. She is robbed of autonomy and true freedom of choice (Stoppard, 2000). The likelihood of internalized guilt and shame increases when women are not exercising their full right to choose. Thus, the economic factor can contribute significantly to choosing abortion, which can complicate how a woman feels about that choice. In other words, her emotional self might not want an abortion but her practical self (her awareness of the hardships of poverty) might see no other alternative, thus creating the internal conflict and distress between two aspects of her personality.

Living with poverty can create daily crisis in the lives of women (Jagannathan, 2005). Diminished levels of economic power can affect a woman's assessment of self-esteem, self-efficacy, and autonomy, which can threaten her mental health and weaken her ability to cope with stressful situations like abortion.

Amy does not know all the reasons her mother forced her to get an abortion. Amy's mother was unmarried and pregnant at age 21. She married her baby's father, but the marriage did not last and ended in a high-conflict divorce. At the time of Amy's abortion, her mother simply told her, "You are not going to end up like me." This may have been her attempt to shield Amy from the experience of having a child out of wedlock, prevent her from marrying at a young age out of necessity, or to protect her from the grim financial future of becoming an unmarried, teenaged parent. Furthermore, Amy came from an economically impoverished home environment. Perhaps Amy's mother did not want to take on the financial burden of a grandchild. These are speculations, but clearly the lack of financial resources may have played a part in her mother's decision to end the pregnancy.

Conflict with Values

Sometimes people make choices and behave in ways that do not reflect their own set of values. A woman may end her pregnancy but then suffer emotional pain because she believes abortion is morally wrong. This dynamic might arise when coercion was used the decision-making process of what to do with an unwanted pregnancy. Having an abortion is therefore upsetting because her behavior does not match her particular set of beliefs and values.

Women's opinions about whether or not abortion reflects their own values can change over time, due to influences from society and also due to complex life experiences of the individual woman. For example, those who strongly oppose abortion and then find themselves with an unwanted pregnancy might start reconsidering their options, especially when the pregnancy is the product of a rape. In reconsidering options, a reassessment of values and beliefs might occur, giving her a wider variety of choices to consider. Another scenario is the woman who has an abortion at a young age, and later in life changes her moral stance, finding it difficult to forgive herself for ending the pregnancy.

This split between the values and behavior of an individual is often the culprit of compromised mental health. Living with guilt, self-loathing, or lack of forgiveness for breaches of moral code can cause tremendous suffering for an individual who is not at peace with her life decisions. Often religious beliefs enter into a woman's ideas of right and wrong. When a woman sees abortion as morally incorrect or religiously sinful, and yet she has one anyway, she may be fearful of social stigma or spiritual punishment. She may have difficulty coming to terms with her emotions without some kind of outside intervention from a mental health worker (Russo & Dabul, 1997).

Amy's comments following her disclosure indicated that abortion would not have been an option for her had she been supported in an alternate choice at the time of her pregnancy. She stated that she holds a personal philosophy that is pro-choice, but she would not have chosen abortion for herself, had her circumstances been different. At 28 years old with no children and no plans to have any in the near future, she grieves what she sees as her lost opportunity to become a parent.

Concealment

Abortion has a history of being one of the most hotly debated moral issues of our modern world (Rubin & Russo, 2004). There are strong voices on both sides, struggling to influence the way we think about abortion. The emotional climate of the debate can be quite frightening, especially when pro-life language refers to abortion as murder. Women who are intimidated by the passionate voices of anti-abortion activists become silent as a way of coping with a hostile environment (a common coping mechanism used by battered women to avoid dangerous conflict or mental abuse) (McCloskey & Fraser, 1997). Women who cannot speak about their experiences suffer greater emotional turmoil than those who are allowed to talk openly about difficult times in their lives. Because abortion is a morally controversial topic in our society, women are likely to silence themselves and conceal thoughts and feelings about their abortion experiences (Major & Gramzow, 1999).

When abortion is referred to as killing, when abortion clinics are picketed by protesters who harass women seeking services, when the media and our political/religious leaders focus on abortion as a pivotal issue defining poor moral judgment, women can feel more disturbed by the experience (Cozzarelli et al., 2000). Even when a woman is acting within her own set of values and within her own moral code, she may feel shamed by society at large and therefore be reluctant to seek out support from others. As described earlier in this essay, a lack of emotional support can lead to distress after abortion. In Amy's case, although we had months of building a strong, trusting, counseling relationship, she was still reluctant to share her abortion story. Although she stated that she knew I would not judge her for having had an abortion, disclosing to me was still extremely difficult for her.

Shame was the single most powerful emotion that Amy reported in reference to her abortion. She had never talked to anyone about her experience for fear of humiliation, criticism, and embarrassment. She assumed she would be judged at least as harshly as she judged herself. Amy was responding to cues from her family, who did not speak of the abortion before or after the event. She was also responding to the values of her small Midwestern town, which was heavily influenced by fundamental Christian theology. Abortion for her was shrouded in family secrecy and was considered socially and morally unacceptable in her immediate cultural environment. Amy responded to these dynamics by silencing herself, relinquishing the power of her own voice and inadvertently eliminating the possibility of emotional support from others.

Other Variables

Many factors influence the effect of abortion on a woman's mental health. Amy's story illustrates some reasons why abortion can be particularly distressing. The factors presented thus far, those evident in Amy's particular situation, are not an exhaustive list. Other variables also may carry significance for an individual, such as race and religion of the abortion patient, although these may be highly individualistic, depending on her support network and internal spiritual views. In a study published in 1997, Russo and Dabul found that regardless of race or religion, abortion did not affect the general well being of women. She found other factors having a more powerful effect on women's well being and self-esteem, including education, income, and having a work role (Russo & Dabul, 1997).

Factors such as how much time has lapsed since the abortion, term of the pregnancy at the time of abortion, history of multiple abortions, or ending a wanted pregnancy (when abortion is chosen for medical reasons) can play into how a woman views her abortion (Major et. al., 2000.) Lack of medical safety from illegal abortions can also create conditions resulting in emotional disturbance after abortion (Stotland, 2007). These are examples of other variables that may complicate how women think and feel about their abortions and determine psychological outcome. All of the factors that surround abortion will determine how counselors and therapists respond to post-abortion women and how they design interventions to assist in healing.

Post-Abortion Intervention

After a close look at some of the factors that might lead to compromised mental health following an abortion, how does a counselor design an effective post-abortion intervention? Women who seek counseling to address adverse psychological responses after abortion need unbiased mental health professionals who can carefully screen to identify precisely what issues are problematic (Rubin & Russo, 2004).

Amy's story presents many factors that can create a complicated, long-term negative impact from the complex issues surrounding abortion. While her experience is not necessarily typical, she represents a portion of women who do suffer from traumatic memories and disturbing thoughts and emotions associated with her abortion. It is not possible to isolate Amy's abortion experience from the social, political, religious, and interpersonal contexts in which it occurred.

In order to design an effective intervention, a counselor must understand the issues inherent in being a woman in our society. When abortion is problematic, the context in which it happens is of utmost relevance. A feminist orientation to counseling is especially helpful in recognizing the cultural dynamics that make abortion an especially difficult experience for some women. Janet Stoppard's text on depression in women (2000) closely examines the social conditions that play a powerful role in creating negative emotional experiences for women.

A treatment plan that can target issues such as depression, anxiety, complicated grieving, PTSD, and other mental illnesses is necessary when counseling women during the post-abortion phase. Screening for pre-existing psychological problems helps determine what events in a woman's history might be contributing to her difficulties after abortion. Careful examination of the events preceding and following an abortion can give clues to underlying issues such as lack of emotional support, coercion, domestic violence, rape, and financial stress. A woman's religious orientation may be creating an impossible inner conflict, which requires intervention from a compassionate and understanding therapist. All of these outside influences affect how women respond emotionally to their abortion experience.

A counseling intervention that allows women to speak about their experiences without being judged can be particularly healing for those who have had an abortion. Women can experience anger and rage that have been suppressed by a society that fails to accept these emotions in women. When a woman expresses anger about those who have taken away power and control, she can begin to reconstruct a solid sense of identity that is congruent with her own sense of reality. Self-blame can create a negative adjustment to abortion, resulting in a prolonged sense of guilt and internalized shame (Mueller & Major, 1989). Shame and guilt decrease when she understands how she has been victimized by circumstances inherent in her cultural and social environment. This reframing of the event has been found to be powerfully healing for post-abortion women (Rubin & Russo, 2004). Counselors who provide emotional support and validation can help ameliorate feelings of isolation and ostracism.

Women who regret abortion and who long for the child that was never born may need grief counseling. The lack of emotional support for post-abortion women, and their tendency to conceal emotions may hinder the ability to grieve the loss and gain a sense of closure. Counselors must possess an understanding of the stages and dynamics of grief in order to guide women toward acceptance and resolution of the loss.

Counselors have a responsibility to educate women, providing accurate information and dispelling myths about abortion. Helping women understand abortion within the context of the social, political, and religious influences of their lives will enable them to appraise their experiences from a broader perspective. Issues that have compromised a woman's ability to cope with abortion can then be revealed and addressed through the counseling process. Women can learn to incorporate new coping skills that will improve self-esteem and build self-efficacy. By doing so, they can rightfully reclaim the power and control they need to direct their own lives.

Amy spent most of her childhood in silence. She learned that speaking up about her needs was not effective or productive, and often created a more dangerous situation, so she silenced her own voice. Healing for her began the day she found the courage to enter counseling and speak about her experiences. In the safety of my small counseling office, she gradually disclosed details about her life that damaged her self-esteem and her ability to cope effectively with life. Talking about the abortion she had when she was a teenager was one of many traumatic memories, all of which resulted at least in part from a lack of power and control in her life. On the day the manuscript for this essay was submitted, Amy brought to my office a collage of images that she had worked on since our last session. These cutout magazine pictures were images that were symbolic of her life and held special meaning. The largest image was a close-up photograph of a woman's open mouth being gagged by a large metal chain. In large print was the word, "survivor." Scattered elsewhere in her collage were pictures of women's mouths. When I asked about this recurring symbol, Amy said the most healing element of counseling thus far has been finding the freedom to speak about her experiences, break away from the bondage of silence, and trust the power of her own voice.

Conclusion

Although research supports the view that abortion generally does not present a significant threat to a woman's mental health, debates exist on whether or not abortion is a direct cause of psychological disturbance in women. When looking at abortion from the perspective of the women's crisis movement, we can see that a lack of power and control over women's reproductive health and other aspects of her life is more likely the cause of emotional disturbance. Social, political, religious and interpersonal factors affecting a woman's experience of abortion must be examined in order to understand the impact they have on her mental health. Awareness of the factors that create a complicated and distressing abortion experience is crucial to counselors who are designing interventions to serve women who seek services for post-abortion emotional difficulties.

References

Adler, N. E., H. P. David, B. N. Major, S. H. Roth, N. F. Russo and G. E. Wyatt (1990). Psychological Responses After Abortion. *Science, 248*, 41–44.

Adler, N. E., E. O. Ozer and J. Tschann (2003). Abortion Among Adolescents. *American Psychologist, 58*, 211–217.

Almeling, R. and L. Tews (1999). Abortion Myths. *National Abortion Federation*.Retrieved July 1, 2007: *www.prochoice.org/about_abortion/myths/post_abortion_syndrome.html*

Bradshaw, Z. and P. Slade (2003). The Effects of Induced Abortion on Emotional Experiences and Relationships: a Critical Review of the Literature. *Clinical Psychology Review, 23*, 929–958.

Brown, L. S. (2004). Feminist Paradigms of Trauma Treatment. *Psychotherapy: Theory, Research, Training, 41*, 464–471.

Cozzarelli, C., B. Major, A. Karrasch and K. Fueen (2000). Women's Experiences of and Reactions to Antiabortion Picketing. *Basic and Applied Social Psychology, 22*, 265–275.

Cozzarelli, C., N. Sumer and B. Major (1998). Mental Models of Attachment and Coping with Abortion. *Journal of Personality and Social Psychology, 74*, 453–467.

Jagannathan, R. (2006). Economic Crisis and Women's Childbearing Motivations: the Induced Abortion Response of Women on Public Assistance. *Brief Treatment and Crisis Intervention, 6*, 52.

Lemkau, J.P. (1991). Post-Abortion Adjustment of Health Care Professionals in Training. *American Journal of Orthopsychiatry, 61,* 92–102.

Major, B. (2003). Psychological Implications of Abortion — Highly Charged and Rife with Misleading Research. *Canadian Medical Association Journal, 168,* 1257.

Major, B., C. Cozzarelli, M. L. Cooper, J. Zubek, C. Richards, M. Wilhite and R. H. Gramzow (2000). Psychological Responses of Women After First-Trimester Abortion. *Archives of General Psychiatry, 57,* 777–784.

Major, B. and R. H. Gramzow (1999). Abortion as Stigma: Cognitive and Emotional Implications of Concealment. *Journal of Personality and Social Psychology, 77,* 735–745.

Major, B., C. Richards, L. M. Cooper, C. Cozzarelli and J. Aubek (1998). Personal Resilience, Cognitive Appraisals, and Coping: An Integrative Model of Adjustment to Abortion. *Journal of Personality and Social Psychology, 74,* 735–752.

McCloskey, K. A. and J. S. Fraser (1997). Using Feminist MRI Brief Therapy During Initialcontact with Victims of Domestic Violence. *Psychotherapy, 34,* 433–446.

Mueller, P., and B. Major (1989). Self-Blame, Self-Efficacy, and Adjustment to Abortion. *Journal of Personality and Social Psychology, 57,* 1059–1068.

Quinton, W. J., B. Major and C. Richards (2001). Adolescents and Adjustment to Abortion: are Minors at Risk? *Psychology, Public Policy, and Law, 3,* 491–514.

Rogers, C. (1965). *Client-Centered Therapy: Its Current Practice, Implications, and Theory.* Boston: Houghton Mifflin.

Rubin, L., and N. F. Russo (2004). Abortion and Mental Health: What Therapists Need to Know. *Women in Therapy, 27,* 69–90.

Russo, N.F. and A. J. Dabul (1997). The Relationship of Abortion to Well-Being: Do Race and Religion Make a Difference? *Professional Psychology: Research and Practice, 28,* 23–31.

Russo, N.F. and J. E. Denious (2001). Violence In the Lives of Women Having Abortions: Implications for Practice and Public Policy. *Professional Psychology: Research and Practice, 32,* 142–150.

Russo, N.F. and K. L. Zierk (1992). Abortion, Childbearing, and Women's Well-Being. *Professional Psychology: Research and Practice, 23,* 269–280.

Smucker, M. R. and C. V. Dancu (1999). *Cognitive-Behavioral Treatment for Adult Survivors of Childhood Trauma.* Northvale, New Jersey: Jason Aronson, Inc.

Stoppard, J.M. (2000). *Understanding Depression: Feminist Social Constructionist Approaches.* New York: Routledge.

Stotland, N. (2007). The Safety of Legal Abortion and the Hazards of Illegal Abortion. *NARAL Pro-Choice America Foundation.* Retrieved June 2, 2007: *www.prochoice america.org/assets/files/Abortion-Access-to-Abortion-Science*

Teichman, Y., S. Shenhar and S. Segal (1993). Emotional Distress In Israeli Women Before and After Abortion. *American Journal of Orthopsychiatry, 63,* 277–288.

Pedagogical Considerations for an Interdisciplinary Course on Abortion

LORI BAKER-SPERRY

In the spring of 2001, the Department of Women's Studies (then a program) offered an interdisciplinary course on abortion. Scheduled as an experimental course, WS391, students enrolled for 3 hours of credit. The course filled quickly. With approximately 25 students, the course was held from 6:30–9:00 on Wednesday evenings in a small classroom. The course was envisioned as one where there would be much dialogue, interest and challenge, as sometimes diverging disciplinary perspectives were addressed. The course goals included the exploration of the issues surrounding abortion and reproduction in the U.S., an examination of the ways that different disciplines address or evaluate a topic, and to possibly produce new knowledge about abortion as a result of the interdisciplinary work of conducting the course and preparing and presenting material.

Upon inception, the professor of record, Baker-Sperry, developed a schedule of disciplines and sent invitations to faculty and professionals in many fields: sociology, feminist study, political science, history, English, philosophy, religion, psychology, community health, and anthropology. She requested that they focus on the application of feminist theory in their respective disciplines as it applied to abortion and reproduction. With representatives from each heartily accepting the invitation, materials were solicited. Many faculty submitted readings to Baker-Sperry prior to each class (some upon acceptance, others about two weeks in advance, in order to copy and distribute in the preceding class). The readings, while no longer current and therefore not included here, were well received by the students. Many faculty contributing to this book have, in fact, utilized the assigned materials in their own chapters, and therefore, each reference section is rich with both classic and current materials that would be suitable for a similar course.

Without a composite text, the readings provided "windows" into the disciplines they represented through the lens of abortion and reproduction. Students were always surprised at how differently disciplines may view a subject that is as "black and white" as abortion. They were also struck by the commonalities, such as the importance of legal and historical constraints. In place of an interdisciplinary text, two books were assigned which supplemented the weekly articles supplied by faculty, "Abortion: Opposing Viewpoints" (1997) and "Controlling Reproduction: An American History" (Tone, 1997). The complete citations are available on the syllabus below.

The class period was set up as a two and a half hour block, with one 15 minute break. Baker-Sperry spent the first half hour addressing course-related concerns, assignments, and preparation for future presenters. She also brought in current events topics as they related to the issues surrounding abortion. For example, it was in spring of 2001 that President Bush reinstated the gag rule, refusing to allow federal funds to be used to provide information about abortion. Students were very receptive to the discussion of current events, and would often bring in materials and sources they had uncovered.

The presenters arrived a few minutes before 7:00. Often, particular contributors attended many classes. Although there were a few faculty or professionals who did not attend but their session, a small group became actively involved in the course. These individuals were very careful not to overrun the group, but sat back, weighed in when referenced, and learned alongside the students, as well. That is one of the beauties of interdisciplinary and multidisciplinary work. Each presenter received a letter of thanks from Baker-Sperry and the class.

Two films were chosen for the course, based upon availability and reviews, *If These Walls Could Talk* and *Leona's Sister Gerri*. These films are summarized in short reviews following the syllabus below. Both films were startlingly effective, sometimes difficult, but very moving. Each featured women with their own personal stories, and both illustrated the phenomenon referenced earlier: when it comes to the personal story, others' opinions about abortion may shift. It was clear that students responded to the individual stories, regardless of their own vocalized perspective on abortion.

There is one caveat, however: these films cover difficult material and they do so in a way that is very real. *If These Walls Could Talk* features representations, i.e. fictional accounts, but they are nonetheless moving, and *Leona's Sister Gerri* captures the essence of a woman dead from an illegal abortion. During the film "Leona's Sister Gerri," one student excused herself and Baker-Sperry walked with her to the hallway. She just "needed a breather," but chose to come back in and finish viewing.

Students did wrestle with the material, but the group was very vocal in class. This helped in terms of processing the material. The class was a mature group of students, both in their perspectives and as a result of the earlier coursework, and managed the subject well. They had, of course, self–selected into the class. Each student worked through their reactions in their response journals, and many made active arguments (across the continuum of opinion) about abortion and reproduction in their final papers and presentations. It was an exciting class and group of students to witness.

The interdisciplinary course on abortion was such a success with students and faculty, the Department of Women's Studies went on to offer two other such courses: "Women and War" and "Women and Mothering." There are many other topics that would be suitable as well, such as "Women and Aging" and a multi–discipline critique of the language used to define and describe women, "Women Defined."

WS 391
SPECIAL TOPICS COURSE: ABORTION

REQUIRED TEXTS:

Abortion: Opposing Viewpoints. California: Greenhaven Press, Inc.
Tone, Andrea, ed. 1997. Controlling Reproduction: An American History. Delaware: Scholarly Resources, Inc.

COURSE DESCRIPTION AND GOALS:

This course offers an in-depth investigation of the social, political, and historical issues surrounding abortion. The course content reflects an academic discussion of the topic, avoiding value-laden, volatile discussion and presentation. This course offers a series of guest lecturers from a range of academic disciplines, as well as film.

The main goal of this course is to emphasize the importance of thinking about a controversial topic in an intellectual way, in light of a wide variety of perspectives. Such an analysis serves to highlight the connected nature of many such social issues to a political and historical time period. Therefore, students are encouraged to approach this controversial issue not only with interest, but a respect for differing viewpoints. Lastly, this course serves to contribute to an interest in further learning in general, about this and other topics.

COURSE REQUIREMENTS:

Attendance and Participation: Attendance is required and constitutes 20% of your overall course grade. Students are expected to come to class on time and with the assigned reading completed. It is imperative that you attend class to fully understand the course requirements and expectations for both the papers and presentations. Any questions or concerns about assigned work should be raised during office hours or in the first half hour of class. You are always free to stop by my office as well.

Class notes are not available to students. Each student is urged to exchange information with class members, in case of missed notes or material.

Response Journals: You are required to submit weekly "journal responses" in this course. Your journal will give you the opportunity to carefully evaluate and constructively respond to the course on a continual basis. The journals are two-part: a 1–2 page evaluation/discussion of the assigned reading for that week and a 1–2 page response/discussion of the presentation from the previous week. The journals are to be typed, double-spaced, twelve point font, standard one-inch margins. There will be a total of 10 response journals throughout the course of the semester for a total of 30% of your overall course grade (see calendar of meetings for due dates, which are indicated by an asterisk).

Since formulating both clear and intelligent arguments is fundamental to sharing our knowledge with others, I expect proper spelling, grammar, sentence formation and writing style. If you are unsure of your writing abilities, I would be glad to assist you if I can or you may always consult the writing center (they are a great resource). That said, this is to be a reflection of your voice; you will not be graded on your opinions, nor how flowery you make it sound. Often the most profound statements are simple and heart-felt. Be honest, you will not be graded down if your opinion is different from mine or another source offered in class. Instead, the majority of your grade will depend upon your grasp of the reading or presentation, how well you formulate your arguments, spelling and grammar, and your ability to convey your interest for the subject.

Late response journals will receive no more than 50% of the original total.

Final Paper/Presentation: The first part of the final assignment is to complete a term paper covering a particular aspect of the abortion issue *from your major discipline*. For example, if you are a political science major, you might discuss how the abortion issue has contributed to the recent election debates. Or, if you are a religion major you might explore the perspective of the Catholic Church in relation to the abortion issue. The final paper is to be 10 pages, double-spaced, twelve-point font, standard one-inch margins. There are to be at least five sources total, with no more than two internet sources (be particularly cautious when using internet sources for any paper — be sure to get the full internet address and critically evaluate the site). This portion of the final assignment is worth 30% of your overall grade.

The second part of the final assignment is to present your paper in class. Each student will have approximately fifteen minutes to present his or her paper and hold discussion. This portion is worth 20% of your overall grade.

Late papers will receive no more than 50% of the original total.

OFFICE HOURS:

Regularly scheduled office hours are from 4:00 P.M. to 6:00 P.M. on Tuesdays and Thursdays. Do not, however, let a time conflict worry you! I will often be in my office during the day, please stop in or schedule an appointment for a convenient time. Do not put off a question or concern because you cannot make office hours.

Please come and see me if you have questions or concerns *at any time*.

POINTS:

Attendance	20%
Response Journals	30%
Final Paper	30%
Final Presentation	20%
Total	100%

TENTATIVE CALENDAR OF MEETINGS — (Subject to Change) and READING LIST:

January 11	Introduction to Course: Discussion of syllabus, overview of course procedure, goals and objectives.
January 18	Presentation: History
January 25	Presentation: Sociology Reading: Controlling Reproduction I: Birth Control and Abortion in Early America *Response Journal #1 due
February 1	Presentation: Anthropology Reading: Abortion: Opposing Viewpoints, Chapter 1: Is Abortion Immoral? *Response Journal #2 due
February 8	Philosophy Reading: Controlling Reproduction II: The Medicalization of Reproduction *Response Journal #3 due
February 15	Political Science Reading: Abortion: Opposing Viewpoints, Chapter 2: Should Abortion Rights Be Restricted? *Response Journal #4 due
February 22	Religion Reading: Controlling Reproduction III: Fertility Control in Nineteenth-Century America *Response Journal #5 due
March 1	Administrative (45 min); mid-semester class discussion (2 hour). Reading: Abortion: Opposing Viewpoints, Chapter 3: Can Abortion Be Justified? *Response Journal #6 due
March 8	Spring Break
March 15	Film — If These Walls Could Talk Reading: Abortion: Opposing Viewpoints, Chapter 4: Is Abortion Safe for Women?

No response Journal due; in-class discussion of reading assignment

March 22   Counseling
            Reading: Controlling Reproduction IV: Regulating Reproduction
            *Response Journal #7 due

March 29   Health
            Reading: Abortion: Opposing Viewpoints, Chapter 5: Is Research Using Aborted Fetal Tissue Ethical?
            *Response Journal #8 due

April 5   English
            Reading: Controlling Reproduction V: Birth Control Revolution
            *Response Journal #9 due

April 12   Open for cancellations; Film: Leona's Sister Gerri; Class Discussion/Wrap Up
            Reading: Controlling Reproduction VI: Reproductive Rights
            *Response Journal #10 due

April 19   Paper Presentations

April 26   Paper Presentations

Finals Week Paper Presentations

*Each response journal is to cover reading assignment for present week (1–2 pages) and presentation from previous week (1–2 pages).

FILM SUMMARY

If These Walls Could Talk (1996)
Directors; Cher, Nancy Savoca
97 minutes

The HBO movie If These Walls Could Talk traces the pregnancy and abortion experiences of three women, who live in the same house: in the 50s, 70s, and 90s. Spanning 40 years, this film addresses multiple issues regarding women's access to abortion such as legality, feasibility of another child, and financial concerns. A nurse, Claire, in 1952 faces social stigma with her unplanned, unwed pregnancy and seeks a quintessential "back-alley" abortion. She dies of hemorrhage at the end of the segment. In 1974, in the same house, a mid-forties wife and mother of four, Barbara, wrestles with the stress of raising another child. She ultimately decides to have the child. The third story concerns the experiences of a college woman, Chris, impregnated by her professor. Chris chooses to access abortion, but is startled by the reality of that choice when the clinic is surrounded by protestors and, once inside, a doctor is killed.

Leona's Sister Gerri (1995)
Jane Gillooly
57 minutes

Leona's Sister Gerri is the story of Gerri Santoro, the victim of an illegal abortion, left dead on a hotel room floor. The photograph of her body was reproduced thousands of times and used to support pro-choice arguments against abortion, particularly in marches and informational literature. The film traces the story of her life, particularly focusing on the events leading to the abortion. It also addresses the experience of her family, in the wake of the public use of and response to her picture. This film is an excellent tool to illuminate the personal, and often conflicted, perspectives on abortion and the abortion experience. The historical nature also helps to situate the issues surrounding abortion in a wider context.

"As heart stopping as any experience of our own, this fine and moving documentary reminds all who see it that life stories, not statistics, contain the truth."
–Gloria Steinem

Concluding Remarks
The Uncertainty of Autonomy and the Assuredness of Vagueness

HEATHER MCILVAINE-NEWSAD

When we began this project so many years ago, we did so for three basic reasons. The first reason was that when the multi-disciplinary course on abortion was conceptualized and subsequently offered, there was no textbook on the market that explored the issue of abortion and reproductive health care in the United States from a truly multi-disciplinary perspective.

As Basu (2003) concluded, the vast majority of texts and scholarly articles concerning abortion fall into three distinct categories:

1. Medical aspects of abortion and reproductive health care
2. Pro-choice versus pro-life arguments based entirely in the United States.
3. Abortion outside the United States, mainly in developing countries, framed within the politicized context of Catholicism.

None of these categories adequately covered the scope of material we were interested in, nor did they do so at a level appropriate for the course. Therefore, the presenters brought readings from their disciplines to the students to supplement what texts were available on the market at the time.

This text attempts to create a new category, covering the most important arguments from the disciplines represented by those who participated in the course. The strength of this book lies in the holistic manner in which the subject is addressed. The professors who taught segments of the course represented a wide variety of disciplinary views, not all of which were easily found in the existing literature. I do not hesitate to write that while each of us we were well versed on the issue of abortion from our own disciplinary perspectives, we learned a great deal from each other. This only rein-forced that notion that a comprehensive text representing multiple perspec-tives on abortion was needed. Upon conclusion of the course, we remained interested in learning from each other and subsequently prepared papers and presented our experience as a peer-reviewed panel at the 24th Annual National Women's Studies Association Conference in New Orleans in 2002. It was at this conference that we were encouraged by numerous feminist scholars to "just write the book" as others too recognized that the need was there. And thus, we embarked on the journey of writing.

The second reason for writing the book is not so straight forward. For the vast majority of the authors in this book, abortion and issues dealing with reproductive health care are not our primary areas of expertise. Yet, as women and feminists we are confronted on a daily basis with these concerns in and out of the classroom. As Aimee Shouse writes in her essay, "The Pol-itics of Abortion: The Impact of Interest Groups," abortion and issues sur-rounding reproductive health care are mentioned in virtually every course we offer from political science, to philosophy, and the health sciences. The fact that so many of our students — male and female alike — appear so unaware of the strides made by their foremothers to earn them the right to choose their reproductive futures is indicative of their lack of knowledge about the complexity — social, cultural, economic, ecological, political, reli-gious, etc. — of the world in which they live. In short, we needed to write this book because while abortion is a complex and uncomfortable issue to explore, it is something that is part of human existence. While not every-one will be directly touched by abortion, there is no escaping its prominence and power in contemporary society.

At this point it should be clear to the reader that this book does not focus on the moral debates about abortion. There are a plethora of schol-arly books that more than adequately address this issue. Because the pro-choice versus pro-life debate dominates virtually all discussions in both the popular media and scholarly texts in the United States, we intended to dis-tance ourselves from this debate somewhat by offering a more complete con-text in which to situate the debate. It is our intention that upon completion of reading this book, students will begin to understand the complex fabric that encompasses a seemingly dichotomous subject.

This leads me to the third and final reason for this project: to pull together recent literature and resources on abortion from a multidisciplinary perspective. Current discussions on abortion have their roots in historical, religious, scientific and cultural understandings of how we have interpreted the question of what it means to be human. Therefore, to have a firm grasp of what each party at the table brings to the dialogue, one needs to be familiar with the historical and contemporary context in which the debate on abortion is situated. As professor of record for the course, Lori Baker-Sperry organized a structure for the class beginning by providing the students with a broad feminist framework through which to view the multiple disciplinary perspectives in the classroom. Each instructor who led a segment of the course supplied readings from his or her discipline to the students for them to read prior to the lectures. As professors at a mainly undergraduate university, we know how time consuming and cumbersome it can be to assemble current readings for a course. We have attempted to eliminate the need for instructors who wish to teach an interdisciplinary course on abortion to do what we had to do, by writing this book. The sample syllabus and the brief list of suggested readings from each discipline offer instructors a platform to begin to craft their own multidisciplinary course on abortion.

In the introduction, my co-editors Martinelli-Fernandez and Baker-Sperry aptly reflected on many of the issues raised by the various essays in the book. In this concluding essay, I would like to do one of the things my discipline does well — identify and address two themes that emerge from each essay. These arguments are often slippery and unwieldy, yet they find themselves at the center of the abortion discussion.

Autonomy and Vagueness

One key question posed in many of the essays is that of female autonomy. Polly Radosh, in her essay, "Abortion: A Sociological Perspective," posits that the change in female autonomy in the late 19th and early 20th century in the United States is related to the shift in medical training at the time. Up until the creation of the American Medical Association (AMA) in 1847, the vast majority of all female reproductive health care issues were attended to by female midwives. Basing their knowledge on traditional healing techniques learned through apprenticeship, midwives used herbs to regulate the menstrual cycle. Patients were cared for at home and the regulation of the menstrual period was a private, not a public matter. Midwives were viewed as the most appropriate choice for reproductive health care because they could relate on a personal and professional level to the issues their patients were confronting.

As the education of physicians became more empirically and scientifically based, learning was undertaken in the public sphere of the university setting, rather than through a more privately supervised apprenticeship. Midwives, who were excluded from this educational realm were viewed as possessing less scientific authority and therefore less valid knowledge about women's health. Female based knowledge — folk medicine and witchcraft — were disregarded as unscientific. As men began to dominate the field of medicine and establish standards to be replicated throughout the United States, they simultaneously co-opted the autonomy of their female patients and practitioners.

As a result of recent shifts in the gender roles in the United States, more women are becoming physicians. According to the Association of American Medical Colleges (2006), approximately 50 percent of all incoming students are female. In addition, according to the American College of Obstetricians and Gynecologists (2008), the vast majority of students enrolled in obstetrics and gynecological training programs in the United States are women. Finally, since the 1970's the value of the nurse-midwife has experienced resurgence in the American medical community. While not permitted to practice independently from a board certified physician, nurse-midwives are currently a popular choice among women seeking medical care during all stages of their reproductive lives.

The creation of a patriarchal system of medical care has drawn what were formerly private knowledge systems into the public domain establishing hierarchical roles of patient and doctor. Patients' "gut instincts" about what may be ailing them are often disregarded as uneducated hunches, as a clear delineation between the knowledge holder and the knowledge seeker has been established. The fact that for a long period of time women have remained absent from the role of doctor and the importance of the nurse-midwife has only recently been acknowledged as valid has reinforced the patriarchal system in which we live.

In their essay, "Health and Medical Aspects of Abortion," Kathy Fisher and Sarah R. Goff emphasize the medical definition of fetal development and highlight the medical aspects of abortion. What this essay along with Althea K. Alton's essay, "Staying Within an "Understanding Distance": One

Feminist's Scientific and Theological Reflections on Pregnancy and Abortion," brings to light is the vagueness of our understanding of human reproduction. As Alton points out in her essay, there is no scientific consensus to when life begins. Nor is there a general socio-cultural consensus as to when life begins or ends. In some cultures, children are not given names or considered humans with souls until they have survived for a significant amount of time outside of the womb. Many anthropologists associate this delayed attachment of personhood to young children to high infant and/or child mortality rates. It is easier (if there is such a notion as ease in losing a child) to lose a young infant or child to disease or illness when one does not yet recognize it as completely human. Contrast this with the rapidly changing conceptualization of personhood within our contemporary high tech culture, where expectant parents can see their unborn children through high level ultrasonic photographs long before the fetus leaves the womb. It is not uncommon for pregnant women to know the sex of their child and have named it while still in *utero*. Changing technology has altered the way in which we view human reproduction, but it has not clarified our understanding of it.

As Basu (2003, p. 251) so aptly writes, a number of questions have arisen as a result of our evolving cultural biomedicine system. These questions include:

1. When is a delayed menstrual period a pregnancy?
2. When is a pregnancy a form of life?
3. When does the life in a womb acquire a "soul"?

One thing that is interesting about all of these questions is the linear progression of thought. By this I mean the Western concept of life as having a beginning, middle, and an end. As Alton mentions in her essay, "from a biological perspective, when life begins is not really the most important issue since, with regards to reproduction, life is a continuum." Exploring varying cultural ideas and understanding the various interpretations of human reproduction and autonomy assist in bringing new voices to the discussion about abortion.

Nowhere is the discussion on feminist autonomy more clearly addressed than in Susan A. Martinelli-Fernandez's essay "Abortion, Polyphonic Narratives and Kantianism: Quality of Life Matters." Autonomy, coming from the Greek *nomos* (meaning the law), is broadly understood as the right to self-govern. When dealing specifically with moral and political issues, it is often used as the basis for determining the moral responsibility for individual actions. In the medical field, doctors and other health care professionals strive to meet the goal of patient autonomy, although it often conflicts with treatments that are "medically" beneficial. Examining the philosophy of autonomy, freedom, care, and respect for humans as well as non-humans allows Martinelli-Fernandez to establish a middle ground among these complicated ideas. By situating individual choice in the web of socio-cultural, religious, economic, and other relationships, she demonstrates how "relational autonomy" is a concept worth investigating, especially within the abortion debate. She clearly demonstrates that Kantian moral obligations actually arise out of particular relationships. Therefore the establishment of arguments for universality, impartiality, and objections of abstraction are clearly not useful for the discussion on abortion.

This notion of universality brings me to the next essay: "Abortion and Mental Health," by Gayla Elliott. In this essay, a case study demonstrates that the notion of universal female autonomy is disputed given individual physical and cultural contexts. Through the presentation of a feminist case study, Elliott reveals how the lack of female autonomy resulted in psychological challenges for one woman.

As a young woman, Amy (the case study subject) while sexually active as a teenager, was unfamiliar with the initial physical signs of pregnancy. It was not until some time later that she realized she was pregnant. Unbeknownst to Amy, her mother did not want Amy to face the challenges of being a single parent as she had. Thus, without the knowledge of her daughter, Amy's mother scheduled an appointment for Amy to have an abortion. It was not until after the procedure was complete that Amy understood what had taken place. Years after the fact, the event continued to plague her in part because she was stripped of any voice in determining her reproductive future and also because she feared that her desire to become a mother at some point in her life might never be realized.

As Elliott writes, for the vast majority of individuals abortion results in no long-term trauma. According to Hern (1995), psychological studies consistently show that women who are healthy can adjust to any outcome of pregnancy, whether it is term birth, induced abortion, or spontaneous abortion (miscarriage). It is preferable, however, as both Elliott and Hern (1995) write, to have strong emotional support not only from friends and

family, but also from a compassionate physician and a lay abortion counselor. Women, who have this kind of female centered support, as well as support from family and friends, generally have few psychological challenges
post-abortion. On the other hand, women like Amy who have received antag-
onistic, negative messages about the pregnancy and abortion are likely to
experience high levels of stress during the abortion and later on in life. It
seems clear that the lack of choice in Amy's situation has contributed to
many of her long-term psychological challenges.

In "The Politics of Abortion: The Impact of Interest Groups," Aimee
D. Shouse deftly lays out the complex system which informs American abortion policy. By providing the reader with an overview of the roles played by
political parties, interest groups and candidates, Shouse provides us with a
synopsis of how abortion policy is formulated. Equally important is the fact
that it is deceptive on the part of American politicians to assume or postu-
late that there is a single public opinion on abortion, since our population
is so diverse. This once again challenges the notion of universality and places
the individual situation within a complex and changing landscape of influential factors.

To illustrate this fact, Shouse offers the recent passage of abortion policies in some states which have enacted guidelines to ostensibly protect the
emotional well-being of a woman who is considering an abortion. As Shouse
notes, "While a woman's health is protected by the state's regulation of abortion providers, the state addresses a woman's emotional health by aiming policies toward the woman herself." I personally find this legislation offensive.
It implies that women are a weaker sex unable to care for their emotional
well being without the guidance of our governing (and largely male) leaders. In short, the passage of this kind of legislation only reinforces the patriarchal society in which we live.

A second example offered by Shouse highlights the use of emerging
technology to test the concept of personhood. According to legislation passed
in Georgia under the "Women's Ultrasound Right to Know Act," all physicians are required to offer women seeking an abortion the chance to view
the ultrasound image and hear the fetal heartbeat before an abortion takes
place. While a woman is not required to submit to the request, the mere
fact that it is required to be offered challenges the concept of female autonomy and personhood. Relying on arguments firmly contradicted by the scientific community, Georgia's law (H.B. 147) seeks to ensure that a woman is

protected from the "devastating psychological consequences" of making an uninformed decision regarding abortion.

Contrast the construction of our contemporary high-tech society reflected in the passage of the Georgia's law H.B. 147 to the society represented in Lori Baker-Sperry's essay, "Orphans, Abortions, and the Public Fetus in *The Cider House Rules*," and we see how making use of a novel can be helpful in illustrating the value of recognizing the influence of time and place on abortion. Baker-Sperry writes that "we construct our terms, name our terms, place value and meaning to those words only in the context of our lives with one another." Nowhere is this argument more true than in the discussion surrounding abortion. Dr. Warren Hern, physician, anthropologist, and founder of the Boulder Abortion Clinic has written numerous scholarly articles and op-ed columns on the use of language in the abortion debate. In a recent contribution to the *Colorado Statesman,* Hern (2007) writes:

> An egg is a person. No, an egg is a chicken. A fertilized human egg is a person. An acorn is a tree. A seed is an apple. A set of plans is a house. A *blastocyst* is a "preborn baby." An adult human being is a "pre-dead corpse."

> The U.S. Constitution refers to "All persons born...," not "all persons conceived..." or "all fertilized eggs...." No live birth, no person.

Hern goes on to write that the construction of personhood and the use of language to illustrate those concepts are of course, relative only in the context of specific times and places. Hern provides an illustration from the Shipibo Indians of the Peruvian Amazon among whom he has worked for more than 40 years. He notes that a baby is not given a name and thereby the status of personhood until it is at least three months old. The reason for this is situated in time and place, because in some Amazon basin villages as many as 20–30 percent of all children die before they reach their first birthday. The death of any child hurts, but the death of a non-person may be slightly less traumatic.

Baker-Sperry's essay poses another important question: "Whose construction of meaning is valued?" And are these voices heard within the abortion debate. The use of *Cider House Rules* in which the voices of those often marginalized from the political arena is a powerful way for students to hear the multitude of voices from our highly stratified and politically apathetic society. Students are challenged to consider if the same women in *The Cider*

House Rules were transported to rural Illinois in 2008 would they be judged in the same manner as they were in the book? The answers are varied, yet useful to demonstrate the power of situating individuals within time, space, and social culture.

An Anthropologist's Story

> We [anthropologists] were the first to insist that we see the lives of others through lenses of our own grinding and that they look back on ours through ones of their own [Geertz 1989].

My own interest in anthropology and women's issues began as a Peace Corps Volunteer in the Dominican Republic in the early 1990s. Living in a rural impoverished village in the mountains off the southern coast, I watched women face a reality much different than that I had ever experienced. Women in the community had little or no options for birth control. The infant mortality rate was astonishingly high. Abortions, while illegal, were available to those with resources. No women in the village where I lived and worked had the resources — social or economic — to obtain an abortion. Yet many women frequented the *curandera,* or local female shaman, to regulate their monthly flow. I watched as the emotional and physical toll of repeated pregnancies and child loss aged women well beyond their biological years.

I started a women's group that met twice a month to discuss how we could make their lives better. Among the many things we talked about were how to grow more nutritious food, how important it was to keep their daughters in school (the vast majority of the women could neither read nor write), and how to have fewer and healthier children. Although I did not realize it at the time, I was already a practicing feminist anthropologist having formed one of my first focus groups which allowed women to voice their concerns in a safe and supportive environment. Some of the suggestions were successfully put into place, while others were unable to be realized given the highly patriarchal and Catholic culture of the island. Most importantly, I learned and continue to learn much from women who are different yet similar to me.

Since completing my time in the Peace Corps, I have been fortunate to continue to find myself surrounded by strong feminists at all stages of my professional career. I have learned many valuable lessons from each of them, yet, the voices of those who are most often marginalized still speak the loudest to me. I hope that in my essay, "Hidden in Plain View: An Overview of Abortion in Rural Illinois and Around the Globe" readers of this book will hear some of those voices and consider the messages they impart to all of us.

In her introductory remarks, Lori Baker-Sperry asked what she as a third wave feminist brings to the discussion about abortion. I have asked myself the same question and only now think I know the answer: I bring the voices and subjective experiences of women who are often excluded from the public debate on abortion to the discussion. Ruth Benedict (1989) famously wrote, "The purpose of anthropology is to make the world safe for human differences." Nowhere does this statement ring more true than in the context of the conversation on abortion. We hope that this volume contributes to the sorting out of some of the ramifications of viewing the abortion debate through a single lens. In recognizing and respecting differing points of view; conceding the influence of social, cultural, economic, religious, and historical variables; and acknowledging the shifting landscape of autonomy and the understanding of personhood we can hopefully establish a discussion resulting in a more effective and sensitive public policy on abortion.

References

American College of Obstetricians and Gynecologists (2008). Retrieved July 11, 2008: *http://www.acog.org/.*

Association of American Medical Colleges (2006). U.S. Medical School Enrollment Continues to Climb: Class Sizes Increase in All Regions for Second Straight Year. Retrieved July 11, 2008: *http://www.aamc.org/newsroom/pressrel/2006/061018.htm.*

Basu, A.M. (2003). Concluding Remarks: The Role of Ambiguity. In Basu, ed. *The Sociocultural and Political Aspects of Abortion* (pp. 249–260). Westport, Connecticut: Praeger.

Benedict, R. (1989). The Chrysanthemum and the Sword: Patterns of Japanese Culture. New York: Mariner Books.

Geertz, C. (1989). Works and Lives: Anthropologist as Author. Stanford, California: Stanford University Press.

Hern, W. (1995). Abortion: Medical and Social Aspects in *Encyclopedia of Marriage and the Family, Volume I.* David Levinson, Editor in Chief. Simon and Schuster MacMillan: New York.

Hern, W. (2007). Would a Fertilized Egg Need a Passport? When Is an Egg Not an Egg? *The Colorado Statesman.* July 27. Retrieved June 8, 2008: *www.coloradostatesman.com*

Rylko-Bauer, B. (1996). Abortion from a Crosscultural Perspective: An Introduction. *Social Science Medicine* 42(4), 479–482.

About the Contributors

Althea K. Alton (Ph.D., Cornell University) is an associate professor of biological sciences and director of the Baccalaureate Degree in Liberal Arts and Sciences at Western Illinois University. Dr. Alton teaches courses in genetics, molecular biology, developmental biology and women's spirituality. She has also lectured on feminist *Middrash* and liberation theology. As part of her doctoral research, Dr. Alton worked on in-vitro fertilization and gamete-intra-fallopian-transfer (GIFT). Althea is completing her master of divinity degree at Garrett-Evangelical Theological Seminary and served as a licensed pastor in the United Methodist Church from 1994 to 2005. She continues to supply pulpits in the Presbyterian Church, the American Baptist Church and the Christian Church (Disciples of Christ). She is currently a candidate for the ordained ministry in the Christian Church (Disciples of Christ).

Lori Baker-Sperry, (Ph.D., sociology, Purdue University), is an associate professor of women's studies at Western Illinois University. Her research focuses on the qualitative study of children and children's literature, particularly focusing on issues of agency and socialization. Baker-Sperry teaches numerous women's studies courses, including introductory and advanced feminist theory, women in popular culture, and intersections of race, class, and gender.

Gayla Elliott (MA, Truman State University) has provided art therapy and counseling services in various mental health settings for over 20 years. For the last seven years, she has worked with the Western Illinois Regional Council Community Action Agency's Victim Services in Macomb, Illinois. In addition to her MA in art therapy, she has a BA in fine arts from Simpson College in Indianola, Iowa, and received professional credentials from the American Art Therapy Association. Gayla is currently pursuing an MA in counseling psychology from Union Institute and University, Vermont College. She lives in Macomb with her daughter, Georgia.

Kathy Fischer (Ph.D., Southern Illinois University) is professor emeritus at Western Illinois University. She graduated from Blessing Hospital School of Nursing in 1970 and worked as an RN for five years in the areas of surgical nursing and campus health center nursing. She subsequently obtained degrees from Western Illinois University (BA and MS) and Southern Illinois University (Ph.D.), all in school health education. She was employed in the Health Sciences Department at WIU for 32 years, teaching courses in the areas of women's health, sex education, mental health, drug education, and school health curriculum. She resides with her husband in Macomb, Illinois. They have three grown children.

Sarah R. Goff is a women's reproductive health care advocate who earned her bachelor of arts degree from the University of Iowa in American studies, with an emphasis in women's studies, and a master of science degree from Western Illinois University in community health education. She has worked in clinical and administrative positions for the Emma Goldman Clinic and two Planned Parenthood affiliates, and currently serves on the board of directors at Planned Parenthood of Southeast Iowa. She resides in Burlington with her husband and son.

Susan A. Martinelli-Fernandez (Ph.D., University of Chicago) is associate dean of the College of Arts and Sciences and professor of philosophy at Western Illinois University. Susan teaches courses in applied ethics, ethical theory, feminism, and philosophy and literature and has delivered papers in these areas at national and international conferences. She has been co-director of the Program for the Study of Ethics at Western Illinois University and is currently faculty advisor to Golden Key International Honour Society, Western Illinois University Chapter. Dr. Martinelli-Fernandez has served as secretary/treasurer and vice-president of the Illinois Philosophical Association and served on the executive board of the Society for Teaching Ethics across the Curriculum. Susan is a member of Delta Kappa Gamma International (Lambda State — Illinois, Theta Chapter), promoting professional and personal growth of women educators and excellence in education, and has served as the co-chair of the International Committee. She has published on Kant, Hume, feminism, and in applied areas of business ethics, reproductive issues, and military ethics.

Heather McIlvaine-Newsad (Ph.D., University of Florida) is an associate professor of anthropology at Western Illinois University. She teaches courses in cultural anthropology; applied anthropological methods; gender, race, and the environment; and disaster studies. Heather has received a number of teaching awards including the Outstanding First Year Experience Faculty Award, Excellence in Multicultural Teaching Award, Outstanding Teaching with Technology Award, and the President's Excellence in Diversity Award for Multicultural Education. She has worked in Germany, the Dominican Republic, and Ecuador with issues pertaining to women, health, and food production systems. She has published numerous articles on gender and the environment, local food systems, and the culture of disaster research and is currently conducting longitudinal research on rural fishing communities on the Gulf Coast under the auspices of National Marine Fisheries, a division of NOAA (the National Oceanic and Atmospheric Administration).

Polly F. Radosh (Ph.D., Southern Illinois University) is the former chair of the Department of Women's Studies at Western Illinois University. While at Western Illinois University she received several awards for excellence in teaching, and was the 2007 recipient of the research honor Distinguished Faculty Lecturer, at Western Illinois University. Dr. Radosh has published numerous articles on women in the criminal justice system. She continues to teach, research, and write about issues affecting women in prison and has recently begun a new trajectory of research on Irish immigrant women. Dr. Radosh recently accepted a position as dean at SUNY Geneseo.

Sue V. Rosser (Ph.D., University of Wisconsin–Madison) is the dean of Ivan Allen College, the liberal arts college at Georgia Institute of Technology, where she is also professor of history, technology, and society. She has edited collections and written approximately 115 journal articles on feminist theory and its application to practical problems of women and science and women's health. She is the author of nine books.

Aimee D. Shouse (Ph.D., Vanderbilt University) is an associate professor of political science at Western Illinois University, where she has been on the faculty since 1993. She received her bachelor's degree in political science from the University of Central Arkansas and completed her doctorate in 1996 at Vanderbilt University. Dr. Shouse teaches courses in the area of American government, including courses on women and politics, the Congress, and interest group politics. Her research interests mirror her teaching interests; she has presented several papers on the political activity of occupational associations, looking specifically at occupations that are overwhelmingly segregated by sex. She has also researched the political activity of lay midwives as well as state policy on the legality of practicing lay midwifery. She has edited several volumes for use in courses on American government and has published on the topic of teaching American government to students majoring in teacher education.

Index